"THERE CAN B… …TEXT OF THE HISTORY OF PH… …LISH."

…cal Bulletin

"We welcome … …e of Father Copleston's cla… history of philosophy. It is marked by solid learning, breadth of view, scientific objectivity and shrewd common sense."

The London *Tablet*

"Father Copleston continues his urbane and very readable account of philosophers and their systems. His book has the consecutiveness and unity of a novel . . . With the two volumes that preceded, it constitutes a remarkable achievement, the most considerable work of scholarship produced by English Scholasticism in our day, a work that has been received with respect by philosophy scholars everywhere."

Book Reviews

"The present volume may be warmly recommended not merely for those academically concerned with the history of philosophy, but for anyone aspiring to a clearer insight into the process by which the European mind cast off the tutelage of the Mediaeval doctors."

Avery R. Dulles, S.J.
Woodstock Letters

"For those who are familiar with the first two volumes of Father Copleston's *History of Philosophy*, it will be sufficient to say that this, the third volume, maintains the same standard of excellence. Father Copleston's work is already recognized as the standard Catholic history of philosophy."

The Catholic World

"In this volume, Father Copleston continues the fine scholarship and good style that characterized his previous two volumes."

Catholic Library World

"Father Copleston's work will rank as the most authoritative and outstanding study in this field by a Catholic scholar and second to none as a book of general reference on the subject."

Homilectic and Pastoral Review

Volumes of A HISTORY OF PHILOSOPHY now available in Image Books:

Volume 1
Parts I & II – Greece & Rome

Volume 2 Mediaeval Philosophy
Part I – Augustine to Bonaventure
Part II – Albert the Great to Duns Scotus

Volume 3 Late Mediaeval and Renaissance Philosophy
Part I – Ockham to the Speculative Mystics
Part II – The Revival of Platonism to Suárez

Volume 4 Modern Philosophy
Descartes to Leibniz

Volume 5 Modern Philosophy – The British Philosophers
Part I – Hobbes to Paley
Part II – Berkeley to Hume

Volume 6 Modern Philosophy
Part I – The French Enlightenment to Kant
Part II – Kant

Volume 7 Modern Philosophy
Part I – Fichte to Hegel
Part II – Schopenhauer to Nietzsche

Volume 8 Modern Philosophy – Bentham to Russell
Part I – British Empiricism and the Idealist Movement in Great Britain
Part II – Idealism in America, The Pragmatist Movement The Revolt against Idealism

Volume 9 Modern Philosophy – Maine de Biran to Sartre
Part I – The Revolution to Henri Bergson
Part II – Bergson to Sartre

A History of Philosophy

VOLUME III

Late Mediaeval and Renaissance Philosophy

PART II

The Revival of Platonism to Suárez

by Frederick Copleston, S.J.

IMAGE BOOKS
A Division of Doubleday & Company, Inc.
Garden City, New York

Image Books Edition 1963
by special arrangement with The Newman Press
Image Books Edition published February, 1963

DE LICENTIA SUPERIORUM ORDINIS:
E. Helsham, S.J.
Praep. Prov. Angliae
NIHIL OBSTAT:
J. L. Russell, S.J.
Censor Deputatus
IMPRIMATUR:
✠ Joseph, Archiepiscopus Birmingamiensis
Birmingamiae die 4 Januarii 1952

Printed in the United States of America
Cover by Ronald Clyne

CONTENTS

Part Two
THE PHILOSOPHY OF THE RENAISSANCE

APPENDICES

Part Two

THE PHILOSOPHY OF THE RENAISSANCE

Chapter Thirteen

THE REVIVAL OF PLATONISM

The Italian Renaissance – The northern Renaissance – The revival of Platonism.

1. The first phase of the Renaissance was the humanistic phase which began in Italy and spread to northern Europe. But it would be absurd to speak as if the Renaissance was a historical period with such clearly-defined temporal limits that one could give the exact dates of its beginning and end. In so far as the Renaissance means or involved a rebirth of literature and a devotion to classical learning and style it may be said to have begun as early as the twelfth century, the century in which John of Salisbury, for example, had declaimed against barbarity in Latin style, the century which saw the humanism of the School of Chartres. It is true that the great theologians and philosophers of the thirteenth century were more concerned with *what* was said and with exactitude of statement than with literary style and grace of expression; but it should not be forgotten that a St. Thomas Aquinas could write hymns which are remarkable for their beauty and that in the same period in which Duns Scotus was composing his somewhat bold and unstylistic commentaries Dante was creating one of the greatest achievements of the Italian language. Dante (1265–1321) certainly wrote from the standpoint of a mediaeval; but in the same century in which Dante died, the fourteenth century, we find Petrarch (1304–74) not only setting himself against the cult of Aristotelian dialectic and promoting the revival of the classical, especially the Ciceronian, style but also favouring through his

vernacular sonnets the growth of the spirit of humanistic individualism. Boccaccio (1313–75) also belonged to the fourteenth century; and at the end of the century, in 1396, Manuel Chrysoloras (d. 1415), the first real teacher of classical Greek in the West, began lecturing at Florence.

The political conditions in Italy favoured the growth of the humanistic Renaissance, inasmuch as princely, ducal and ecclesiastical patrons were able to spend large sums of money on the purchase and copying of manuscripts and on the foundation of libraries; and by the time the Renaissance made itself felt in northern Europe the greater part of the Greek and Latin classics had been recovered and made known. But the Italian Renaissance was by no means confined to the recovery and dissemination of texts. A most important feature was the rise of a new style and ideal of education, represented by teachers like Vittorino da Feltre (1378–1446) and Guarino of Verona (1370–1460). The humanistic educational ideal at its best was that of developing the human personality to the full. Ancient literature was regarded as the chief means of education; but moral training, development of character, physical development and awakening of the aesthetic sensibility were not neglected; nor was the ideal of liberal education regarded as in any way incompatible with the acceptance and practice of Christianity.[1] This, however, was the humanistic ideal at its best. In practice the Italian Renaissance became associated to a certain extent with a growth of moral or amoral individualism and with the pursuit of fame; while in the later stages of the Renaissance the cult of classical literature degenerated into 'Ciceronianism', which meant the substitution of the tyranny of Cicero for that of Aristotle. The exchange was scarcely a change for the better. Moreover, while a man like Vittorino da Feltre was a convinced and devout Christian, many figures of the Renaissance were influenced by a spirit of scepticism. While it would be ridiculous to belittle the achievements of the Italian Renaissance at its best, other aspects were symptomatic of the disintegration rather than of the enrichment of the preceding cultural phase. And the degenerate phase of 'Ciceronianism' was no improvement on the broader outlook fostered by a theological and philosophical education.

2. In the Italian Renaissance the ideas of self-develop-

ment and self-culture were marked features: it was, in large part, an individualistic movement, in the sense that the ideal of social and moral reform was not conspicuous: indeed, some of the humanists were 'pagan' in outlook. The ideal of reform, when it came, did not spring from the Renaissance as such, which was predominantly cultural, aesthetic and literary in character. In northern Europe, however, the literary Renaissance was allied with efforts to achieve moral and social reformation, and there was a greater emphasis on popular education. The northern Renaissance lacked much of the splendour of the Italian Renaissance and it was less 'aristocratic' in character; but it was more obviously allied with religious and moral purposes and, arising at a later date than the Italian movement, it tended to merge with the Reformation, at least if 'Reformation' is understood in a very broad sense and not merely in the sectarian sense. But though both movements had their peculiar strong points, both tended to lose their original inspiration in the course of time, the Italian movement degenerating into 'Ciceronianism', the northern movement tending to pedantry and 'grammaticism', divorced from a living appreciation of the humanistic aspects of classical literature and culture.

Among the scholars associated with the Renaissance in northern Europe one may mention Rudolf Agricola (1443–85), Hegius (1420–95), who was for a time headmaster of a school at Deventer founded in the fourteenth century by the Brethren of the Common Life, and Jacob Wimpfeling (1450–1528), who made of the university of Heidelberg a centre of humanism in western Germany. But the greatest figure of the northern Renaissance was Erasmus (1467–1536), who promoted the study of Greek and Latin literature, including the Scriptures and the writings of the Fathers, and gave a great impetus to the development of humanistic education. In Great Britain there were ecclesiastics like William of Waynflete (*c.* 1395–1486), St. John Fisher (1459–1535), who brought Erasmus to Cambridge, John Colet (*c.* 1467–1519), who founded St. Paul's School in 1512, and Thomas Linacre (*c.* 1460–1524); and laymen like St. Thomas More (1478–1535). Winchester College was founded in 1382 and Eton in 1440.

The Reformers stressed the need of education; but they

were led by religious motives rather than by devotion to the humanistic ideal as such. John Calvin (1509–64), who had studied the humanities in France, drew up an educational curriculum for the schools of Geneva and, since he was religious autocrat of the city, he was able to enforce a system of education on Calvinistic lines. But the most humanistically-minded of the famous continental reformers was Philip Melanchthon (1497–1560), the foremost disciple of Martin Luther (1483–1546). In 1518 Melanchthon became professor of Greek at the university of Wittenberg. The humanism of the Reformers, which was hindered rather than promoted by the religious tenets of strict Protestantism, was not, however, their own discovery; it was derived from the impetus of the Italian Renaissance. And in the Counter-Reformation the humanistic ideal was prominent in the educational system developed by the Society of Jesus, which was founded in 1540 and produced the *Ratio Studiorum* in a definite form in 1599.

3. Through the interest and enthusiasm which it aroused for the literature of Greece and Rome the humanistic phase of the Renaissance not unnaturally inspired a revival of ancient philosophy in its various forms. Of these revived philosophies one of the most influential was Platonism or, to speak more accurately, neo-Platonism. The most remarkable centre of Platonic studies in Italy was the Platonic Academy of Florence, founded by Cosimo de' Medici under the influence of George Gemistus Plethon (d. 1464) who arrived in Italy from Byzantium in 1438. Plethon was an enthusiastic adherent of the Platonic or neo-Platonic tradition, and he composed in Greek a work on the difference between the Platonic and Aristotelian philosophies. His main work, of which only parts have survived, was his νόμων συγγραφή. A kindred spirit was John Argyropoulos (d. 1486), who occupied the chair of Greek at Florence from 1456 until 1471, when he left for Rome, where he numbered Reuchlin among his pupils. One must also mention John Bessarion of Trebizond (1395–1472), who was sent from Byzantium together with Plethon to take part in the Council of Florence (1438–45), at which he laboured to achieve the reunion of the Eastern Church with Rome. Bessarion, who became a cardinal, composed among other works an *Adversus calumnia-*

torem Platonis, in which he defended Plethon and Platonism against the Aristotelian George of Trebizond, who had written a *Comparatio Aristotelis et Platonis* in answer to Plethon.

It must not be thought that these Platonists were all determined haters of Scholasticism. John Argyropoulos translated into Greek St. Thomas Aquinas's *De ente et essentia*, and Bessarion too had a great respect for the Angelic Doctor. For these Platonists it was not so much a question of setting one philosopher against another, Plato against Aristotle, as of renewing a Platonic, or rather neo-Platonic, view of reality which would unite in itself the valuable elements of pagan antiquity and yet at the same time be Christian. It was the religious side of neo-Platonism, as well as its philosophy of beauty and harmony, which particularly appealed to the Platonists and what they particularly disliked in Aristotelianism was the tendency to naturalism which they detected therein. Plethon looked to the renewal of the Platonic tradition for a renewal of life or a reform in Church and State; and if his enthusiasm for Platonism led him into an attack on Aristotle which even Bessarion considered to be somewhat immoderate, it was what he regarded as the spirit of Platonism and its potentialities for spiritual, moral and cultural renewal which inspired him, rather than a purely academic interest in, for example, the Platonic affirmation and the Aristotelian denial of the theory of Ideas. The Platonists considered that the world of the humanistic Renaissance would greatly benefit in practice by absorbing such a doctrine as that of Man as the microcosm and as the ontological bond between the spiritual and the material.

One of the most eminent scholars of the neo-Platonic movement was Marsilius Ficinus (1433–99). As a young man he composed two works, the *De laudibus philosophiae* and the *Institutiones platonicae* and these were followed in 1457 by the *De amore divino* and the *Liber de voluptate*. But in 1458 his father sent him to Bologna, to study medicine. Cosimo de' Medici, however, recalled him to Florence and had him taught Greek. In 1462 Marsilius translated the Orphic Hymns and in the following years he translated, at Cosimo's request, the Dialogues and Epistles of Plato and works by Hermes Trismegistus, Iamblichus (*De Secta Pythagorica*), Theo of Smyrna (*Mathematica*) and others. In 1469 appeared the first edition of his commentary on Plato's *Symposium* and commentaries on the *Philebus*, the *Parmenides* and the *Timaeus*. In 1474 he published his *De religione christiana* and his most important philosophical work, the *Theologia platonica*. In the following year appeared the commentary on the *Phaedrus* and the second edition of the commentary on the *Symposium*. The translations of and commentaries on the *Enneads* of Plotinus were published in 1485 and 1486; and in 1489 the *De triplici vita*, Marsilius' last work. Marsilius was an indefatigable worker, and in his translations he aimed above all at literal fidelity to the original: even though he sometimes made mistakes in his translation, there can be no doubt of the benefit he conferred on the men of his age.[2]

Marsilius Ficinus became a priest when he was forty years old, and he dreamed of drawing atheists and sceptics to Christ by means of the Platonic philosophy. In his commentary on the *Phaedrus* he declares that the love spoken of by Plato and that spoken of by St. Paul are one and the same, namely the love of the absolute Beauty, which is God. God is both absolute Beauty and the absolute Good; and on this theme Plato and Dionysius the Areopagite (the Pseudo-Dionysius) are in accord. Again, when Plato insisted that we are 'reminded of' eternal objects, the Ideas, by the sight of their temporal and material imitations, was he not saying the same as St. Paul when the latter declares that the invisible things of God are understood by means of creatures? In the *Theologia platonica* the universe is depicted according to the neo-Platonic spirit as a harmonious and beautiful system, consisting of degrees of being which extend from corporeal things up to God, the absolute Unity or One. The place of man as the bond between the spiritual and the material is emphasized; and, though Marsilius thought of Aristotelianism as springing from the same philosophical tradition and inspiration as Platonism, he insisted, both as Christian and as Platonist, on the immortality and divine vocation of the human soul. He naturally adopted leading ideas from St. Augustine, developing the Platonic theory of Ideas (or better, Forms) in an Augustinian sense and insisting on Illumination. We learn nothing save in and through God, who is the light of the soul.

A strongly-marked syncretistic element appears in Marsilius' philosophy, as in that of other Platonists like Plethon. It is not only Plato, Plotinus, Iamblichus and Proclus whose thought is synthesized with that of St. John, St. Paul and St. Augustine, but also Hermes Trismegistus[3] and other pagan figures make their appearance as bearers of the spiritual movement which sprang from an original primitive revelation of the beauty and harmoniously ordered and graded system of reality. Marsilius Ficinus, like other Christian Platonists of the Italian Renaissance, was not only personally captivated by Platonism (in a very wide sense), but he also thought that those minds which had become alienated from Christianity could be brought back to it by being led to view Platonism as a stage in divine revelation. In other words, there was no need to choose between the beauty of classical thought on the one hand and Christianity on the other; one could enjoy both. One could not, however, enjoy the Platonic-Christian heritage if one fell a victim to Aristotelianism as interpreted by those who set Aristotle against Plato, understood him in a naturalistic sense and denied the immortality of the human soul.

The best-known member of the circle which was influenced by Marsilius Ficinus was probably John Pico della Mirandola (1463–94). John possessed a knowledge of both Greek and Hebrew, and when twenty-four years old he planned to defend at Rome 900 theses against all comers, his object being to show how Hellenism and Judaism (in the form of the Cabbala) can be synthesized in a Platonic-Christian system. The disputation was, however, forbidden by the ecclesiastical authorities. John's tendency to syncretism showed itself also in the composition of an (unfinished) work, *De concordia Platonis et Aristotelis*.

John Pico della Mirandola was strongly influenced by the 'negative theology' of neo-Platonism and the Pseudo-Dionysius. God is the One; but He is above being rather than being.[4] He is indeed all things, in the sense that He comprises in Himself all perfections; but He comprises these perfections in His undivided unity in an ineffable manner which exceeds our understanding.[5] As far as we are concerned, God is in darkness; we approach Him philosophically by denying the limitations of creaturely perfections. Life is one perfection; wisdom is another perfection. Think away the particularity and limitations of these and all other perfections and 'that which remains is God'. This is not to be understood pantheistically, of course; God is the One, transcending the world which He has created.

The world is a harmonious system, consisting of beings belonging to different levels of reality; and John Pico della Mirandola speaks of God as having desired to create someone to contemplate the nature of the world, to love its beauty and to admire its greatness. 'Therefore, all things having been already completed (as Moses and Timaeus testify), He took thought finally to produce man.'[6] But God did not assign to man a fixed and peculiar place in the universe or laws which he was unable to contravene. 'I placed thee in the middle of the world, that thence thou mightest see more easily all that is in the world. We made thee neither a heavenly being nor an earthly being, neither mortal nor immortal, in order that thou, as the free and sovereign artificer of thyself, mightest mould and sculpture thyself in the form which thou shouldest prefer. Thou wilt be able to degenerate to (the level of) the lower things, the brutes; thou wilt be able, according to thy will, to be reborn into (the level of) the higher things, the divine.'[7] Man is the microcosm; but he has the gift of freedom, which enables him to descend or to ascend. John was, therefore, hostile to the determinism of the astrologers, against whom he wrote his *In astrologiam libri XII*. His view of man, moreover, is a Christian view. There are three 'worlds' within the world or universe; the infralunar world, 'which brutes and men inhabit'; the celestial world, 'in which the planets shine'; and the super-celestial world, 'the abode of the angels'. But Christ, through the Passion, has opened to man the way into the super-celestial world, the way even to God Himself.[8] Man is the head and synthesis of the lower creation, and Christ is the head of the human race.[9] He is also, as divine Word, the 'beginning in which God made heaven and earth'.[10]

In his work against the astrologers John Pico della Mirandola opposed the magical conception of nature. In so far as astrology involved a belief in the harmonious system of nature and in the interrelatedness of all events, it was, whether true or false, a rational system. But it was not rationally grounded, and it involved, moreover, the belief that every earthly event was determined by the heavenly bodies and the belief that he who possessed a knowledge of certain symbols could by the right use of those symbols influence things. It was against the deterministic view of human actions and against the belief in magic that John set himself. Events are causally governed; but the causes are to be looked for in the natures and forms of the various things in the world, not in the stars, and a magical knowledge and use of symbol is ignorant superstition.

Finally one may mention that John's enthusiasm for Plato and his fondness for citing not only Greek and Islamic authors but also Oriental figures did not mean that he was without any appreciation of Aristotle. As already mentioned, he wrote a work on the agreement of Plato and Aristotle, and in the *Procemium* to the *De ente et uno* he asserts his belief in this agreement. In the fourth chapter of this work he remarks, for instance, that those who think that Aristotle did not realize, as Plato did, that being is subordinate to the One and does not include God 'have not read Aristotle', who expressed this truth 'much more clearly than Plato'. Whether John interpreted Aristotle correctly is, of course, another question; but he was certainly no fanatical anti-Aristotelian. As to the Scholastics, he cites them and he speaks of St. Thomas as 'the splendour of our theology'.[11] John was far too much of a syncretist to be exclusive.

In the last years of his life John Pico della Mirandola was influenced by Savonarola (1452–98), who also influenced the former's nephew, John Francis Pico della Mirandola (1469–1533). In his *De praenotionibus* John Francis discussed the criteria of divine revelation, finding the chief criterion in an 'inner light'. In regard to philosophy as such he did not follow his uncle's example of attempting to reconcile Aristotle and Plato: on the contrary, he sharply attacked the Aristotelian theory of knowledge in his *Examen vanitatis doctrinae gentium et veritatis Christianae disciplinae*. He argued that the Aristotelian bases his philosophy on sense-experience, which is supposed to be the source even of those most general principles which are employed in the process of proof. But sense-experience informs one about the conditions of the percipient subject rather than about objects themselves, and the

Aristotelian can never proceed from his empiricist basis to a knowledge of substances or essences.

Among other Platonists one may mention Leo Hebraeus (*c.* 1460–*c.* 1530), a Portuguese Jew who came to Italy and wrote *Dialoghi d'amore* on the intellectual love of God whereby one apprehends beauty as the reflection of absolute Beauty. His views on love in general gave an impetus to the Renaissance literature on this subject, while his idea of the love of God in particular was not without influence on Spinoza. John Reuchlin (1455–1522) may also be mentioned here. This learned German, who not only was a master of the Latin and Greek languages but also introduced into Germany and promoted the study of Hebrew, studied in France and Italy, where, at Rome, he came under the influence of John Pico della Mirandola. In 1520 he became professor of Hebrew and Greek at Ingolstadt; but in 1521 he moved to Tübingen. Looking on the function of philosophy as the winning of happiness in this life and the next, he had little use for the Aristotelian logic and philosophy of nature. Strongly attracted by the Jewish Cabbala, he considered that a profound knowledge of the divine mysteries is to be obtained from that source; and he combined his enthusiasm for the Cabbala with an enthusiasm for neo-Pythagorean number-mysticism. In his view Pythagoras had drawn his wisdom from Jewish sources. In other words, Reuchlin, though an eminent scholar, fell a victim to the attractions of the Cabbala and of the fantasies of number-mysticism; and in this respect he is more akin to the German theosophists and occultists of the Renaissance than to the Italian Platonists. However, he was certainly influenced by the Platonic circle at Florence and by John Pico della Mirandola, who also thought highly of Pythagoreanism, and on this account he can be mentioned in relation with Italian Platonism.

It is clear that the revived Platonism of Italy might just as well, or better, be called neo-Platonism. But the inspiration of Italian Platonism was not primarily an interest in scholarship, in distinguishing, for example, the doctrines of Plato from those of Plotinus and in critically reconstituting and interpreting their ideas. The Platonic tradition stimulated and provided a framework for the expression of the Renaissance Platonists' belief in the fullest possible development of man's higher potentialities and in their belief in Nature as the expression of the divine. But though they had a strong belief in the value and possibilities of the human personality as such they did not separate man either from God or from his fellow-men. Their humanism involved neither irreligion nor exaggerated individualism. And though they had a strong feeling for Nature and for beauty, they did not deify Nature or identify it with God. They were not pantheists. Their humanism and their feeling for Nature were characteristic of the Renaissance; but for a pantheistic view of Nature we have to turn to other phases of Renaissance thought and not to the Florentine Academy nor, in general, to Italian Platonism. Nor do we find in the Italian Platonists an individualism which discards the ideas of Christian revelation and of the Church.

Chapter Fourteen

ARISTOTELIANISM

Critics of the Aristotelian logic – Aristotelianism – Stoicism and scepticism.

1. The Scholastic method and the Aristotelian logic were made objects of attack by a number of humanists. Thus Laurentius Valla or Lorenzo della Valle (1407–57) attacked the Aristotelian logic as an abstruse, artificial and abstract scheme which is able neither to express nor to lead to concrete and real knowledge. In his *Dialecticae disputationes contra Aristotelicos* he carried on a polemic against what he regarded as the empty abstractions of the Aristotelian-Scholastic logic and metaphysic. The Aristotelian logic, in Valla's opinion, is sophistry, depending largely on linguistic barbarism. The purpose of thought is to know things, and knowledge of things is expressed in speech, the function of words being to express in determinate form insight into the determinations of things. Many of the terms employed in the Aristotelian logic, however, do not express insight into the concrete characteristics of things, but are artificial constructions which do not express reality at all. A reform of speech is needed, and logic must be recognized as subordinate to 'rhetoric'. The orators treat all subjects much more clearly and in a profounder and sublimer manner than the confused, bloodless and dry dialecticians.[1] Rhetoric is not for Laurentius Valla simply the art of expressing ideas in beautiful or appropriate language; still less is it the art of persuading others 'rhetorically'; it denotes the linguistic expression of real insight into concrete reality.

Paying more attention to the Stoics and Epicureans than to Plato and Aristotle, Laurentius Valla maintained in his *De voluptate* that the Epicureans were right in emphasizing human striving after pleasure and happiness. But as a Christian he added that the complete happiness of man is not to be found in this life. Faith is necessary for life. For instance, man is conscious of freedom; but human freedom, according to Valla in his *De libero arbitrio*, is, as far as the natural light of reason can see, incompatible with the divine omnipotence. Their reconciliation is a mystery which must be accepted on faith.

Laurentius Valla's ideas on logic were taken up by Rudolf Agricola (1443–85) in his *De inventione dialectica;* and a somewhat similar view was maintained by the Spanish humanist Luis Vives (1492–1540). But Vives also deserves mention for his rejection of any slavish adherence to the scientific, medical or mathematical ideas of Aristotle and for his insistence that progress in science depends on direct observation of phenomena. In his *De anima et vita* he demanded recognition of the value of observation in psychology: one should not be content with what the ancients said about the soul. He himself treated in an independent way of memory, affections, etc., and stated, for example, the principle of association.

The importance of 'rhetoric' as a general science was strongly emphasized by Marius Nizolius (1488–1566 or 1498–1576), the author of a famous *Thesaurus Ciceronianus*. In philosophical writings like the *Antibarbarus philosophicus sive de veris principiis et vera ratione philosophandi contra pseudophilosophos* he rejected all undue deference to former philosophers in favour of independence of judgment. Philosophy in the narrow sense is concerned with the characteristics of things and comprises physics and politics, while rhetoric is a general science which is concerned with the meaning and right use of words. Rhetoric thus stands to other sciences as soul to body; it is their principle. It does not mean for Nizolius the theory and art of public speaking; it is the general science of 'meaning', and it is independent of all metaphysics and ontology. Rhetoric shows, for instance, how the meaning of general words, of universal terms, is independent of, or does not demand, the objective existence of universals. The universal term expresses a mental operation by which the human mind 'comprehends' all individual members of a class. There is no abstraction, in the sense of a mental operation whereby the mind apprehends the metaphysical essence of things in the universal concept; rather does the mind express in a universal term its experience of individuals of the same class. In the deductive syllogism the mind does not reason from the general or universal to the particular but rather from the whole to the part; and in induction the mind passes from the parts to the whole rather than from particulars to the universal. In 1670 Leibniz republished Nizolius' *De veris principiis et vera ratione philosophandi contra pseudophilosophos*, praising the author's attempt to free the general forms of thought from ontological presuppositions but criticizing his inadequate notion of induction. Even if, however, Nizolius did attempt to purify logic from metaphysics and to treat it from the linguistic point of view, it seems to me that his substitution of *comprehensio* for *abstractio* and of the relation of part to whole for the relation of particular to universal contributed very little, if anything, to the discussion concerning universals. That it is individuals alone which exist would have been agreed to by all mediaeval anti-realists; but it is not enlightening to say that universals are collective terms which arise by a mental act called *comprehensio*. What is it which enables the mind to 'comprehend' groups of individuals as belonging to definite classes? Is it simply the presence of similar qualities? If this is what Nizolius meant, he cannot be said to have added anything which was not already present in terminism. But he did insist that for factual knowledge we have to go to things themselves and that it is useless to look to formal logic for information about the nature or character of things. In this way his logical views contributed to the growth of the empiricist movement.

The artificial character of the Aristotelian-Scholastic logic was also insisted on by the famous French humanist Petrus Ramus or Pierre de la Ramée (1515–72), who became a Calvinist and perished in the massacre of St. Bartholomew's Eve. True logic is a natural logic; it formulates the laws which govern man's spontaneous and natural thinking and reasoning as expressed in correct speech. It is thus the *ars disserendi* and is closely allied with rhetoric. In his *Institutionum dialecticarum libri III* Petrus Ramus divided this natural logic into two parts, the first concerning 'discovery' (*De inventione*), the second dealing with the judgment (*De iudicio*). As the function of natural logic is to enable one to answer questions concerning things, the first stage of the process of logical thought consists in discovering the points of view or categories which will enable the inquiring mind to solve the question raised. These points of view or categories (Ramus calls them *loci*) include original or underived categories like cause and effect and derived or secondary categories like genus, species, division, definition, etc. The second stage consists in applying these categories in such a way that the mind can arrive at the judgment which answers the question raised. In his treatment of the judgment Petrus Ramus distinguishes three stages: first, the syllogism; secondly, the system, the forming, that is to say, of a systematic chain of conclusions; and thirdly, the bringing of all sciences and knowledge into relation with God. Ramus' logic consisted, therefore, of two main sections, one concerning the concept, the other concerning the judgment; he had little new to offer and as his ideal was that of deductive reasoning, he was unable to make any very positive contribution to the advance of the logic of discovery. His lack of real originality did not, however, prevent his logical writings winning widespread popularity, especially in Germany, where Ramists, anti-Ramists and semi-Ramists carried on a lively controversy.

Men like Laurentius Valla, Nizolius, and Petrus Ramus were strongly influenced by their reading of the classics, especially of Cicero's writings. In comparison with Cicero's orations the logical works of Aristotle and the Scholastics seemed to them dry, abstruse and artificial. In the speeches of Cicero, on the other hand, the natural logic of the human mind was expressed in relation to concrete questions. They stressed, therefore, 'natural' logic and its close association with rhetoric or speech. They certainly contrasted the Platonic dialectic with the Aristotelian logic; but in the formation of their ideas on logic, which should be regarded as expressing a humanistic reaction against Scholasticism, Cicero was actually of greater importance than Plato. Their emphasis on rhetoric, however, coupled with the fact that they retained in practice a good deal of the outlook of the formal logician, meant that they did little to develop the method or logic of science. It is true that one of their watchwords was 'things' rather than abstract concepts; and in this respect they may be said to have encouraged the empiricist outlook; but, in general, their attitude was aesthetic rather than scientific. They were humanists, and their projected reform of logic was conceived in the interests of humanism, that is, of cultured expression and, at a deeper level, of the development of personality, rather than in the interests of empirical science.

2. Turning from the opponents of the Aristotelian-Scholastic logic to the Aristotelians themselves, one may mention first one or two scholars who promoted the study of the writings of Aristotle and opposed the Italian Platonists. George of Trebizond (1395–1484), for instance, translated and commented on a number of Aristotle's works and he attacked Plethon as the would-be founder of a new neo-Platonic pagan religion. Theodore of Gaza (1400–78), who, like George of Trebizond, became a convert to Catholicism, was also an opponent of Plethon. He translated works of Aristotle and Theophrastus; and in his ὅτι ἡ φύσις οὐ βουλεύεται he discussed the question whether the finality which exists according to Aristotle in nature is really to be ascribed to nature. Hermolaus Barbarus (1454–93) also translated works by Aristotle and commentaries by Themistius. Aristotelian scholars of this sort were for the most part opponents of Scholasticism as well as of Platonism. In the opinion of Hermolaus Barbarus, for example, St. Albert, St. Thomas and Averroes were all philosophical 'barbarians'.

The Aristotelian camp became divided between those who interpreted Aristotle according to the mind of Averroes and those who interpreted him according to the mind of Alexander of Aphrodisias. The difference between them which most excited the attention of their contemporaries was that the Averroists maintained that there is only one immortal intellect in all men while the Alexandrists contended there is no immortal intellect in man. As both parties thus denied personal immortality they excited the hostility of the Platonists. Marsilius Ficinus, for example, declared that both parties did away with religion by denying immortality and divine providence. At the fifth Lateran Council (1512–17) the doctrines of both Averroists and Alexandrists concerning man's rational soul were condemned. In the course of time, however, the former greatly modified the theologically objectionable aspects of Averroism, which tended to become a matter of scholarship rather than of any strict adherence to Averroes's peculiar philosophical ideas.

The centre of the Averroist party was at Padua. Nicoletto Vernias, who lectured at Padua from 1471 to 1499, at first maintained the Averroistic doctrine of one immortal reason in all men; but later on he abandoned his theologically unorthodox view and defended the position that each man has an individual immortal rational soul. The same is true of Agostino Nipho or Augustinus Niphus (1473–1546), a pupil of Vernias and author of commentaries on Aristotle, who first defended the Averroistic doctrine in his *De intellectu et daemonibus* and then later abandoned it. In his *De immortalitate animae*, written in 1518 against Pomponazzi, he maintained the truth of the Thomist interpretation of Aristotle's doctrine against the interpretation given by Alexander of Aphrodisias. One may also mention Alexander Achillini (1463–1512), who taught first at Padua and afterwards at Bologna, and Marcus Antonius Zimara (1460–1532). Achillini declared that Aristotle must be corrected where he differs from the orthodox teaching of the Church, while Zimara, who commented on both Aristotle and Averroes, interpreted the latter's doctrine concerning the human intellect as referring to the unity of the most general principles of knowledge which are recognized by all men in common.

The most important figure of the Alexandrist group was Pietro Pomponazzi (1462–1525), a native of Mantua, who taught successively at Padua, Ferrara and Bologna. But if one wishes to represent Pomponazzi as a follower of Alexander of Aphrodisias, one must add that it was the Aristotelian elements of Alexander's teaching which exercised a distinctive influence on him, rather than Alexander's own developments of Aristotle's doctrine. The aim Pomponazzi seems to have had in mind was to purify Aristotle of non-Aristotelian accretions. That is why he attacked Averroism, which he regarded as a perversion of genuine Aristotelianism. Thus in his *De immortalitate animae* (1516) he takes his stand on the Aristotelian idea of the soul as the form or entelechy of the body and uses it not only against the Averroists but also against those who, like the Thomists, try to show that the human soul is naturally separable from the body and immortal. His main point is that the human soul, in its rational as in its sensitive operations, depends on the body; and in support of his argument and of the conclusion he draws from it he appeals, in accordance with Aristotle's practice, to the observable facts. This is not to say, of course, that Aristotle drew the same conclusion from the observable facts that Pomponazzi drew; but the latter followed Aristotle in appealing to empirical evidence. It was largely because of its incompatibility with the observable facts that he rejected the Averroistic hypothesis concerning the rational soul of man.

Pomponazzi argued that it is an empirically supported fact that all knowledge originates in sense-perception and that human intellection always needs an image or phantasm. In other words, even those intellectual operations which transcend the power of animals are nevertheless dependent on the body; and there is no evidence to show that while the sensitive soul of the animal is intrinsically dependent on the body man's rational soul is only extrinsically dependent. It is perfectly true that the human soul can exercise functions which the animal soul is incapable of exercising; but there is no empirical evidence to show that those higher functions of the human soul can be exercised apart from the body. The human mind, for instance, is certainly characterized by the power of self-consciousness; but it does not possess this power in the way that an independent intelligent substance would possess it, namely as a power of direct and immediate intuition of itself; the human mind knows itself only in knowing something other than itself.[2] Even the beasts enjoy some self-knowledge. 'Nor must we deny that the beasts know themselves. For it seems to be altogether stupid and irrational to say that they do not know themselves, when they love themselves and their species.'[3] Human self-consciousness transcends the rudimentary self-consciousness of the brutes; but it is none the less dependent on the soul's union with the body. Pomponazzi did not deny that intellection is itself non-quantitative and non-corporeal; on the contrary, he affirmed it;[4] but he argued that the human soul's 'participation in immateriality' does not involve its separability from the body. His main objection against the Thomists was that they in his view asserted both that the soul is and that it is not the form of the body. He considered that they did not take seriously the Aristotelian doctrine which they professed to accept; they endeavoured to have it both ways. The Platonists were at least consistent, even if they paid scant attention to the facts of psychology. Pomponazzi's own theory, however, can scarcely be considered immune from inconsistency. While rejecting a materialistic view of the rational soul,[5] he yet refused to allow that one can argue from the immaterial character of the soul's intelligent life to its capacity for existing in a state of separation from the body. Nor is it easy to understand precisely what was meant by phrases like 'participation in immateriality' or *immaterialis secundum quid*. Possibly Pomponazzi's view, if translated into more modern terms, would be that of epiphenomenalism. In any case, his main point was that investigation of the empirical facts does not permit one to state that the human soul possesses any mode of cognition or volition which it can exercise in independence of the body and that its status as form of the body precludes its natural immortality. In order to possess natural immortality its relation to the body would have to be that accepted by the Platonists, and for the truth of the Platonic theory there is no empirical evidence. To this Pomponazzi added some considerations deduced from his acceptance of the notion of a hierarchy of beings. The human rational soul stands midway in the scale; like the lower souls it is the form of the body, though unlike them it transcends matter in its higher operations; like the separate Intelligences it understands essences, though unlike them it can do so only in and with reference to the concrete particular.[6] It depends for its materials of knowledge on the body, though in its use of the material supplied by sense-perception it transcends matter.

The inconsistency of Pomponazzi's doctrine has been mentioned above; and I do not see how this inconsistency can be denied. It must be remembered, however, that he demanded the fulfilment of two conditions before he would recognize the soul's immortality as rationally established.[7] First of all it must be shown that the intelligence as such, in its nature as intelligence, transcends matter. Secondly it must be shown that it is independent of the body in its acquisition of the materials of knowledge. The first position Pomponazzi accepted; the second he regarded as contrary to the empirical facts. The soul's natural immortality cannot, therefore, be proved by mere reason, since, in order for it to be proved, *both* positions would have to be established.

Pomponazzi also gave consideration to the moral objections which were brought against his doctrine, namely that it was destructive of morality by denying sanctions in the future life, by confining the operation of divine justice to the present life, in which it is obviously not always fulfilled, and, most important of all, by depriving man of the possibility of attaining his last end. As regards the first point Pomponazzi argued that virtue is in itself preferable to all other things and that it is its own reward. In dying for his country or in dying rather than commit an act of injustice or sin a man gains virtue. In choosing sin or dishonour in place of death a man does not win immortality, except perhaps an immortality of shame and contempt in the mind of posterity, even if the coming of inevitable death is postponed a little longer.[8] It is true that many people would prefer dishonour or vice to death if they thought that death ended all; but this shows simply that they do not understand the true nature of virtue and vice.[9] Moreover, this is the reason why legislators and rulers have to have recourse to sanctions. In any case, says Pomponazzi, virtue is its own reward, and the essential reward (*praemium essentiale*), which is virtue itself, is diminished in proportion as the accidental reward (*praemium accidentale*, a reward extrinsic to virtue itself) is increased. This is presumably a clumsy way of saying that virtue is diminished in proportion as it is sought with a view to obtaining something other than virtue itself. In regard to the difficulty about divine justice, he asserts that no good action ever goes unrewarded and no vicious action unpunished, since virtue is its own reward and vice its own punishment.[10]

As regards the end of man or purpose of human existence, Pomponazzi insists that it is a moral end. It cannot be theoretical contemplation, which is vouchsafed to few men; nor can it consist in mechanical skill. To be a philosopher or to be a house-builder is not within the power of all;[11] but to become virtuous is within everyone's power. Moral perfection is the common end of the human race; 'for the universe would be completely preserved (*perfectissime conservaretur*) if all men were zealous and perfectly moral, but not if all were philosophers or smiths or house-builders'.[12] This moral end is sufficiently attainable within the bounds of mortal life: the idea of Kant that the attainment of the complete good of man postulates immortality was foreign to the mind of Pomponazzi. And to the argument that man has a natural desire for immortality and that this desire cannot be doomed to frustration, he answers that in so far as there is really a natural desire in man not to die, it is in no way fundamentally different from the animal's instinct to shun death, while if an elicited or intellectual desire is meant, the presence of such a desire cannot be used as an argument for immortality, for it has first to be shown that the desire is not unreasonable. One can conceive a desire for all sorts of divine privileges; but it does not follow that such a desire will be fulfilled.[13]

In his *De naturalium effectuum admirandorum causis sive de incantationibus* (generally known as the *De incantationibus*) Pomponazzi endeavours to give a natural explanation of miracles and wonders. He makes a great deal of astral influences; but his astrological explanations are, of course, naturalistic in character, even if they are erroneous. He also accepted a cyclic theory of history and historical institutions, a theory which he apparently applied even to Christianity itself. But in spite of his philosophical ideas Pomponazzi reckoned himself a true Christian. Philosophy, for example, shows that there is no evidence for the immortality of the human soul; on the contrary, it would lead us to postulate the soul's mortal character; but we know by revelation that the human soul is immortal. As already mentioned, Pomponazzi's doctrine concerning the soul's mortality was condemned at the fifth Lateran Council and he was attacked in writing by Niphus and others; but he was never involved in any more serious trouble.

Simon Porta of Naples (d. 1555), in his *De rerum naturalibus principiis, De anima et mente humana*, followed Pomponazzi's doctrine concerning the mortality of the human soul; but not all the latter's disciples did so. And we have seen that the Averroist school also tended to modify its original position. Finally we find a group of Aristotelians who can be classified neither as Averroists nor as Alexandrists. Thus Andrew Cesalpino (1519–1603) tried to reconcile the two parties. He is perhaps chiefly remarkable for his botanical work; in 1583 he published a *De plantis libri XVI*. Jacobus Zabarella (1532–89), though a devoted Aristotelian, left many important questions undecided. For instance, if one accepts the eternity of motion and of the world, one can accept an eternal first mover; but if one denies the eternity of motion and of the world, one has no adequate philosophical reason for accepting an eternal first mover. In any case it cannot be demonstrated that the heaven itself is not the supreme being. Similarly, if one regards the soul's nature as form of the body, one will judge it to be mortal; but if one regards its intellectual operations, one will see that it transcends matter. On the other hand, the active intellect is God Himself, using the human passive intellect as an instrument; and the question whether the human soul is immortal or not is left undecided as far as philosophy is concerned. Zabarella was succeeded in his chair at Padua by Caesar Cremoninus (1550–1631) who also refused to allow that one can argue with certainty from the movement of the heaven to the existence of God as mover. In other words the idea of Nature as a more or less independent system was gaining ground; and, indeed, Cremoninus insisted on the autonomy of physical science. He based his own scientific ideas, however, on those of Aristotle and rejected the newer ideas in physics, including the Copernican astronomy. He is said to have been the friend of Galileo who refused to look through a telescope in case he should find it necessary to abandon the Aristotelian astronomy.

The influence of Pomponazzi was strongly felt by Lucilius Vanini (1585–1619), who was strangled and burnt as a heretic at Toulouse. He was the author of an *Amphitheatrum aeternae providentiae* (1615) and of a *De admirandis naturae reginae deaeque mortalium arcanis libri quatuor* (1616). He seems to have embraced a kind of pantheism, though he was accused of atheism, which he was said to have dissembled in his first work.

Apart from the work done by scholars in connection with the text of Aristotle, it cannot, I think, be said that the Aristotelians of the Renaissance contributed much that was valuable to philosophy. In the case of Pomponazzi and kindred figures they may be said to have encouraged a 'naturalistic' outlook; but the growth of the new physics can scarcely be attributed to the influence of the Aristotelians. It was made possible very largely by mathematical developments, and it grew in spite of, rather than because of, the Aristotelians.

In northern Europe Philip Melanchthon (1497–1560), although an associate and collaborator of Martin Luther, who was a determined enemy of Scholastic Aristotelianism, distinguished himself as a humanist. Educated in the spirit of the humanistic movement, he then fell under Luther's influence and rejected humanism; but the fact that this narrowness of outlook did not last very long shows that he was always a humanist at heart. He became the leading humanist of the early Protestant movement and was known as the *Praeceptor Germaniae* because of his educational work. For the philosophy of Aristotle he had a lively admiration, though as a thinker he was somewhat eclectic, his ideal being that of moral progress through the study of classical writers and of the Gospels. He had little interest in metaphysics, and his idea of logic, as given in his logical text-books, was influenced by that of Rudolf Agricola. Aristotle he interpreted in a nominalistic sense; and, though he freely utilized Aristotle in his *Commentarius de anima* (in which ideas drawn indirectly from Galen also make their appearance) and in his *Philosophiae moralis epitome* and *Ethicae doctrinae elementa*, he endeavoured to bring Aristotelianism into harmony with revelation and to supplement it by Christian teaching. A salient aspect of Melanchthon's teaching was his doctrine of innate principles, particularly moral principles, and of the innate character of the idea of God, both of which are intuited by means of the *lumen naturale*. This doctrine was opposed to the Aristotelian view of the mind as a *tabula rasa*.

Melanchthon's utilization of Aristotle was influential in the Lutheran universities, though it did not commend itself to all Protestant thinkers, and there occurred some lively disputes, among which may be mentioned the week's debate at Weimar in 1560 between Flacius and Strigel on freedom of the will. Melanchthon maintained the freedom of the will; but Flacius (Illyricus) considered that this doctrine, supported by Strigel, was at variance with the true theory of original sin. In spite of Melanchthon's great influence there was always a certain tension between rigid Protestant theology and the Aristotelian philosophy. Luther himself did not deny all human freedom; but he did not consider that the freedom left to man after the Fall is sufficient to enable him to achieve moral reform. It was only natural, then, that controversy should arise between those who deemed themselves genuine disciples of Luther and those who followed Melanchthon in his Aristotelianism, which was somewhat of a strange bedfellow for orthodox Lutheranism. In addition, of course, there were, as has been mentioned earlier, the disputes between the Ramists, anti-Ramists and semi-Ramists.

3. Among other revivers of ancient philosophical traditions one may mention Justus Lipsius (1547–1606), author of a *Manuductio ad stoicam philosophiam* and a *Physiologia Stoicorum*, who revived Stoicism, and the famous French man of letters, Michel de Montaigne (1533–92), who revived Pyrrhonic scepticism. In his *Essais* Montaigne revived the ancient arguments for scepticism; the relativity of sense-experience, the impossibility of the intellect's rising above this relativity to the sure attainment of absolute truth, the constant change in both object and subject, the relativity of value-judgments, and so on. Man is, in fine, a poor sort of creature whose boasted superiority to the animals is, to a great extent, a vain and hollow pretension. He should, therefore, submit himself to divine revelation, which alone gives certainty. At the same time Montaigne came to attribute considerable importance to the idea of 'nature'. Nature gives to each man a dominant type of character which is fundamentally unchangeable; and the task of moral education is to awaken and preserve the spontaneity and originality of this endowment of nature rather than to attempt to mould it into a stereotyped pattern by the methods of Scholasticism. But Montaigne was no revolutionary; he thought rather that the form of life embodied in the social and political structure of one's country represents a law of nature to which one should submit oneself. The same is true of religion. The theoretical basis of any given religion cannot be rationally established; but the moral consciousness and obedience to

nature form the heart of religion, and these will only be injured by religious anarchy. In this practical conservatism Montaigne was, of course, faithful to the spirit of Pyrrhonic scepticism, which found in the consciousness of one's ignorance an added reason for adhering to traditional social, political and religious forms. A sceptical attitude in regard to metaphysics in general might seem calculated to lead to an emphasis on empirical science; but, as far as Montaigne himself was concerned, his scepticism was rather that of a cultivated man of letters, though he was influenced too by the moral ideal of Socrates and by the Stoic ideals of tranquillity and of obedience to nature.

Among Montaigne's friends was Pierre Charron (1541–1603), who became a lawyer and later a priest. In his *Trois vérités contre tous les athées, idolâtres, juifs, Mohamétans, hérétiques et schismatiques* (1593) he maintained that the existence of one God, the truth of the Christian religion and the truth of Catholicism in particular are three proved truths; but in his main work, *De la sagesse* (1601), he adopted from Montaigne a sceptical position, though he modified it in the second edition. Man is unable to reach certainty concerning metaphysical and theological truths; but human self-knowledge, which reveals to us our ignorance, reveals to us also our possession of a free will by which we can win moral independence and dominion over the passions. The recognition and realization of the moral ideal is true wisdom, and this true wisdom is independent of dogmatic religion. 'I desire that one should be a good man without paradise and hell; these words are, in my view, horrible and abominable, "if I were not a Christian, if I did not fear God and damnation, I should do this or that".'[14]

Another Pyrrhonist was Francis Sanchez (*c.* 1552–1632), a Portuguese by birth, who studied at Bordeaux and in Italy and taught medicine first at Montpellier and afterwards at Toulouse. In his *Quod nihil scitur*, which appeared in 1580, Sanchez maintained that the human being can know nothing, if the word 'know' is understood in its full sense, that is to say, as referring to the perfect ideal of knowledge. God alone, who has created all things, knows all things. Human knowledge is based either on sense-perception or on introspection. The former is not reliable, while the latter, though assuring us of the existence of the self, can give no clear idea of it; our knowledge of the self is indefinite and indeterminate. Introspection gives us no picture of the self, and without a picture or image we can have no clear idea. On the other hand though sense-perception provides us with definite images, these images are far from giving a perfect knowledge of things. Moreover, as the multiplicity of things forms a unified system, no one thing can be perfectly known unless the whole system is known; and this we cannot know.

But though Sanchez denied that the human mind can attain perfect knowledge of anything, he insisted that it can attain an approximate knowledge of some things and that the way to do so is through observation rather than through the Aristotelian-Scholastic logic. The latter makes use of definitions which are purely verbal, and syllogistic demonstration presupposes principles the truth of which is by no means clear. Of the leading sceptics Sanchez probably came nearest to anticipating the direction which philosophy and science were to take; but he was prevented by his sceptical attitude from making positive and constructive suggestions. For example, his strictures on the old deductive logic would lead one to expect a clear emphasis on the empirical investigation of nature; but his sceptical attitude in regard to sense-perception was a hindrance to his making any valuable positive contribution to the development of natural philosophy. The scepticism of these Renaissance thinkers was doubtless a symptom of the period of transition between mediaeval thought and the constructive systems of the 'modern' era; but in itself it was a blind alley.

Chapter Fifteen

NICHOLAS OF CUSA

Life and works – The influence of Nicholas's leading idea on his practical activity – The coincidentia oppositorum *– 'Instructed ignorance' – The relation of God to the world – The 'infinity' of the world – The world-system and the soul of the world – Man, the microcosm; Christ – Nicholas's philosophical affiliations.*

1. Nicholas of Cusa is not an easy figure to classify. His philosophy is frequently included under the heading 'mediaeval philosophy', and there are, of course, some good reasons for doing this. The background of his thought was formed by the doctrines of Catholicism and by the Scholastic tradition, and he was undoubtedly strongly influenced by a number of mediaeval thinkers. It was possible, then, for Maurice De Wulf to say of him, when outlining his ideas in the third volume of his history of mediaeval philosophy, that 'in spite of his audacious theories he is only a continuer of the past',[1] and that he 'remains a mediaeval and a Scholastic'.[2] On the other hand, Nicholas lived in the fifteenth century and for some thirty years his life overlapped that of Marsilius Ficinus. Moreover, although one can emphasize the traditional elements in his philosophy and push him back, as it were, into the Middle Ages, one can equally well emphasize the forward-looking elements of his thought and associate him with the beginnings of 'modern' philosophy. But it seems to me preferable to see in him a transition-thinker, a philosopher of the Renaissance, who combined the old with the new. To treat him simply as a mediaeval thinker seems to me to involve the neglect of those elements in his philosophy which

have clear affinities with the philosophical movements of thought at the time of the Renaissance and those elements which reappear at a later date in the system of a thinker like Leibniz. Yet even if one decides to classify Nicholas of Cusa as a Renaissance philosopher, there still remains the difficulty of deciding to which Renaissance current of thought his philosophy should be assigned. Is he to be associated with the Platonists on the ground that he was influenced by the neo-Platonic tradition? Or does his view of Nature as in some sense 'infinite' suggest rather that he should be associated with a philosopher like Giordano Bruno? There are doubtless grounds for calling him a Platonist, if one understands the term in a sufficiently generous way; but it would be peculiar if one included him in the same chapter as the Italian Platonists. And there are doubtless grounds for calling him a philosopher of Nature; but he was before all things a Christian, and he was no pantheist like Bruno. He in no way deified Nature. And he cannot be classified with the scientists, even if he was interested in mathematics. I have therefore adopted the solution of giving him a chapter to himself. And this is, in my opinion, what he deserves. Though having many affiliations, he stands more or less by himself.

Nicholas Kryfts or Krebs was born at Cusa on the Moselle in 1401. Educated as a boy by the Brothers of the Common Life at Deventer, he subsequently studied at the universities of Heidelberg (1416) and Padua (1417–23) and received the doctorate in Canon Law. Ordained priest in 1426, he took up a post at Coblenz; but in 1432 he was sent to the Council of Basle on the business of the Count von Manderscheid, who wanted to become bishop of Trier. Becoming involved in the deliberations of the Council, Nicholas showed himself a moderate adherent of the conciliar party. Later, however, he changed his attitude to the position of the papacy and fulfilled a number of missions on behalf of the Holy See. For example, he went to Byzantium in connection with the negotiations for the reunion of the Eastern Church with Rome, which was accomplished (temporarily) at the Council of Florence. In 1448 he was created cardinal and in 1450 he was appointed to the bishopric of Brixen, while from 1451 to 1452 he acted as Papal Legate in Germany. He died in the August of 1464 at Todi in Umbria.

In spite of his ecclesiastical activities Nicholas wrote a considerable number of works, of which the first important one was the *De concordantia catholica* (1433–4). His philosophical writings include the *De docta ignorantia* and the *De coniecturis* (1440), the *De Deo abscondito* (1444) and the *De quaerendo Deum* (1445), the *De Genesi* (1447), the *Apologia doctae ignorantiae* (1449), the *Idiotae libri* (1450), the *De visione Dei* (1453), the *De possest* (1460), the *Tetralogus de non aliud* (1462), the *De venatione sapientiae* (1463) and the *De apice theoriae* (1464). In addition he composed works on mathematical subjects, like the *De transmutationibus geometricis* (1450), the *De mathematicis complementis* (1453) and the *De mathematica perfectione* (1458), and on theological subjects.

2. The thought of Nicholas of Cusa was governed by the idea of unity as the harmonious synthesis of differences. On the metaphysical plane this idea is presented in his idea of God as the *coincidentia oppositorum*, the synthesis of opposites, which transcends and yet includes the distinct perfections of creatures. But the idea of unity as the harmonious reconciliation or synthesis of opposites was not confined to the field of speculative philosophy: it exercised a powerful influence on Nicholas's practical activity, and it goes a long way towards explaining his change of front in regard to the position in the Church of the Holy See. I think that it is worth while to show how this is the case.

At the time when Nicholas went to the Council of Basle and published his *De concordantia catholica* he saw the unity of Christendom threatened, and he was inspired by the ideal of preserving that unity. In common with a number of other sincere Catholics he believed that the best way of preserving or restoring that unity lay in emphasizing the position and rights of General Councils. Like other members of the conciliar party, he was encouraged in this belief by the part played by the Council of Constance (1414–18) in putting an end to the Great Schism which had divided Christendom and caused so much scandal. He was convinced at that time of the natural rights of popular sovereignty not only in the State but also in the Church; and, indeed, despotism and anarchy were always abhorrent to him. In the State the monarch does not receive his authority directly and immediately from God, but rather from or through the people. In the Church, he thought, a General Council, representing the faithful, is superior to the pope, who possesses only an administrative primacy and may for adequate reasons be deposed by a Council. Though he maintained the idea of the empire, his ideal was not that of a monolithic empire which would override or annul the rights and duties of national monarchs and princes: it was rather that of a federation. In an analogous manner, though he was a passionate believer in the unity of the Church, he believed that the cause of this unity would be better served by a moderate conciliar theory than by an insistence on the supreme position of the Holy See. By saying this I do not mean to imply that Nicholas did not at that time believe that the conciliar theory was theoretically justified or that he supported it only for practical reasons, because he considered that the Church's unity would thus be best preserved and that ecclesiastical reform would stand a better chance of being realized if the supremacy of General Councils was recognized. But these practical considerations certainly weighed with him. Moreover, a 'democratic' view of the Church as a harmonious unity in multiplicity, expressed juridically in the conciliar theory, undoubtedly possessed a strong attraction for him. He aimed at unity in the Church and in the State and between Church and State; but the unity at which he aimed, whether in the Church or in the State, or between Church and State, was not a unity resulting from the annulment of differences.

Nicholas came to abandon the conciliar theory and to act as a champion of the Holy See. This change of view was certainly the expression of a change in his theoretical convictions concerning the papacy as a divine institution possessing supreme ecclesiastical authority and jurisdiction. But at the same time he was certainly influenced by the conviction that the cause which he had at heart, namely the unity of the Church, would not in fact be promoted by belittling the position of the pope in the Church. He came to think that an effective implementation of the conciliar theory would be more likely to result in another schism than in unity, and he came to look on the supreme position of the Holy See as the expression of the essential unity of the Church. All the limited authorities in the Church receive their authority from the absolute or sovereign authority, the Holy See, in a manner analogous to the way in which finite, limited beings receive their being from the absolute infinite, God.

This change of view did not involve the acceptance of extravagant theories, like those of Giles of Rome. Nicholas did not envisage, for example, the subordination of State to Church, but rather a harmonious and peaceful relation between the two powers. It was always at reconciliation, harmony, unity in difference that he aimed. In this ideal of unity without suppression of differences he is akin to Leibniz. It is true that Nicholas's attempts to secure harmonious unity were by no means always successful. His attempts to secure harmony in his own diocese were not altogether felicitous; and the reunion of the Eastern Church with Rome, in which he co-operated, was of brief duration. But Leibniz's somewhat unpractical, and sometimes indeed superficial, plans and ideals of unity were also unrealized in practice.

3. God is, for Nicholas, the *coincidentia oppositorum*, the synthesis of opposites in a unique and absolutely infinite being. Finite things are multiple and distinct, possessing their different natures and qualities while God transcends all the distinctions and oppositions which are found in creatures. But God transcends these distinctions and oppositions by uniting them in Himself in an incomprehensible manner. The distinction of essence and existence, for example, which is found in all creatures, cannot be in God as a distinction: in the actual infinite, essence and existence coincide and are one. Again, in creatures we distinguish greatness and smallness, and we speak of them as possessing attributes in different degrees, as being more or less this or that. But in God all these distinctions coincide. If we say that God is the greatest being (*maximum*), we must also say that He is the least being (*minimum*), for God cannot possess size or what we ordinarily call 'greatness'. In Him *maximum* and *minimum* coincide.[3] But we cannot comprehend this synthesis of distinctions and oppositions. If we say that God is the *complicatio oppositorum et eorum coincidentia*,[4] we must realize that we cannot have a positive understanding of what this means. We come to know a finite thing by bringing it into relation to or comparing it with the already known: we

come to know a thing by means of comparison, similarity, dissimilarity and distinction. But God, being infinite, is like to no finite thing; and to apply definite predicates to God is to liken Him to things and to bring Him into a relation of similarity with them. In reality the distinct predicates which we apply to finite things coincide in God in a manner which surpasses our knowledge.

4. It is clear, then, that Nicholas of Cusa laid emphasis on the *via negativa*, the way of negation in our intellectual approach to God. If the process of getting to know or becoming acquainted with a thing involves bringing the hitherto unknown thing into relation with, or comparing it with, the already known, and if God is unlike every creature, it follows that the discursive reason cannot penetrate God's nature. We know of God what He is not rather than what He is. In regard, therefore, to positive knowledge of the divine nature our minds are in a state of 'ignorance'. On the other hand, this 'ignorance' of which Nicholas speaks is not the ignorance of someone who has no knowledge of God or who has never made the effort to understand what God is. It is, of course, the result of human psychology and of the limitations which necessarily affect a finite mind when confronted by an infinite object which is not an empirically given object. But, in order to possess a real value it must be apprehended as the result of these factors, or at any rate as the result of the infinity of God and the finitude of the human mind. The 'ignorance' in question is not the result of a refusal to make an intellectual effort or of religious indifference: it proceeds from the realization of God's infinity and transcendence. It is thus 'learned' or 'instructed ignorance'. Hence the title of Nicholas's most famous work, *De docta ignorantia.*

It may appear inconsistent to stress the 'negative way' and at the same time to affirm positively that God is the *coincidentia oppositorum*. But Nicholas did not reject the 'affirmative way' altogether. For example, since God transcends the sphere of numbers He cannot be called 'one' in the sense in which a finite thing, as distinct from other finite things, is called 'one'. On the other hand, God is the infinite Being and the source of all multiplicity in the created world; and as such He is the infinite unity. But we cannot have a positive understanding of what this unity is in itself. We do make positive affirmations about God, and we are justified in doing so; but there is no positive affirmation about the divine nature which does not need to be qualified by a negation. If we think of God in terms simply of ideas drawn from creatures our notion of Him is less adequate than the realization that He transcends all our concepts of Him: negative theology is superior to positive or affirmative theology. Superior to both, however, is 'copulative' theology by which God is apprehended as the *coincidentia oppositorum*. God is rightly recognized as the supreme and absolutely greatest Being: He cannot be greater than He is. And as the greatest Being He is perfect unity.[5] But we can also say of God that He cannot be smaller than He is. We can say, therefore, that He is the *minimum*. In fact, He is both the greatest and the smallest in a perfect *coincidentia oppositorum*. All theology is 'circular', in the sense that the attributes which we rightly predicate of God coincide in the divine essence in a manner which surpasses the understanding of the human mind.[6]

The lowest stage of human knowledge is sense-perception. The senses by themselves simply affirm. It is when we come to the level of reason (*ratio*) that there is both affirmation and denial. The discursive reason is governed by the principle of contradiction, the principle of the incompatibility or mutual exclusion of opposites; and the activity of the reason cannot bring us to anything more than an approximate knowledge of God. In accordance with his fondness for mathematical analogies Nicholas compares the reason's knowledge of God to a polygon inscribed in a circle. However many sides one adds to the polygon it will not coincide with the circle, even though it may approximate more and more to doing so. What is more, our knowledge of creatures also is only approximate, for their 'truth' is hidden in God. In fine, all knowledge by means of the discursive reason is approximate, and all science is 'conjecture'.[7] This theory of knowledge was developed in the *De coniecturis*; and Nicholas explained that the highest possible natural knowledge of God is attained not by discursive reasoning (*ratio*) but by intellect (*intellectus*), a superior activity of the mind. Whereas sense-perception affirms and reason affirms and denies, intellect denies the oppositions of reason. Reason affirms X and denies Y, but intellect denies X and Y both disjunctively and together; it apprehends God as the *coincidentia oppositorum*. This apprehension or intuition cannot, however, be properly stated in language, which is the instrument of reason rather than of intellect. In its activity as intellect the mind uses language to suggest meaning rather than to state it; and Nicholas employs mathematical analogies and symbols for this purpose. For example, if one side of a triangle is extended to infinity, the other two sides will coincide with it. Again, if the diameter of a circle is extended to infinity the circumference will coincide in the end with the diameter. The infinite straight line is thus at the same time a triangle and a circle. Needless to say, Nicholas regarded these mathematical speculations as no more than symbols; the mathematical infinite and the absolutely infinite being are not the same, though the former can both serve as a symbol for the latter and constitute an aid to thought in metaphysical theology.[8]

The leading ideas of the *De docta ignorantia* were resumed in the writings which compose the *Idiotae*, and in the *De venatione sapientiae* Nicholas reaffirmed his belief in the idea of 'learned' or 'instructed ignorance'. In this work he reaffirmed also the doctrine contained in the *De non aliud*. God cannot be defined by other terms: He is His own definition. Again, God is not other than anything else, for He defines everything else, in the sense that He alone is the source and conserver of the existence of all things.[9] Nicholas also reaffirmed the central idea which he had developed in the *De possest*. 'God alone is *Possest*, because He is in act what He can be.'[10] He is eternal act. This idea he took up again in the *De apice theoriae*, his last work, in which God is represented as *posse ipsum*, the absolute power which reveals itself in creatures. The emphasis laid on this idea has suggested to students of Nicholas's works a change of view on the part of the author. And there is, indeed, a good deal to be said in favour of this interpretation. Nicholas says expressly in *De apice theoriae* that he once thought that the truth about God is found better in darkness or obscurity than in clarity and he adds that the idea of *posse*, of power or being able, is easy to understand. What boy or youth is ignorant of the nature of *posse*, when he knows very well that he can eat, run and speak? And if he were asked whether he could do anything, carry a stone, for example, without the power to do so, he would judge such a question to be entirely superfluous. Now, God is the absolute *posse ipsum*. It would appear, then, that Nicholas felt the need of counterbalancing the negative theology on which he had formerly laid such stress. And we may say perhaps that the idea of *posse*, together with other positive ideas like that of light, of which he made use in his natural theology, expressed his conviction of the divine immanence, while the emphasis on negative theology represented rather his belief in the divine transcendence. But it would be wrong to suggest that Nicholas abandoned the negative for the affirmative way. He makes it quite clear in his last work that the divine *posse ipsum* is in itself incomprehensible and that it is incommensurable with created power. In the *Compendium*,[11] which he wrote a year before the *De apice theoriae*, Nicholas says that the incomprehensible Being, while remaining always the same, shows Himself in a variety of ways, in a variety of 'signs'. It is as though one face appeared in different ways in a number of mirrors. The face is one and the same, but its appearances, which are all distinct from itself, are various. Nicholas may have described the divine nature in various ways, and he may very well have thought that he had overdone the way of negation; but it does not seem that there was any fundamental change in his point of view. God was always for him transcendent, infinite and incomprehensible, even though He was also immanent and even though Nicholas may have come to see the desirability of bringing this aspect of God into greater prominence.

5. In speaking of the relation between God and the world Nicholas used phrases which have suggested to some readers a pantheistic interpretation. God contains all things; He is *omnia complicans*. All things are contained in the divine simplicity, and without Him they are nothing. God is also *omnia explicans*, the source of the multiple things which reveal something of Him. *Deus ergo est omnia complicans, in hoc quod omnia in eo; est omnia explicans, in hoc quia ipse in omnibus.*[12] But Nicholas protested that he was no pantheist. God contains all things in that He is the cause of all things: He contains them *complicative*, as one in His

divine and simple essence. He is in all things *explicative*, in the sense that He is immanent in all things and that all things are essentially dependent on Him. When he states that God is both the centre and the circumference of the world[13] he is to be interpreted neither in a pantheistic nor in an acosmistic sense. The world is not, says Nicholas, a limited sphere with a definite centre and circumference. Any point can be taken and considered as the world's centre, and it has no circumference. God, then, can be called the centre of the world in view of the fact that He is everywhere or omnipresent and the circumference of the world in that He is nowhere, that is, by local presence. Nicholas was certainly influenced by writers like John Scotus Eriugena, and he employed the same type of bold phrases and statements which Meister Eckhart had employed. But in spite of a strong tendency to acosmism, as far as the literal meaning of some of his statements is concerned, it is clear that he insisted strongly on the distinction between the finite creature and the infinite Godhead.

In phrases which recall to mind the doctrine of John Scotus Eriugena Nicholas explains that the world is a theophany; a 'contraction' of the divine being. The universe is the *contractum maximum* which came into existence through emanation from the *absolutum maximum*.[14] Every creature is, as it were, a created God or God created (*quasi Deus creatus*).[15] Nicholas even goes so far as to say that God is the absolute essence of the world or universe, and that the universe is that very essence in a state of 'contraction' (*Est enim Deus quidditas absoluta mundi seu universi. Universum vero est ipsa quidditas contracta*).[16] Similarly, in the *De coniecturis*[17] Nicholas declares that to say that God is in the world is also to say that the world is in God, while in the *De visione Dei*[18] he speaks of God as invisible in Himself but visible *uti creatura est*. Statements of this sort certainly lend themselves to a pantheistic interpretation; but Nicholas makes it clear on occasion that it is a mistake to interpret them in this way. For example, in the *De coniecturis*[19] he asserts that 'man is God, but not absolutely, since he is man. He is therefore a human God (*humanus est igitur Deus*).' He goes on to assert that 'man is also the world' and explains that man is the microcosm or 'a certain human world'. His statements are bold, it is true; but by saying that man is God, though not absolutely, he does not appear to mean more than other writers meant when they called man the image of God. It is clear that Nicholas was deeply convinced of the world's nothingness apart from God and of its relation to God as a mirror of the divine. The world is the *infinitas contracta* and the *contracta unitas*.[20] But this does not mean that the world is God in a literal sense; and in the *Apologia doctae ignorantiae* Nicholas explicitly rejects the charge of pantheism. In the *explicatio Dei* or creation of the world unity is 'contracted' into plurality, infinity into finitude, simplicity into composition, eternity into succession, necessity into possibility.[21] On the plane of creation the divine infinity expresses or reveals itself in the multiplicity of finite things, while the divine eternity expresses or reveals itself in temporal succession. The relation of creatures to the Creator surpasses our understanding; but Nicholas, according to his wont, frequently provides analogies from geometry and arithmetic, which, he believed, made things a bit clearer.

6. But though the world consists of finite things it is in a sense infinite. For example, the world is endless or indeterminate in respect of time. Nicholas agrees with Plato that time is the image of eternity,[22] and he insists that since before creation there was no time we must say that time proceeded from eternity. And if time proceeded from eternity it participates in eternity. 'I do not think that anyone who understands denies that the world is eternal, although it is not eternity.'[23] 'Thus the world is eternal because it comes from eternity and not from time. But the name "eternal" belongs much more to the world than to time since the duration of the world does not depend on time. For if the motion of the heaven and time, which is the measure of motion, were to cease, the world would not cease to exist.'[24] Nicholas thus makes a distinction between time and duration, though he does not develop the theme. Time is the measure of motion, and it is thus the instrument of the measuring mind and depends on the mind.[25] If motion disappeared, there would be no time; but there would still be duration. Successive duration is the copy or image of the absolute duration which is eternity. We can conceive eternity only as endless duration. The duration of the world is thus the image

of the divine eternity and can be called in some sense 'infinite'. This is a curious line of argument, and it is not easy to see precisely what is meant; but presumably Nicholas meant, in part at least, that the world's duration is potentially endless. It is not the absolute eternity of God, but it has not of itself any necessary limits.

The universe is one, unbounded by any other universe. It is, therefore, in some sense spatially 'infinite'. It is without any fixed centre, and there is no point which one could not choose to regard as the world's centre. There is, of course, no absolute 'up' or 'down' either. The earth is neither the centre of the world nor its lowest and least honourable part; nor has the sun any privileged position. Our judgments in these matters are relative. Everything in the universe moves, and so does the earth. 'The earth, which cannot be the centre, cannot be without any motion.'[26] It is smaller than the sun, but it is larger than the moon, as we know from observation of eclipses.[27] Nicholas does not appear to say explicitly that the earth rotates round the sun, but he makes it clear that both the sun and the earth move, together with all the other bodies, though their velocities are not the same. The fact that we do not perceive the earth's motion is no valid argument against its motion. We perceive motion only in relation to fixed points; and if a man in a boat on a river were unable to see the banks and did not know that the water itself was moving he would imagine that the boat was stationary.[28] A man stationed on the earth may think that the earth is stationary and that the other heavenly bodies are in motion, but if he were on the sun or the moon or Mars he would think the same of the body on which he was stationed.[29] Our judgments about motion are relative: we cannot attain 'absolute truth' in these astronomical matters. In order to compare the movements of the heavenly bodies we have to do so in relation to selected fixed points; but there are no fixed points in actuality. We can, therefore, attain only an approximate or relative knowledge in astronomy.

7. The idea of a hierarchy of levels of reality from matter, through organisms, animals and man, up to pure spirits was a leading feature both of Aristotelianism and of the Platonic tradition. But Nicholas, while retaining this idea, laid particular emphasis on the individual thing as a unique mani-

festation of God. In the first place, no two individual things are exactly alike. By saying this Nicholas did not mean to deny the reality of species. The Peripatetics, he says,[30] are right in saying that universals do not actually exist: only individual things exist, and universals as such belong to the conceptual order. None the less members of a species have a common specific nature which exists in each of them in a 'contracted' state, that is to say, as an individual nature.[31] No individual thing, however, realizes fully the perfection of its species; and each member of a species has its own distinct characteristics.[32]

In the second place, each individual thing mirrors the whole universe. Every existent thing 'contracts' all other things, so that the universe exists *contracte* in every finite thing.[33] Moreover, as God is in the universe and the universe in God, and as the universe is in each thing, to say that everything is in each thing is also to say that God is in each thing and each thing in God. In other words, the universe is a 'contraction' of the divine being, and each finite thing is a 'contraction' of the universe.

The world is therefore a harmonious system. It consists of a multiplicity of finite things; but its members are so related to one another and to the whole that there is a 'unity in plurality'.[34] The one universe is the unfolding of the absolute and simple divine unity, and the whole universe is reflected or mirrored in each individual part. According to Nicholas, there is a soul of the world (*anima mundi*); but he rejects the Platonic view of this soul. It is not an actually existent being distinct from God on the one hand and from the finite things in the world on the other hand. If the soul of the world is regarded as a universal form containing in itself all forms, it has no separate existence of its own. The forms exist actually in the divine Word, as identical with the divine Word, and they exist in things *contracte*,[35] that is, as the individual forms of things. Nicholas evidently understood the Platonists as teaching that universal forms exist in a soul of the world, which is distinct from God, and this view he rejected. In the *Idiotae*[36] he says that what Plato called the 'soul of the world' Aristotle called 'nature', and he adds that in his opinion the 'soul of the world' or 'nature' is God, 'who works all things in all things'. It is clear, then, that although Nicholas borrowed from Platonism the phrase 'soul of the world' he did not understand by this an existent being distinct from God and intermediate between God and the world. In his cosmology there is no intermediary stage in creation between the actual infinite, God, and the potential infinite, the created world.

8. Although each finite thing mirrors the whole universe, this is particularly true of man who combines in himself matter, organic life, sensitive animal life and spiritual rationality. Man is the microcosm, a little world, embracing in himself the intellectual and material spheres of reality.[37] 'We cannot deny that man is called the microcosm, that is, a little world'; and just as the great world, the universe, has its soul, so has man his soul.[38] The universe is mirrored in every part, and this is true analogously of man, who is the little universe or world. The nature of man is mirrored in a part like the hand, but it is mirrored more perfectly in the head. So the universe, though mirrored in every part, is mirrored more perfectly in man. Therefore man can be called a 'perfect world, although he is a little world and a part of the great world'.[39] In fact, as uniting in himself attributes which are found separately in other beings man is a finite representation of the divine *coincidentia oppositorum*.

The universe is the *concretum maximum*, while God is the *absolutum maximum*, absolute greatness. But the universe does not exist apart from individual things; and no individual thing embodies all the perfections of its species. The absolute greatness is thus never fully 'contracted' or rendered 'concrete'. We can conceive, however, a *maximum contractum* or *concretum* which would unite in itself not only the various levels of created existence, as man does, but also the Godhead itself together with created nature, though this union 'would exceed all our understanding'.[40] But though the mode of union is a mystery, we know that in Christ divine and human nature have been united without confusion of natures or distinction of persons. Christ, then, is the *maximum concretum*. He is also the *medium absolutum*, not only in the sense that in Him there is a unique and perfect union of the uncreated and the created, of the divine and human nature, but also in the sense that He is the unique and necessary means by which human beings can be united to God.[41] Without Christ it is impossible for man to achieve eternal happiness. He is the ultimate perfection of the universe,[42] and in particular of man, who can realize his highest potentialities only through incorporation with Christ. And we cannot be incorporated with Christ or transformed into His image save through the Church, which is His body.[43] The *Dialogus de pace seu concordantia fidei* shows that Nicholas was by no means narrow in his outlook and that he was quite prepared for concessions to the Eastern Church for the sake of unity; but his works in general by no means suggest that he favoured sacrificing the integrity of the Catholic faith in order to obtain external unity, profoundly concerned though he was about unity and deeply conscious of the fact that such unity could be obtained only through peaceful agreement.

9. It is clear enough that Nicholas of Cusa made copious use of the writings of preceding philosophers. For example, he often quotes the Pseudo-Dionysius; and it is obvious that he was strongly influenced by the latter's insistence on negative theology and on the use of symbols. He knew, too, the *De divisione naturae* of John Scotus Eriugena, and though Eriugena's influence on his thought was doubtless less than that exercised by the Pseudo-Dionysius (whom he thought of, of course, as the disciple of St. Paul) it is reasonable to suppose that some of his bold statements on the way in which God becomes 'visible' in creatures were prompted by a reading of the ninth-century philosopher's work. Again, Nicholas was certainly influenced by the writings of Meister Eckhart and by the latter's use of startling antinomies. Indeed, a great deal of Nicholas's philosophy, his theory of *docta ignorantia*, for example, his idea of God as the *coincidentia oppositorum*, his insistence on the world as a divine self-manifestation and as the *explicatio Dei*, his notion of man as the microcosm, can be regarded as a development of earlier philosophies, particularly those belonging in a wide sense to the Platonic tradition and those which may be classed as in some sense 'mystical'. His fondness for mathematical analogies and symbolism recalls not only the writings of Platonists and Pythagoreans in the ancient world but also those of St. Augustine and other Christian writers. It is considerations of this sort which provide much justification for

those who would class Nicholas of Cusa as a mediaeval thinker. His preoccupation with our knowledge of God and with the world's relation to God points backward, it might be maintained, to the Middle Ages. His whole thought moves, some historians would say, in mediaeval categories and bears the imprint of mediaeval Catholicism. Even his more startling utterances can be paralleled in the case of writers whom everyone would class as mediaevals.

On the other hand, it is possible to go to the opposite extreme and to attempt to push Nicholas forward into the modern period. His insistence on negative theology, for example, and his doctrine of God as the *coincidentia oppositorum* can be assimilated to Schelling's theory of the Absolute as the vanishing-point of all differences and distinctions, while his view of the world as the *explicatio Dei* can be regarded as a foretaste of Hegel's theory of Nature as God-in-His-otherness, as the concrete manifestation or embodiment of the abstract Idea. His philosophy can, that is to say, be considered as an anticipation of German idealism. In addition it is obvious that Nicholas's idea of the mirroring of the universe in each finite thing and of the qualitative difference which exists between any two things reappeared in the philosophy of Leibniz.

It can hardly be denied, I think, that there is truth in both these conflicting points of view. Nicholas's philosophy undoubtedly depended on or utilized to a great extent preceding systems. On the other hand, to point out the similarities between certain aspects of his thought and the philosophy of Leibniz is by no means to indulge in far-fetched analogies. When it comes to connecting Nicholas of Cusa with post-Kantian German speculative idealism the links are clearly more tenuous, and there is more chance of anachronistic assimilations; but it is true that interest in his writings began to show itself in the nineteenth century and that this was largely due to the direction taken in that century by German thought. But if there is truth in both points of view, that is all the more reason, I think, for recognizing in Nicholas a transition-thinker, a figure of the Renaissance. His philosophy of Nature, for example, certainly contained elements from the past, but it represented also the growing interest in the system of Nature and what one may perhaps call the growing feeling for the universe as a developing and self-unfolding system. Nicholas's idea of the 'infinity' of the world influenced other Renaissance thinkers, especially Giordano Bruno, even though Bruno developed Nicholas's ideas in a direction which was alien to the latter's mind and convictions. Again, however much Nicholas's theory of Nature as the *explicatio Dei* may have been dependent on the Platonic or neo-Platonic tradition, we find in that theory an insistence on the individual thing and on Nature as a system of individual things, none of which are exactly alike, that looks forward, as has already been mentioned, to the Leibnizian philosophy. Furthermore, his rejection of the idea that anything in the world can properly be called stationary and of the notions of any absolute 'centre' or 'up' and 'down' links him with the cosmologists and scientists of the Renaissance rather than with the Middle Ages. It is perfectly true, of course, that Nicholas's conception of the relation of the world to God was a theistic conception; but if Nature is looked on as a harmonious system which is in some sense 'infinite' and which is a developing or progressive manifestation of God, this idea facilitates and encourages the investigation of Nature for its own sake and not simply as a stepping-stone to the metaphysical knowledge of God. Nicholas was not a pantheist, but his philosophy, in regard to certain aspects at least, can be grouped with that of Bruno and other Renaissance philosophers of Nature; and it was against the background of these speculative philosophies that the scientists of the Renaissance thought and worked. One may remark in this connection that Nicholas's mathematical speculations provided a stimulus for Leonardo da Vinci.

In conclusion we may perhaps remind ourselves that though Nicholas's idea of the infinite system of Nature was developed by philosophers like Giordano Bruno and though these speculative natural philosophies formed a background for and stimulus to the scientific investigation of Nature, Nicholas himself was not only a Christian but also an essentially Christian thinker who was preoccupied with the search for the hidden God and whose thought was definitely Christocentric in character. It was in order to illustrate this last point that in dealing with his theory of man as the microcosm I mentioned his doctrine of Christ as the *maxi-*

mum contractum and the *medium absolutum*. In his humanistic interests, in his insistence on individuality, in the value he attached to fresh mathematical and scientific studies, and in the combination of a critical spirit with a marked mystical bent he was akin to a number of other Renaissance thinkers; but he continued into the Renaissance the faith which had animated and inspired the great thinkers of the Middle Ages. In a sense his mind was steeped in the new ideas which were fermenting at the time; but the religious outlook which permeated his thought saved him from the wilder extravagances into which some of the Renaissance philosophers fell.

Chapter Sixteen

PHILOSOPHY OF NATURE (1)

General remarks – Girolamo Cardano – Bernardino Telesio – Francesco Patrizzi – Tommaso Campanella – Giordano Bruno – Pierre Gassendi.

1. In the last chapter mention was made of the link between Nicholas of Cusa's idea of Nature and the other philosophies of Nature which appeared at the time of the Renaissance. Nicholas's idea of Nature was theocentric; and in this aspect of his philosophy he stands close to the leading philosophers of the Middle Ages; but we have seen how in his thought the idea of Nature as an infinite system, in which the earth occupies no privileged position, came to the fore. With a number of other Renaissance thinkers there arose the idea of Nature considered as a self-sufficient unity, as a system unified by all-pervading forces of sympathy and attraction and animated by a world-soul, rather than, as with Nicholas of Cusa, as an external manifestation of God. By these philosophers Nature was regarded practically as an organism, in regard to which the sharp distinctions, characteristic of mediaeval thought, between living and non-living and between spirit and matter, lost their meaning and application. Philosophies of this type naturally tended to be pantheistic in character. In certain respects they had an affinity with aspects of the revived Platonism or neo-Platonism of the Renaissance; but whereas the Platonists laid emphasis on the supernatural and on the soul's ascent to God, the philosophers of Nature emphasized rather Nature itself considered as a self-sufficient system. This is not to say that all the Renaissance

thinkers who are usually regarded as 'natural philosophers' abandoned Christian theology or looked on themselves as revolutionaries; but the tendency of their thought was to loosen the bonds which bound nature to the supernatural. They tended to 'naturalism'.

It is, however, rather difficult to make general judgments about those Renaissance thinkers whom historians are accustomed to classify as 'natural philosophers' or 'philosophers of Nature'; or perhaps one should say rather that it is dangerous to do so. Among the Italians, for example, one can certainly find affinities between the philosophy of Giordano Bruno and the German romantic philosophy of the nineteenth century. But 'romanticism' is not exactly a characteristic which one would naturally attribute to the thought of Girolamo Fracastoro (1483–1553), who was physician to Pope Paul III and who wrote on medical subjects, as well as composing a work on astronomy, the *Homocentricorum seu de stellis liber* (1535). In his *De sympathia et antipathia rerum* (1542) he postulated the existence of 'sympathies' and 'antipathies' between objects, that is, of forces of attraction and repulsion, to explain the movements of bodies in their relations to one another. The names 'sympathy' and 'antipathy' may appear perhaps to be symptomatic of a romantic outlook; but Fracastoro explained the mode of operation of these forces by postulating *corpuscula* or *corpora sensibilia* which are emitted by bodies and enter through the pores of other bodies. Applying this line of thought to the problem of perception, he postulated the emission of *species* or images which enter the percipient subject. This theory obviously renewed the mechanical theories of perception put forward in ancient times by Empedocles, Democritus and Epicurus, even though Fracastoro did not adopt the general atomistic theory of Democritus. A view of this kind emphasizes the passivity of the subject in its perception of external objects, and in his *Turrius sive de intellectione* (published 1555) he says that understanding (*intellectio*) is but the representation of an object to the mind, the result of the reception of a *species* of the object. From this he drew the conclusion that understanding is probably purely passive. It is true that he also postulated a special power, which he named *subnotio*, of experiencing or apprehending the various impressions of a thing as a totality possessing relations which are present in the object itself or as a meaningful whole. So one is not entitled to say that he denied any activity on the part of the mind. He did not deny the mind's reflective power nor its power to construct universal concepts or terms. Moreover, the use of the term *species* was obviously derived from the Aristotelian-Scholastic tradition. None the less, Fracastoro's theory of perception has a strongly marked 'naturalistic' character. Perhaps it is to be associated with his interests as a medical man.

Fracastoro was a physician, while Cardano was a mathematician and Telesio possessed a wide interest in scientific matters. But though a man like Telesio stressed the need for empirical investigation and research in science he certainly did not confine himself to hypotheses which could be empirically verified but advanced philosophical speculations of his own. It is not always easy to decide whether a given Renaissance thinker should be classified as a philosopher or a scientist: a number of philosophers of the time were interested in science and in scientific investigation, while the scientists were by no means always averse to philosophic speculation. However, those whose personal scientific work was of importance in the development of scientific studies are very reasonably classed as scientists, while those who are noteworthy rather for their speculation than for their personal contribution to scientific studies are classed as philosophers of Nature, even though they may have contributed indirectly to scientific advance by anticipating speculatively some of the hypotheses which the scientists attempted to verify. But the union of philosophic speculation with an interest in scientific matters, sometimes combined with an interest in alchemy and even in magic, was characteristic of the Renaissance thinkers. They had a profound belief in the free development of man and in his creative power and they sought to promote human development and power by varied means. Their minds delighted in free intellectual speculation, in the development of fresh hypotheses and in the ascertaining of new facts about the world; and the not uncommon interest in alchemy was due rather to the hope of thus extending man's power, control and wealth than to mere superstition. With the necessary qualifications one can say that the Renaissance spirit expressed a shift of emphasis from the other-worldly to the this-worldly, from transcendence to immanence, and from man's dependence to man's creative power. The Renaissance was a time of transition from a period in which the science of theology formed the mental background and stimulated men's minds to a period in which the growth of the particular natural sciences was to influence more and more the human mind and human civilization; and some at least of the Renaissance philosophies were fertilizing agents for the growth of science rather than systems of thought which one could be expected to treat very seriously as philosophies.

In this chapter I propose to deal briefly with some of the Italian philosophers of Nature and with the French philosopher, Pierre Gassendi. In the next chapter I shall treat of German philosophers of Nature, excluding Nicholas of Cusa, who has been considered separately.

2. Girolamo Cardano (1501–76) was a mathematician of note and a celebrated physician, who became professor of medicine at Pavia in 1547. A typically Renaissance figure he combined his mathematical studies and the practice of medicine with an interest in astrology and a strong bent towards philosophical speculation. His philosophy was a doctrine of hylozoism. There is an original, indeterminate matter, filling all space. In addition it is necessary to postulate a principle of production and movement, which is the world-soul. The latter becomes a factor in the empirical world in the form of 'warmth' or light; and from the operation of the world-soul in matter empirical objects are produced, all of which are en-souled and between which there exist relations of sympathy and antipathy. In the process of the world's formation the heaven, the seat of warmth, was first separated from the sublunary world, which is the place of the wet and the cold elements. Cardano's enthusiasm for astrology was expressed in his conviction that the heavens influence the course of events in the sublunary world. Metals are produced in the interior of the earth through the mutual reactions of the three elements of earth, water and air; and not only are they living things but they all tend towards the form of gold. As for what are normally called living things, animals were produced from worms, and the forms of worms proceed from the natural warmth in the earth.

This view of the world as an animate organism or as a unified system animated by a world-soul obviously owed a good deal to the *Timaeus* of Plato, while some ideas, like those of indeterminate matter and of 'forms', derived from the Aristotelian tradition. It might be expected perhaps that Cardano would develop these ideas in a purely naturalistic direction, but he was not a materialist. There is in man an immortal rational principle, *mens*, which enters into a temporary union with the mortal soul and the body. God created a definite number of these immortal souls, and immortality involves metempsychosis. In this view of the immortal mind as something separable from the mortal soul of man one can see the influence of Averroism; and one can probably see the same influence in Cardano's refusal to admit that God created the world freely. If creation was due simply and solely to the divine choice, there was no reason or ground for creation: it was a necessary process rather than the result of God's choice.

But there was more in Cardano's philosophy than a mere antiquarianism or a patching-together of elements taken from different philosophies of the past to make a hylozoistic and animistic system. It is clear that he laid great emphasis on the idea of natural law and on the unity of Nature as a law-governed system; and in this respect his thought was in tune with the scientific movement of the Renaissance, even though he expressed his belief in natural law in terms of ideas and theories taken from philosophies of the past. This conviction in regard to the reign of law comes out clearly in his insistence that God has subjected the heavenly bodies, and bodies in general, to mathematical laws and that the possession of mathematical knowledge is a form of true wisdom. It is represented even by his belief in 'natural magic', for the power of magic rests on the unity of all that is. Naturally, the sense in which words can be said to 'be' and to belong to the realm of causes needs a far clearer analysis than Cardano attempted; but the interest in magic which was one of the characteristics of some of the Renaissance thinkers expresses their belief in the causal system of the universe, even though to us it may seem fantastic.

3. A hylozoistic theory was also maintained by Bernardino Telesio (1509–88) of Cosenza in Calabria, the author

of *De natura rerum iuxta propria principia* and the founder of the *Academia Telesiana* or *Cosentina* at Naples. According to Telesio, the fundamental causes of natural events are the warm and cold elements, the opposition between which is concretely represented by the traditional antithesis between heaven and earth. In addition to these two elements Telesio postulated a third, passive matter, which becomes distended or rarefied through the activity of the warm and compressed through the activity of the cold element. In the bodies of animals and men there is present the 'spirit', a fine emanation of the warm element, which passes throughout the body by means of the nerves though it is properly situated in the brain. This idea of 'spirit' goes back to the Stoic theory of the *pneuma* which was itself derived from the medical schools of Greece, and it reappears in the philosophy of Descartes under the name 'animal spirits'.

The 'spirit', which is a kind of psychological substance, can receive impressions produced by external things and can renew them in the memory. The spirit has thus the function of receiving sense-impressions and of anticipating future sense-impressions; and analogical reasoning from case to case is grounded in sense-perception and memory. Reasoning begins, then, with sense-perception and its function is to anticipate sense-perception, in that its conclusions or anticipations of future experience must be empirically verified. Telesio does not hesitate to draw the conclusion that *intellectio longe est sensu imperfectior.*[1] He interpreted geometry, for example, in the light of this theory, namely as a sublimated form of analogical reasoning based on sense-perception. On the other hand, he admitted the idea of empty space, which is not a thing but rather the system of relations between things. Places are modifications of this general order or system of relations.

The fundamental natural drive or instinct in man is that of self-preservation. This is the ruling instinct in animals as well, and even in anorganic matter, which is non-living only in a comparative sense, as is shown by the omnipresence of motion, a symptom of life. (Indeed, all things are gifted with 'perception' in some degree, an idea which was later developed by Leibniz.) It was in terms of this fundamental instinct that Telesio analysed man's emotional life. Thus love and hate are feelings directed respectively towards that which promotes and that which hinders self-preservation, while joy is the feeling attendant on self-preservation. The cardinal virtues, prudence, for example, and fortitude, are all various forms in which the fundamental instinct expresses itself in its fulfilment, whereas sadness and kindred emotions reflect a weakening of the vital impulse. We have here an obvious anticipation of Spinoza's analysis of the emotions.

Telesio did not think, however, that man can be analysed and explained exclusively in biological terms. For man is able to transcend the biological urge to self-preservation: he can even neglect his own happiness and expose himself freely to death. He can also strive after union with God and contemplate the divine. One must postulate, therefore, the presence in man of a *forma superaddita*, the immortal soul, which informs body and 'spirit', and which is capable of union with God.

The professed method of Telesio was the empirical method; for he looked to sense-experience for knowledge of the world and regarded reasoning as little more than a process of anticipating future sense-experience on the basis of past experience. He may thus be regarded as having outlined, even if somewhat crudely, one aspect of scientific method. At the same time he propounded a philosophy which went far beyond what could be empirically verified by sense-perception. This point was emphasized by Patrizzi, to whom I shall turn next. But the combination of a hostility towards Scholastic abstractions not only with an enthusiasm for immediate sense-experience but also with insufficiently-grounded philosophical speculations was not uncharacteristic of Renaissance thought, which was in many respects both rich and undisciplined.

4. Although Francesco Patrizzi (1529–97) observed that Telesio did not conform in his philosophical speculations to his own canons of verification he himself was much more given to speculation than was Telesio, the essence of whose philosophy may very possibly lie in its naturalistic aspect. Born in Dalmatia, Patrizzi ended his life, after many wanderings, as professor of the Platonic philosophy at Rome. He was the author of *Discussionum peripateticarum libri* XV (1571) and *Nova de universis philosophia* (1591), in addition to a number of other works, including fifteen books on geometry. A determined enemy of Aristotle, he considered that Platonism was far more compatible with Christianity

and that his own system was eminently adapted for winning heretics back to the Church. He dedicated his *Nova philosophia* to Pope Gregory XIV. Patrizzi might thus very well have been treated in the chapter on the revival of Platonism; but he expounded a general philosophy of Nature, and so I have chosen to deal briefly with his thought here.

Patrizzi had recourse to the ancient light-theme of the Platonic tradition. God is the original and uncreated light, from which proceeds the visible light. This light is the active, formative principle in Nature, and as such it cannot be called wholly material. Indeed, it is a kind of intermediary being which constitutes a bond between the purely spiritual and the purely material and inert. But besides light it is necessary to postulate other fundamental factors in Nature. One of these is space, which Patrizzi describes in a rather baffling manner. Space is subsistent existence, inhering in nothing. Is it, then, a substance? It is not, says Patrizzi, an individual substance composed of matter and form, and it does not fall within the category of substance. On the other hand it is a substance in some sense; for it inheres in nothing else. It cannot therefore be identified with quantity. Or, if it is, it is not to be identified with any quantity which falls under the category of quantity: it is the source and origin of all empirical quantity. Patrizzi's description of space reminds one rather of that given by Plato in the *Timaeus*. It cannot be called anything definite. It is neither purely spiritual; nor is it on the other hand a corporeal substance: rather is it 'incorporeal body', abstract extension which precedes, logically at least, the production of distinct bodies and which can be logically constructed out of *minima* or points. The idea of the *minimum*, which is neither great nor small but is potentially either, was utilized by Giordano Bruno. Space is filled, according to Patrizzi, by another fundamental factor in the constitution of the world, namely 'fluidity'. Light, warmth, space and fluidity are the four elementary factors or principles.

Patrizzi's philosophy was a curious and bizarre amalgam of neo-Platonic speculation and an attempt to explain the empirical world by reference to certain fundamental material or quasi-material factors. Light was for him partly the visible light, but it was also a metaphysical principle or being which emanates from God and animates all things. It is the principle of multiplicity, bringing the multiple into existence;

but it is also the principle of unity which binds all things into a unity. And it is by means of light that the mind is enabled to ascend to God.

5. Another strange mixture of various elements was provided by Tommaso Campanella (1568–1639), a member of the Dominican Order and author of the famous political Utopia, the *City of the Sun* (*Civitas solis*, 1623), in which he proposed, whether seriously or not, a communistic arrangement of society obviously suggested by Plato's *Republic*. Campanella spent a very considerable portion of his life in prison, mainly on account of charges of heresy; but he composed a number of philosophical works, including *Philosophia sensibus demonstrata* (1591), *De sensu rerum* (1620), *Atheismus triumphatus* (1631) and *Philosophia universalis seu metaphysica* (1637). In politics he upheld the ideal of a universal monarchy under the spiritual headship of the pope and the temporal leadership of the Spanish monarchy. The very man who had to undergo a term of imprisonment on the accusation of conspiring against the king of Spain lauded the Spanish monarchy in his *De monarchia hispanica* (1640).

Campanella was strongly influenced by Telesio, and he insisted on the direct investigation of Nature as the source of our knowledge about the world. He tended also to interpret reasoning on the same lines as those laid down by Telesio. But the inspiration of his thought was different. If he emphasized sense-perception and the empirical study of Nature, he did so because Nature is, as he put it, the living statue of God, the mirror or image of God. There are two main ways of coming to a knowledge of God, first the study with the aid of the senses of God's self-revelation in Nature, and secondly the Bible. That Nature is to be regarded as a manifestation of God was, of course, a familiar theme in mediaeval thought. We have only to think of St. Bonaventure's doctrine of the material world as the *vestigium* or *umbra Dei*; and Nicholas of Cusa, who influenced Campanella, had developed this line of thought. But the Renaissance Dominican laid stress on the actual observation of Nature. It is not primarily a question of finding mystical analogies in Nature, as with St. Bonaventure, but rather of reading the book of Nature as it lies open to sense-perception.

That God's existence can be proved was a matter of which Campanella felt quite certain. And the way he set about proving it is interesting, if only because of its obvious affinity with the teaching of Descartes in the seventeenth century. Arguing against scepticism, Campanella maintained that we can at least know that we do not know this or that, or that we doubt whether this or that is the case. Moreover, in the act of doubting one's own existence is revealed. On this point Campanella is a kind of link between St. Augustine with his *Si fallor, sum*, and Descartes, with his *Cogito, ergo sum*. Again, in the consciousness of one's own existence there is also given the consciousness of what is other than oneself: in the experience of finitude is given the knowledge that other being exists. In love, too, is given the consciousness of the existence of the other. (Perhaps Descartes might have adopted and utilized this point of view to advantage.) I, therefore, exist, and I am finite; but I possess, or can possess, the idea of the infinite reality. This idea cannot be my own arbitrary construction or indeed my construction at all: it must be the effect of God's operation in me. Through reflection on the idea of infinite and independent being I see that God actually exists. In this way knowledge of my own existence as a finite being and knowledge of God's existence as infinite being are closely linked. But it is possible also for man to have an immediate contact with God, which affords the highest possible knowledge open to man and at the same time involves love of God; and this loving knowledge of God is the best way of knowing God.

God is the Creator of all finite beings, and these are composed, according to Campanella, of being and not-being, the proportion of not-being increasing as one descends the scale of perfection. This is certainly a very peculiar way of speaking; but the main idea was derived from the Platonic tradition and was not Campanella's invention. The chief attributes (*primalitates*) of being are power, wisdom and love; and the more not-being is mixed with being, the weaker is the participation in these attributes. As one descends the scale of perfection, therefore, one finds an increasing proportion of impotence or lack of power, of unwisdom and of hatred. But every creature is animate in some sense, and nothing is without some degree of perception and feeling.

Moreover, all finite things together form a system, the precondition of which is provided by space; and they are related to one another by mutual sympathies and antipathies. Everywhere we find the fundamental instinct of self-preservation. But this instinct or drive is not to be interpreted in a narrowly and exclusively egoistic sense. Man, for example, is a social being, adapted to life in society. Furthermore, he is able to rise above love of self in the narrow sense to love of God, which expresses his tendency to return to his origin and source.

We come to recognize the primary attributes of being through reflection on ourselves. Every man is aware that he can act or that he has some power (*posse*), that he can know something and that he wills or has love. We then ascribe these attributes of power, wisdom and love to God, the infinite being, in the highest possible degree, and we find them in non-human finite things in varying degrees. This is an interesting point because it illustrates Campanella's tendency to imply that we interpret Nature on an analogy with ourselves. In a sense all knowledge is knowledge of ourselves. We perceive the effects of things on ourselves, and we find ourselves limited and conditioned by things other than ourselves. We attribute to them, therefore, activities and functions analogous to those we perceive in ourselves. Whether this point of view is consistent with Campanella's insistence, under the influence of Telesio, on direct sense-knowledge of Nature is perhaps questionable; but the justification for our interpretation of Nature on an analogy with ourselves he found in the doctrine of man as the microcosm. If man is the microcosm or little world, the world in miniature, the attributes of being as found in man are also the attributes of being in general. If this way of thinking really represents Campanella's mind, it is open to the obvious objection that the theory of man as the microcosm should be a conclusion and not a premiss. But Campanella started, of course, from the view that God is revealed in every creature as in a mirror. If this point of view is adopted, it follows that knowledge of the being best known to us is the key to the knowledge of being in general.

6. The most celebrated of the Italian philosophers of Nature is Giordano Bruno. Born at Nola near Naples in 1548

(hence sometimes called 'the Nolan') he entered the Dominican Order at Naples; but in 1576 he laid aside the habit at Rome after he had been accused of holding heterodox opinions. He then began a life of wandering which took him from Italy to Geneva, from Geneva to France, from France to England, where he gave some lectures at Oxford, from England back again to France and then to Germany. Returning rashly to Italy, he was arrested by the Venetian Inquisition in 1592, and in the following year he was handed over to the Roman Inquisition and spent some years in prison. Finally, as he continued to stand by his opinions, he was burned at Rome on February 17th, 1600.

Bruno's writings include *De umbris idearum* (1582) and the following works in dialogue form: *La cena de le ceneri* (1584), *Della causa, principio e uno* (1584), *De l'infinito, universo e mondi* (1584), *Spaccio della bestia trionfante* (1584), *Cabala del cavallo pegaseo con l'agguiunta dell'asino cillenico* (1585) and *Degl' eroici furori* (1585). Among his other works are three Latin poems, published in 1591, the *De triplici minimo et mensura ad trium speculativarum scientiarum et multarum activarum artium principia libri* V, the *De monade, numero et figura, secretioris nempe physicae, mathematicae et metaphysicae elementa* and the *De immenso et innumerabilibus, seu de universo et mundis libri* VIII.

The starting-point and the terminology of Bruno's thought were furnished, very naturally, by preceding philosophies. He took over the neo-Platonic metaphysical scheme, as mediated by the Italian Platonists and by Nicholas of Cusa. Thus in his *De umbris idearum* he represented Nature with its multiplicity of beings as proceeding from the divine supersubstantial unity. There is a hierarchy in Nature from matter upwards to the immaterial, from darkness to light; and Nature is intelligible in so far as it is the expression of the divine ideas. Human ideas, however, are simply shadows or reflections of the divine ideas, though human knowledge is capable of advancement and deepening in proportion as the mind moves upwards from the objects of sense-perception towards the divine and original unity, which in itself, however, is impenetrable by the human intellect.

But this traditional scheme formed little more than the

background of Bruno's thought, against which his own philosophy developed. Though neo-Platonism had always represented the world as a divine 'emanation' or creation and as the reflection of God, it had always stressed the divine transcendence and incomprehensibility. But the inner movement of Bruno's speculation was towards the idea of the divine immanence, and so towards pantheism. He never achieved a complete conciliation of the two points of view; nor did he ever carry through a definite exclusion of one point of view in favour of the other.

In his *Della causa, principio e uno* Bruno asserts God's transcendence and incomprehensibility and His creation of things which are distinct from Him. 'From the knowledge of all dependent things we cannot infer any other knowledge of the first cause and principle than by the rather inefficacious way of traces (*de vestigio*). . . . So that to know the universe is like knowing nothing of the being and substance of the first principle. . . . Behold, then, about the divine substance, both because of its infinity and because of its being extremely remote from its effects . . . we can know nothing save by way of traces, as the Platonists say, or by remote effects, as the Peripatetics say. . . .'[2] The interest soon shifts, however, to the principles and causes in the world, and Bruno brings into prominence the idea of the world-soul as the immanent causal and moving agent. The primary and principal faculty of the world-soul is the universal intellect, which is 'the universal physical efficient agent' and 'the universal form' of the world.[3] It produces natural forms in the world, while our intellects produce universal ideas of these forms. It is the universal form of the world in that it is everywhere present and animates everything. Leather as leather or glass as glass, says Bruno, is not in itself animate in the ordinary sense; but it is united to and informed by the world-soul and it has, as matter, the potentiality of forming part of an organism. Matter, in the sense of Aristotle's 'first matter', is indeed, considered from one point of view, a formless and potential substrate; but considered as the fountain-head and source of forms it cannot be regarded as an unintelligible substrate; ultimately pure matter is the same thing as pure act. Bruno used Nicholas of Cusa's doctrine of the *coincidentia oppositorum* in regard to the world.

Starting with the assertion of distinctions he went on to show their relative character. The world consists of distinct things and factors, but in the end it is seen to be 'one, infinite, immobile' (that is, incapable of local motion), one being, one substance.[4] The idea, taken over from Nicholas of Cusa, that the world is infinite is supported by arguments in the *De l'infinito, universo e mondi*. 'I call the universe *tutto infinito*, because it has no margin, limit or surface; I do not call the universe *totalmente infinito*, because any part that we take is finite, and of the innumerable worlds which it contains each is finite. I call God *tutto infinito* because He excludes of Himself all limits and because each of His attributes is one and infinite; and I call God *totalmente infinito* because He is wholly in the whole world and infinitely and totally in each of its parts, in distinction from the infinity of the universe which is totally in the whole but not in the parts, if indeed, in reference to the infinite, they can be called parts.'[5]

Here Bruno draws a distinction between God and the world. He also speaks of God, using the phrases of Nicholas of Cusa, as being the infinite *complicatamente e totalmente* whereas the world is the infinite *explicatamente e non totalmente*. But the tendency of his thought is always to weaken these distinctions or to synthesize the 'antitheses'. In the *De triplici minimo* he speaks of the *minimum* which is found on the mathematical, physical and metaphysical planes. The mathematical *minimum* is the *monas* or unit; the physical *minimum* is the atom or monad, indivisible and in some sense animate, and immortal souls are also 'monads'. Nature is the harmonious self-unfolding system of atoms and monads in their interrelations. Here we have a pluralistic view of the universe, conceived in terms of monads, each of which is in some sense gifted with perception and appetition; and this aspect of Bruno's philosophy anticipates the monadology of Leibniz. But we have already noted his remark that one can hardly speak of 'parts' in relation to the infinite world; and the complementary aspect of his philosophy is represented by his idea of finite things as accidents or *circonstanzie* of the one infinite substance. Again, God is called *Natura naturans* in so far as He is considered in distinction from His manifestations, while He is called *Natura naturata* when considered in His self-manifestation. Here we have the monistic aspect of Bruno's thought which anticipated the philosophy of Spinoza. But as has been already remarked, Bruno never positively abandoned pluralism in favour of monism. It is reasonable to say that the tendency of his thought lay in the direction of monism; but in actual fact he continued to believe in the transcendent God. He considered, however, that philosophy deals with Nature and that God in Himself is a subject which can be properly treated only in theology, above all by the method of negative theology. One is not justified, then, in stating roundly that Bruno was a pantheist. One can say, if one likes, that his mind tended to move away from the categories of neo-Platonism and of Nicholas of Cusa in the direction of a greater insistence on the divine immanence; but there is no real reason for supposing that his retention of the doctrine of the divine transcendence was a mere formality. His philosophy may be a stage on the road from Nicholas of Cusa to Spinoza; but Bruno himself did not travel to the end of that road.

But Bruno's thought was not inspired simply by the neo-Platonic tradition interpreted in a pantheistic sense; it was also deeply influenced by the astronomical hypothesis of Copernicus. Bruno was not a scientist, and he cannot be said to have contributed to the scientific verification of the hypothesis; but he developed speculative conclusions from it with characteristic boldness, and his ideas acted as a stimulus on other thinkers. He envisaged a multitude of solar systems in limitless space. Our sun is simply one star among others, and it occupies no privileged position: still less does the earth. Indeed, all judgments about position are, as Nicholas of Cusa said, relative; and no one star or planet can be called the centre of the universe in an absolute sense. There is no centre, and there is no absolute up or down. Moreover, from the fact that the earth is inhabited by rational beings we are not entitled to draw the conclusion that it is unique in dignity or that it is the centre of the universe from the valuational point of view: for all we know, the presence of life, even of rational beings like ourselves, may not be confined to this planet. The solar systems rise and perish, but all together they form one developing system, indeed one organism animated by the world-soul. Bruno did not confine himself to maintaining that the earth moves and that judgments of position are relative: he linked up the Copernican hypothesis of the earth's movement round the sun with his own metaphysical cosmology. He thus entirely rejected the geocentric and anthropocentric conception of the universe both from the astronomical point of view and in the wider perspective of speculative philosophy. In his system it is Nature considered as an organic whole which stands in the centre of the picture, and not terrestrial human beings who are *circonstanzie* or accidents of the one living world-substance, even if from another point of view each is a monad, mirroring the whole universe.

In some early writings Bruno dealt with questions concerning memory and logic under the influence of the doctrines of Raymond Lull (d. 1315). We can distinguish ideas in the universal intelligence, in the physical order as forms and in the logical order as symbols or concepts. The task of a developed logic would be to show how the plurality of ideas emerge from the 'one'. But though he may be regarded as in some sense a link between Lull and Leibniz, Bruno is best known for his doctrines of the infinite world-substance and of monads and for his speculative use of the Copernican hypothesis. In regard to the first doctrine he probably exercised some influence upon Spinoza, and he was certainly acclaimed as a prophet by later German philosophers like Jacobi and Hegel. In regard to the theory of monads, which is more apparent in his later works, he certainly anticipated Leibniz in some important points, even though it seems improbable that Leibniz received any substantial direct influence from Bruno in the formation of his ideas.[6] Bruno adopted and utilized many ideas taken from Greek, mediaeval and Renaissance thinkers, especially from Nicholas of Cusa; but he possessed an original mind with a strong speculative bent. His ideas were often far-fetched and fantastic and his thought undisciplined, though he was certainly capable of methodical thinking when he chose; and he played the rôle not only of philosopher but also of poet and seer. We have seen that he cannot be called a pantheist in an unqualified manner; but this does not mean that his attitude towards Christian dogmas was either favourable or respectful. He aroused the disapproval and hostility not only of Catholic theologians but also of Calvinists and Lutherans, and his unhappy end was due not to his championship of the Copernican hypothesis, nor to his attacks on Aristotelian Scholasticism, but to his apparent denial of some central theological dogmas. He did make an attempt to explain away his unorthodoxy by reference to a kind of 'double-truth' theory; but his condemnation for heresy was perfectly understandable, whatever one may think of the physical treatment meted out to him. His ultimate fate has, of course, led some writers to attribute to him a greater philosophic importance than he possesses; but though some of the encomia which have sometimes been lavished upon him in an uncritical manner were exaggerated, he nevertheless remains one of the leading and most influential thinkers of the Renaissance.

7. The date of Pierre Gassendi's death, 1655, coupled with the fact that he carried on a controversy with Descartes, offers a very good reason for considering his philosophy at a later stage. On the other hand, his revival of Epicureanism justifies one, I think, in including it under the general heading of Renaissance philosophy.

Born in Provence in 1592, Pierre Gassendi studied philosophy there at Aix. Turning to theology, he lectured for a time on the subject and was ordained priest; but in 1617 he accepted the chair of philosophy at Aix, where he expounded more or less traditional Aristotelianism. His interest in the discoveries of the Renaissance scientists, however, led his thought into other paths, and in 1624 there appeared the first book of his *Exercitationes paradoxicae adversus Aristotelicos*. He was at this time a canon of Grenoble. The work was to have been composed of seven books; but, apart from a portion of the second book, which appeared posthumously in 1659, no more than the first book was written. In 1631 he published a work against the English philosopher Robert Fludd (1574–1637), who had been influenced by Nicholas of Cusa and Paracelsus, and in 1642 his objections against Descartes's system were published.[7] In 1645 he was appointed professor of mathematics at the Collège Royal in Paris. While occupying this post he wrote on some physical and astronomical questions, but he is best known for the works which he wrote under the influence of the Epicurean philosophy. His treatise *De vita, moribus et doctrina Epicuri libri VIII* appeared in 1647, and this was followed in 1649 by the *Commentarius de vita, moribus et placitis Epicuri seu animadversiones in decimum librum Diogenis Laertii.* This was a Latin translation of and commentary on the tenth book of Diogenes Laërtius's *Lives of the Philosophers.* In the same year he published his *Syntagma philosophiae Epicuri.* His *Syntagma philosophicum* was published posthumously in the edition of his works (1658). In addition he wrote a number of *Lives,* of Copernicus and Tycho Brahe for example.

Gassendi followed the Epicureans in dividing philosophy into logic, physics and ethics. In his logic, which includes his theory of knowledge, his eclecticism at once becomes apparent. In company with many other philosophers of the time he insisted on the sense-origin of all our natural knowledge: *nihil in intellectu quod non prius fuerit in sensu.* And it was from an empiricist standpoint that he criticized Descartes. But although he spoke as if the senses were the only criterion of evidence he also admitted, as one might well expect of a mathematician, the evidence of the deductive reason. As to his 'physics', this was clearly a combination of very different elements. On the one hand, he revived the Epicurean atomism. Atoms, possessing size, shape and weight (interpreted as an inner propensity to movement) move in empty space. According to Gassendi, these atoms come from a material principle, the substrate of all becoming, which, with Aristotle, he described as 'prime matter'. With the help of atoms, space and motion he gave a mechanistic account of Nature. Sensation, for example, is to be explained mechanically. On the other hand, man possesses a rational and immortal soul, the existence of which is revealed by the facts of self-consciousness and by man's power of forming general ideas and apprehending spiritual objects and moral values. Moreover, the system, harmony and beauty of Nature furnish a proof of the existence of God, who is incorporeal, infinite and perfect. Man, as a being who is both spiritual and material and who can know both the material and the spiritual, is the microcosm. Finally, the ethical end of man is happiness, and this is to be understood as absence of pain in the body and tranquillity in the soul. But this end cannot be fully achieved in this life; it can be perfectly attained only in the life after death.

The philosophy of Gassendi may be regarded as an adaptation of Epicureanism to the requirements of Christian orthodoxy. But there is no good reason for saying that the spiritualistic side of his philosophy was inspired simply by motives of diplomatic prudence and that he was insincere in his acceptance of theism and of the spirituality and immortality of the soul. It may well be that the historical importance of his philosophy, so far as it possesses historical importance, lies in the impulse it gave to a mechanistic view of Nature. But this does not alter the fact that his philosophy, considered in itself, is a curious amalgam of Epicurean materialism with spiritualism and theism and of a rather crude empiricism with rationalism. His philosophizing exercised a considerable influence in the seventeenth century, but it was too unsystematic, too much of a patchwork, and too unoriginal to exercise any lasting influence.

Chapter Seventeen

PHILOSOPHY OF NATURE (2)

Agrippa von Nettesheim – Paracelsus – The two Van Helmonts – Sebastian Franck and Valentine Weigel – Jakob Böhme – General remarks.

In this chapter I propose to outline the ideas not only of men like Paracelsus, who are naturally labelled philosophers of Nature, but also of the German mystic, Jakob Böhme. The latter would possibly be more accurately classified as a theosophist than as a philosopher; but he certainly had a philosophy of Nature, which in some respects resembles that of Bruno. Böhme was doubtless much more religiously-minded than Bruno, and to classify him as a philosopher of Nature may involve placing the accent in the wrong place; but, as we have already seen, the term 'Nature' often meant a great deal more for a Renaissance philosopher than the system of empirically-given distinct things which are capable of being investigated systematically.

1. The theme of microcosm and macrocosm, which is prominent in the Italian philosophies of Nature, occupies a prominent place in the German philosophies of the Renaissance. A feature of the neo-Platonic tradition, it became one of the cardinal points in the system of Nicholas of Cusa, and his profound influence on Giordano Bruno has already been mentioned. His influence was naturally also felt by the German thinkers. Thus according to Heinrich Cornelius Agrippa von Nettesheim (1486–1535) man unites in himself the three worlds, namely the terrestrial world of the elements, the world of the heavenly bodies and the spiritual world. Man

is the ontological bond between these worlds, and this fact explains his ability to know all three worlds: man's range of knowledge depends on his ontological character. Further, the harmonious unity of the three worlds in man, the microcosm, reflects the harmonious unity which exists between them in the macrocosm. Man has his soul, and the universe possesses its soul or spirit (*spiritus mundi*), which is responsible for all production. There are, indeed, sympathies and antipathies between distinct things; but they are due to the presence in things of immanent vital principles which are effluences from the *spiritus mundi*. Finally, the affinities and connections between things and the presence in them of latent powers form the basis for the magical art: man can discover and utilize these powers in his service. In 1510 Agrippa von Nettesheim published his *De occulta philosophia* and though he decried the sciences, including magic, in his *Declamatio de vanitate et incertitudine scientiarum* (1527), he republished the work on occultism in a revised form in 1533. Like Cardano, he was a physician and, like Cardano again, he was interested in magic. It is not an interest which one would associate with modern doctors; but the combination of medicine with magic in an earlier age is understandable. The physician was conscious of powers and healing properties of herbs and minerals and of his ability to utilize them to a certain extent. But it does not follow that he had a scientific understanding of the processes which he himself employed; and it is hardly to be wondered at if he was attracted by the idea of wresting nature's secrets from her by occult means and employing the hidden powers and forces thus discovered. Magic would appear to him as a kind of extension of 'science', a short-cut to the acquisition of further knowledge and skill.

2. This view of the matter is borne out by the example of that strange figure, Theophrastus Bombast von Hohenheim, commonly known as Paracelsus. Born at Einsiedeln in 1493, he was for a time professor of medicine at Basle. He died at Salzburg in 1541. Medical science, which promotes human happiness and well-being, was for him the highest of the sciences. It depends, indeed, on observation and experiment; but an empirical method does not by itself constitute medicine a science. The data of experience must be systematized. Furthermore, the true physician will take account of other

sciences like philosophy, astrology and theology; for man, with whom medical science is concerned, participates in three worlds. Through his visible body he participates in the terrestrial world, the world of the elements, through his astral body in the sidereal world and through his immortal soul (the *mens* or *Fünklein*) in the spiritual and divine world. Man is thus the microcosm, the meeting-place of the three worlds which compose the macrocosm; and the physician will have to take this into account. The world at large is animated by its immanent vital principle, the *archeus*, and an individual organism like man develops under the impulse of its own vital principle. Medical treatment should consist essentially in stimulating the activity of the *archeus*, a principle which obviously embodies the truth that the task of the physician is to assist nature to do her work. Indeed, Paracelsus put forward some perfectly sensible medical views. Thus he laid considerable emphasis on the individual and on individual factors in the treatment of disease; no disease, he thought, is ever found in exactly the same form or runs precisely the same course in any two individuals. For the matter of that, his idea that the physician should widen his field of view and take other sciences into account was by no means devoid of value. For it means essentially that the physician should consider man as a whole and should not confine his attention exclusively to physical symptoms and causes and treatment.

In some respects, then, Paracelsus was an enlightened theorist; and he attacked violently the medical practice of the time. In particular, he had no use for slavish adherence to the teaching of Galen. His own methods of procedure were highly empirical, and he can hardly be called a scientific chemist, even though he was interested in chemical specifics and drugs, but he had at least an independent mind and an enthusiasm for the progress of medicine. With this interest in medicine, however, he combined an interest in astrology and in alchemy. Original matter consists of or contains three fundamental elements or substances, sulphur, mercury and salt. Metals are distinguished from one another through the predominance of this element rather than that; but since they all consist ultimately of the same element it is possible to transform any metal into any other metal. The possibility of alchemy is thus a consequence of the original constitution of matter.

Although Paracelsus may have tended to mix up philosophical speculation with 'science' and also with astrology and alchemy in a fantastic manner, he drew a sharp distinction between theology on the one hand and philosophy on the other. The latter is the study of Nature, not of God Himself. Yet Nature is a self-revelation of God; and we are thus able to attain to some philosophical knowledge of Him. Nature was originally present in God, in the 'great mystery' or 'divine abyss'; and the process by which the world is built up is one of differentiation, that is, of the production of distinctions and oppositions. We come to know only in terms of oppositions. For example, we come to know joy in its opposition to sorrow, health in its opposition to sickness. Similarly, we come to know good only in opposition to evil and God only in opposition to Satan. The term of the world's development will be the absolute division between good and evil, which will constitute the last judgment.

3. Paracelsus' ideas were developed by the Belgian chemist and physician, John Baptist van Helmont (1577–1644). The two primary elements are water and air, and the fundamental substances, namely sulphur, mercury and salt, proceed from water and can be transmuted into water. Van Helmont made a real discovery, however, when he realized that there are gases which are different from atmospheric air. He discovered that what he called *gas sylvestre* (carbon dioxide), which is emitted by burning charcoal, is the same as the gas given off by fermenting must. He is, therefore, of some importance in the history of chemistry. Further, his interest in this science, combined with his interests in physiology and medicine, prompted him to experiment in the application of chemical methods in preparing drugs. In this matter he carried on the work of Paracelsus. Van Helmont was much more of a careful experimenter than Paracelsus had been; but he shared the latter's belief in and enthusiasm for alchemy. In addition, he took up and developed Paracelsus' vitalistic theory. Each organism has its own general *archeus* or *aura vitalis*, on which are dependent the *archei* of the different parts or members of the organism. Not content with the vital principles, however, he also postulated a power

of movement, which he called *blas*. This is of various kinds. There is, for instance, a *blas* peculiar to the heavenly bodies (*blas stellarum*) and another which is found in man, the relation between the *blas humanum* and the human *archeus* being left rather obscure.

John Baptist van Helmont did indeed indulge in speculations about the Fall and its effects on human psychology; but he was concerned primarily with chemistry, medicine and physiology, to which one must add alchemy. His son, however, Francis Mercury van Helmont (1618–99), with whom Leibniz was acquainted,[1] developed a monadology according to which there are a finite number of imperishable monads. Each monad may be called corporeal in so far as it is passive, and spiritual in so far as it is active and endowed with some degree of perception. The inner sympathies and attractions between monads cause groups of them to form complex structures, each of which is governed by a central monad. In man, for example, there is a central monad, the soul, which rules the whole organism. This soul shares in the imperishable character of all monads; but it cannot achieve the perfection of its development in one lifetime, that is to say, in the period in which it is the controlling and directing power in one particular set or series of monads. It therefore enters into union with other bodies or sets of monads until it has perfected itself. It then returns to God, who is the *monas monadum* and the author of the universal harmony of creation. The mediator between God and creatures is Christ.

The younger Van Helmont regarded his philosophy as a valuable antidote to the mechanistic interpretation of Nature, as represented by Descartes (in regard to the material world) and by the philosophy of Thomas Hobbes. His monadology was a development of Bruno's ideas, though it was doubtless also influenced by the vitalistic doctrines of Paracelsus and the elder Van Helmont. It is obvious that it anticipated in many respects the monadology of a much more talented man, Leibniz, though it would appear that Leibniz arrived independently at his fundamental ideas. There was, however, a second link between Van Helmont and Leibniz, and that was a common interest in occultism and alchemy, though in Leibniz's case this interest was perhaps simply one way in which his insatiable curiosity showed itself.

4. The German mystical tradition found a continuation in Protestantism with men like Sebastian Franck (1499–1542) and Valentine Weigel (1533–88). The former, however, would not normally be called a philosopher. At first a Catholic, he became a Protestant minister, only to abandon his charge and lead a restless and wandering life. He was hostile not only to Catholicism but also to official Protestantism. God is the eternal goodness and love which are present to all men, and the true Church, he thought, is the spiritual company of all those who allow God to operate within them. Men like Socrates and Seneca belonged to the 'Church'. Redemption is not a historical event, and doctrines like those of the Fall and the redemption by Christ on Calvary are no more than figures or symbols of eternal truths. This point of view was obviously theological in character.

Valentine Weigel, however, attempted to combine the mystical tradition with the philosophy of Nature as found in Paracelsus. He followed Nicholas of Cusa in teaching that God is all things *complicite* and that the distinctions and oppositions which are found in creatures are one in Him. But to this he added the curious notion that God becomes personal in and through creation, in the sense that He comes to know Himself in and through man, in so far as man rises above his egotism and shares in the divine life. All creatures, including man, receive their being from God, but all have an admixture of not-being, of darkness, and this explains man's power of rejecting God. The being of man tends necessarily towards God, turning to its source and origin and ground; but the will can turn away from God. When this happens, the resulting inner tension is what is known as 'hell'.

Accepting from Paracelsus the division of the universe into three worlds, the terrestrial, the sidereal or astral and the heavenly, Weigel also accepted the doctrine of the astral body of man. Man has a mortal body, which is the seat of the senses, but he has also an astral body, which is the seat of reason. In addition he has an immortal soul or part to which belongs the *Fünklein* or *Gemüt*, the *oculus intellectualis* or *oculus mentis*. This is the recipient of supernatural knowledge of God, though this does not mean that the knowledge comes from without; it comes from God present in the soul, knowing Himself in and through man. And it is in the reception of this knowledge, and not in any external rite or in any historical event, that regeneration consists.

It is clear, then, that Weigel attempted a fusion of Nicholas of Cusa's metaphysic and Paracelsus' philosophy of Nature with a religious mysticism which owed something to the tradition represented by Meister Eckhart (as is shown by the use of the term *Fünklein*, the spark of the soul) but which was strongly coloured by an individualistic and anti-ecclesiastical type of Protestant piety and which also tended in a pantheistic direction. In some respects his philosophy puts one in mind of themes of later German speculative idealism, though in the case of the latter the markedly religious and pietistic element of Weigel's thought was comparatively absent.

5. The man who attempted in a much more complete and influential manner to combine the philosophy of Nature with the mystical tradition as represented in German Protestantism was that remarkable figure, Jakob Böhme. Born in 1575 at Altseidenberg in Silesia, he at first tended cattle, though he received some education at the town-school at Seidenberg. After a period of wandering he settled at Görlitz in 1599, where he pursued the trade of a shoemaker. He married and attained a considerable degree of prosperity, which enabled him to retire from his shoemaking business though he subsequently took to making woollen gloves. His first treatise, *Aurora*, was written in 1612, though it was not then published. Indeed, the only works which were published in his lifetime were some devotional writings, which appeared at the beginning of 1624. His *Aurora* was, however, circulated in manuscript, and while this brought him a local reputation it also brought upon him from the Protestant clergy a charge of heresy. His other works include, for example, *Die drei Prinzipien des göttlichen Wesens*, *Vom dreifachen Leben der Menschen*, *Von der Gnadenwahl*, *Signatura rerum* and *Mysterium magnum*. An edition of his works was published at Amsterdam in 1675, considerably later than the year of Böhme's death, which occurred in 1624.

God considered in Himself is beyond all differentiations and distinctions: He is the *Ungrund*,[2] the original ground of all things: He is 'neither light, nor darkness, neither love nor wrath, but the eternal One', an incomprehensible will, which is neither evil nor good.[3] But if God is conceived as the *Ungrund* or Abyss, 'the nothing and the all',[4] the problem arises of explaining the emergence of multiplicity, of distinct existent things. First of all Böhme postulates a process of self-manifestation within the inner life of God. The original will is a will to self-intuition, and it wills its own centre, which Böhme calls the 'heart' or 'eternal mind' of the will.[5] Thus the Deity discovers itself; and in the discovery there arises a power emanating from the will and the heart of the will, which is the moving life in the original will and in the power (or second will) that arises from, but is identical with, the heart of the original will. The three movements of the inner life of God are correlated by Böhme with the three Persons of the Trinity. The original will is the Father; the heart of the will, which is the Father's 'discovery and power', is the Son; and the 'moving life' emanating from Father and Son is the Holy Spirit. Having dealt with these obscure matters in a very obscure way Böhme goes on to show how Nature came into being as an expression or manifestation of God in visible variety. The impulse of the divine will to self-revelation leads to the birth of Nature as it exists in God. In this ideal or spiritual state Nature is called the *mysterium magnum.* It emerges in visible and tangible form in the actual world, which is external to God and is animated by the *spiritus mundi.* Böhme proceeds to give a spiritual interpretation of the ultimate principles of the world and of the various elements, including Paracelsus' sulphur, mercury and salt.

As Böhme was convinced that God in Himself is good and that the *mysterium magnum* is also good, he found himself confronted with the task of explaining the evil in the actual world. His solution of this problem was not always the same. In the *Aurora* he maintained that only what is good proceeds from God; but there is a good which remains steadfast (Christ) and a good which falls away from goodness, typified by Satan. The end of history is, therefore, the rectification of this falling-away. Later, however, Böhme stated that the external manifestation of God must be expressed in contraries, which are natural concomitants of life. The *mysterium magnum,* when it unfolds itself in visible variety, expresses itself in contrary qualities:[6] light and darkness, good and evil, are correlative. There is, then, a dualism in the world. Christ reconciled man to God, but it is possible for men to refuse salvation Finally, Böhme tried to relate evil to a movement in the divine life, which he called the wrath of God. The end of history will then be the triumph of love, involving the triumph of the good.

Böhme's ideas were derived in part from a number of different sources. His meditations on the Scriptures were coloured by the mysticism of Kaspar von Schwenckfeld (1490–1561) and of Valentine Weigel; and we find in his writings a deep piety and an insistence on the individual's relation to God. For the idea of a visible and unified authoritative Church he had evidently little sympathy: he laid all the emphasis on personal experience and inner light. This aspect of his thought would not by itself entitle him to be called a philosopher. So far as he can properly be called a philosopher, the name is justified mainly by his having grappled with two problems of theistic philosophy, namely the problem of the relation of the world to God and the problem of evil. Böhme was obviously no trained philosopher, and he was aware of the inadequacy and obscurity of his language. Moreover, he evidently picked up terms and phrases from his friends and from his reading, which derived mainly from the philosophy of Paracelsus, but which he used to express the ideas fermenting in his own mind. None the less, even though the shoemaker of Görlitz was no trained philosopher, he can be said to have carried on the speculative tradition coming from Meister Eckhart and Nicholas of Cusa through the German philosophers of Nature, particularly Paracelsus, a tradition which he impregnated with a strong infusion of Protestant piety. Yet even if one makes due allowance for the handicaps under which he laboured, and even though one has not the slightest intention of questioning his deep piety and the sincerity of his convictions, it may be doubted whether his obscure and oracular utterances throw much light on the problems with which he dealt. No doubt the obscurity is broken through from time to time by rays of light; but his thought as a whole is unlikely to commend itself to those who are not theosophically inclined. It might be said, of course, that Böhme's obscure utterances represent the attempt of a higher kind of knowledge to express itself in inadequate language. But if one means by this that Böhme was struggling to convey solutions to philosophical problems, it has yet to be shown that he actually possessed those solutions. His writings leave one in considerable doubt at any rate whether this could properly be affirmed.

But to cast doubt upon the philosophical value of Böhme's utterances is not to deny their influence. He exercised an influence on men like Pierre Poiret (1646–1719) in France, John Pordage (1607–81) and William Law (1686–1761) in England. More important, however, is his influence on post-Kantian German idealism. Böhme's triadic schemes and his idea of the self-unfolding of God reappear, indeed, in Hegel, though minus Böhme's intense piety and devotion; but it was probably Schelling who, in the later phase of his philosophical development, was most influenced by him. For the German idealist drew on Böhme's theosophy and on his ideas about creation and the origin of evil. Schelling was led to Böhme partly by Franz von Baader (1765–1841), who had himself been influenced by Saint-Martin (1743–1803), an opponent of the Revolution who had translated Böhme's *Aurora* into French. There are always some minds for whom Böhme's teaching possesses an appeal, though many others not unnaturally fail to share this sympathy.

6. We have seen how the Renaissance philosophies of Nature varied considerably in tone and emphasis, ranging from the professedly empiricist theories of some of the Italian philosophers to the theosophy of a Jakob Böhme. We find, indeed, a common emphasis on Nature as the manifestation of the divine and as a revelation of God which is deserving of study. But whereas in one philosophy the accent may be laid predominantly on the empirical study of Nature itself as given to the senses, in another the accent may be laid on metaphysical themes. For Bruno Nature was an infinite system which can be studied in itself, so to speak; and we saw how he championed enthusiastically the Copernican hypothesis. Yet Bruno was above all things a speculative philosopher. And with Böhme we find the emphasis laid on theosophy and on man's relation to God. It is desirable, indeed, to speak of 'accent' and 'emphasis', since the philosophers not infrequently combined an interest in empirical problems with a bent for somewhat ill-grounded speculations.

Furthermore, they often combined with these interests an interest in alchemy, in astrology and in magic. They express the feeling for Nature which was one characteristic of the Renaissance; but in their study of Nature they were inclined to take attractive short-cuts, whether by bold and often bizarre philosophical speculations or by means of occultism or by both. The philosophies of Nature acted as a kind of background and stimulus to the scientific study of Nature; but for the actual development of the sciences other methods were required.

Chapter Eighteen

THE SCIENTIFIC MOVEMENT OF THE RENAISSANCE

General remarks on the influence of science on philosophy – Renaissance science; the empirical basis of science, controlled experiment, hypothesis and astronomy, mathematics, the mechanistic view of the world – The influence of Renaissance science on philosophy.

1. We have seen that even in the thirteenth century there was a certain amount of scientific development and that in the following century there was an increased interest in scientific problems. But the results of scholarly researches into mediaeval science have not been such as to necessitate any substantial change of view in regard to the importance of Renaissance science. They have shown that interest in scientific matters was not so alien to the mediaeval mind as has been sometimes supposed, and they have shown that the Aristotelian physics and the Ptolemaic astronomy did not possess that firm and universal hold on the mind of the mediaeval physicist with which they have often been credited; but all this does not alter the fact that science underwent a remarkable development at the time of the Renaissance and that this development has exercised a profound influence on European life and thought.

It is not the business of the historian of philosophy to give a detailed account of the discoveries and achievements of the Renaissance scientists. The reader who desires to acquaint himself with the history of science as such must obviously turn to the relevant literature on the subject. But it would be impossible to by-pass the development of science at the time of the Renaissance, if for no other reason than that it exercised a powerful influence upon philosophy. Philosophy does not pursue an isolated path of its own, without any contact with other factors of human culture. It is simply an undeniable historical fact that philosophic reflection has been influenced by science both in regard to subject-matter and also in regard to method and aims. In so far as philosophy involves reflection on the world philosophic thought will obviously be influenced in some way by the picture of the world that is painted by science and by the concrete achievements of science. This is likely to be the case in some degree in all phases of philosophic development. As to scientific method, when the use of a certain method is seen to lead to striking results it is likely that the thought will occur to some philosophers that the adoption of an analogous method in philosophy might also produce striking results in the way of established conclusions. And this thought is one which actually did influence certain philosophers of the Renaissance period. When, however, it is seen that philosophy does not develop in the same way as science, the realization of the fact is likely to give rise to the question whether the prevalent conception of philosophy should not be revised. Why is it, as Kant asked, that science progresses and that universal and necessary scientific judgments can be made and are made (or seemed to Kant to be made), while philosophy in its traditional form does not lead to comparable results and does not seem to progress in the way that science progresses? Is not our whole conception of philosophy wrong? Are we not expecting of philosophy what philosophy of its very nature cannot give? We should expect of philosophy only what it can give, and in order to see what it can give we have to inquire more closely into the nature and functions of philosophic thought. Again, as the particular sciences develop, each with its particular method, reflection will naturally suggest to some minds that these sciences have successively wrested from philosophy her various chosen fields. It may very understandably appear that cosmology or natural philosophy has given way to physics, the philosophy of the organism to biology, philosophical psychology to scientific psychology, and perhaps even moral philosophy to sociology. In other words, it may appear that for all factual information about the world and existent reality we must turn to direct observation and to the sciences. The philosopher, it may appear, cannot increase our knowledge of things in the way that the scientist can, though he may still perform a useful function in the province of logical analysis. And this is, roughly, what a considerable number of modern philosophers think. It is also possible, of course, to accept the idea that all that can be definitely known falls within the province of the sciences and yet at the same time to maintain that it is the special function of philosophy to raise those ultimate problems which cannot be answered by the scientist or in the way that the scientist answers his problems. And then one gets a different conception, or different conceptions, of philosophy.

Again, as science develops, reflection on the methods of science will also develop. Philosophers will be stimulated to analyse scientific method and to do for induction what Aristotle did for syllogistic deduction. And so we get the reflections of Francis Bacon at the time of the Renaissance and of John Stuart Mill in the nineteenth century and of many other philosophers in more recent times. Thus the concrete progress of the sciences may lead to the development of a new field of philosophic analysis, which could not have been developed apart from actual scientific studies and achievements, since it takes the form of reflection on the method actually used in science.

Further, one can trace the influence of a particular science on a particular philosopher's thought. One can trace, for example, the influence of mathematics on Descartes, of mechanics on Hobbes, the rise of historical science on Hegel or of biology and the evolutionary hypothesis on Bergson.

In the foregoing sketchy remarks I have strayed rather far from the Renaissance and have introduced philosophers and philosophical ideas which will have to be discussed in later volumes of this history. But my object in making these remarks was simply the general one of illustrating, even if in an inevitably inadequate manner, the influence of science upon philosophy. Science is not, of course, the only extra-philosophical factor which exercises an influence upon philosophic thought. Philosophy is influenced also by other factors in human culture and civilization. So, too, is science for the matter of that. Nor is one entitled to conclude from the influence of science and other factors upon philosophy that philosophic thought is itself powerless to exercise any influence upon other cultural elements. I do not think that this is in fact the case. But the point which is relevant to my present purpose is the influence of science upon philosophy, and it is for this reason that I have stressed it here. Before, however, anything very definite can be said about the influence of Renaissance science in particular on philosophic thought something must be said about the nature of Renaissance science, even though I am only too conscious of the handicaps under which I labour in attempting to discuss the matter.

2. (i) The 'vulgar' notion of the cause which brought about the flowering of Renaissance science is still, I suppose, that at that period men began for the first time, since the beginning of the Middle Ages at any rate, to use their eyes and to investigate Nature for themselves. Direct observation of the facts took the place of reliance on the texts of Aristotle and other ancient writers, and theological prejudice gave place to immediate acquaintance with the empirical data. Yet only a little reflection is needed to realize the inadequacy of this view. The dispute between Galileo and the theologians is considered, perhaps inevitably, as the representative symbol of the struggle between direct recourse to the empirical data on the one hand and theological prejudice and Aristotelian obscurantism on the other. But it is obvious that ordinary observation will not suffice to convince anyone that the earth moves round the sun: ordinary observation would suggest the contrary. The heliocentric hypothesis doubtless 'saved the appearances' better than the geocentric hypothesis did; but it was a hypothesis. Moreover, it was a hypothesis which could not be verified by the type of controlled experiment which is possible in some other sciences. It was not possible for astronomy to advance very much on the basis of observation alone; the use of hypothesis and of mathematical deduction were also required. It argues, then, a short-sighted view of the achievements of Renaissance science if one ascribes those achievements simply to observation and experiment. As Roger Bacon, the thirteenth-century Franciscan, had insisted, astronomy requires the aid of mathematics.

Yet every science is based in some way on observation and has some connection with the empirical data. It is obvious that a physicist who sets out to ascertain the laws of motion starts in a sense with observed movements; for it is the laws exemplified by movements which he wishes to ascertain. And if the laws which he eventually formulates are entirely incompatible with the observed movements, in the sense that if the laws were true the observed movements would not happen, he knows that he will have to revise his theory of motion. The astronomer does not proceed without any reference at all to empirical data: the chemist starts with the empirical data and makes experiments with existent things: the biologist would not get very far if he paid no attention to the actual behaviour of organisms. The development of physics in comparatively recent times, as interpreted by Eddington, for example, may tend to give the impression that science is not concerned with anything so plebeian as empirical data and that it is a pure construction of the human mind which is imposed upon Nature and constitutes the 'facts'; but unless one is dealing with pure mathematics, from which one cannot expect factual information about the world, one can say that every science rests ultimately on a basis of observation of the empirical data. When a science reaches a high degree of development, the empirical basis may not be so immediately obvious; but it is there none the less. The scientist does not set out to evolve a purely arbitrary theory: rather does he set out to 'explain' phenomena and, where possible, he will test or verify his theory, mediately if not immediately.

The connection of scientific theory with the empirical data is probably always obvious in the case of some sciences, whereas in the case of other sciences it may become far from obvious as the science reaches a high degree of development. But it is likely to be insisted on in the earlier stages of the development of any science, and this is especially the case when explanatory theories and hypotheses are put forward which conflict with long established notions. Thus at the time of the Renaissance, when the Aristotelian physics were being discarded in favour of fresh scientific conceptions, appeal was frequently made to the empirical data and to 'saving the appearances'. We have seen how the philosophers of

Nature often stressed the need for the empirical study of the facts, and it scarcely needs pointing out that medicine and anatomy, not to speak of technology and geography, would not have made the progress which they actually did make in the sixteenth and seventeenth centuries without the aid of empirical investigation. One cannot construct a useful map of the world or give a valid account and explanation of the circulation of the blood by purely *a priori* reasoning.

The results of actual observation may be seen particularly in the advance of anatomy and physiology. Leonardo da Vinci (1452–1519), the great artist who was also deeply interested in scientific and mechanical problems and experiments, was gifted with a remarkable flair for anticipating future discoveries, inventions and theories. Thus he anticipated speculatively the discovery of the circulation of the blood, which was made by William Harvey about 1615; and in optics he anticipated the undulatory theory of light. He is also well known for his plans for flying-machines, parachutes and improved artillery. But it is his anatomical observation which is relevant in the present context. The results of this observation were portrayed in a large number of drawings; but as they were not published they did not exercise the influence which they might have done. The influential book in this connection was the *De fabrica humani corporis* (1543) by Andreas Vesalius, in which he recorded his study of anatomy. This work was of considerable importance for the development of anatomy, since Vesalius did not set out to find evidence in support of traditional theories but was concerned to observe for himself and to record his observations. The book was illustrated, and it also contained accounts of experiments made by the author on animals.

(ii) The discoveries in anatomy and physiology by men like Vesalius and Harvey were naturally powerful influences in undermining men's trust in traditional theories and assertions and in directing their minds to empirical investigation. The fact that the blood circulates is a commonplace for us; but it was not by any means a commonplace then. The ancient authorities, like Galen and Hippocrates, knew nothing of it. But the scientific advance of the Renaissance cannot be ascribed simply to 'observation' in the narrow sense: one has to take into account the increased use of controlled experiment. For example, in 1586 Simon Stevin published the account of a deliberately contrived experiment with leaden balls, which refuted Aristotle's assertion that the velocity of falling bodies is proportional to the weight of the bodies. Again, William Gilbert, who published his *De magnete* in 1600, confirmed by experiment his theory that the earth is a magnet possessing poles which are near its geographical poles, though not coincident with them, and that it is to these magnetic poles that the needle of the compass is attracted. He took a spherical loadstone and observed the behaviour of a needle or a piece of iron wire placed on it in successively different positions. On each occasion he marked on the stone the direction in which the wire came to rest, and by completing the circles he was able to show that the wire or needle always came to rest pointing to the magnetic pole.

It was Galileo Galilei (1564–1642), however, who was the foremost exponent of the experimental method among the Renaissance scientists. Born at Pisa, he studied at the university of that city, exchanging the study of medicine, with which he started, for the study of mathematics. After lecturing at Florence he became professor of mathematics first at Pisa (1589) and then at Padua (1592), occupying this last place for eighteen years. In 1610 he went to Florence as mathematician and philosopher to the Grand Duke of Tuscany and as *mathematicus primarius* in the university, though he was free from the obligation of giving courses of lectures in the university. In 1616 began the celebrated affair with the Inquisition about his astronomical views, which ended with Galileo's formal recantation in 1633. The great scientist was indeed held in detention for a time; but his scientific studies were not stopped, and he was able to continue working until he became blind in 1637. He died in 1642, the year in which Isaac Newton was born.

Galileo's name is universally associated with astronomy; but his work was also of great importance in the development of hydrostatics and mechanics. For example, whereas the Aristotelians maintained that it was a body's shape which decided whether it would sink or float in water, Galileo tried to show experimentally that Archimedes was right in saying that it was the density or specific gravity of a body, and not its shape, which determined whether it would sink or float. He also tried to show experimentally that it was not simply the body's density which decided the matter but rather its density as relative to that of the fluids in which it was placed. Again, while at Pisa he confirmed by experiment the discovery already made by Stevin that bodies of different weight take the same time to fall a given distance and that they do not, as the Aristotelians thought, reach the ground at different times. He also endeavoured to establish experimentally the law of uniform acceleration, which had indeed been anticipated by other physicists, according to which the speed of a body's fall increases uniformly with the time, and the law that a moving body, unless acted upon by friction, the resistance of the air or gravity, continues to move in the same direction at a uniform speed. Galileo was especially influenced by his conviction that Nature is essentially mathematical, and hence that under ideal conditions an ideal law would be 'obeyed'. His relatively crude experimental results suggested a simple law, even if they could hardly be said to 'prove' it. They also tended to suggest the falsity of the Aristotelian notion that no body would move unless acted upon by an external force. Indeed, Galileo's discoveries were one of the most powerful influences which discredited the Aristotelian physics. He also gave an impetus to technical advance by, for example, his plans for a pendulum clock, which was later constructed and patented by Huygens (1629–95), and by his invention, or reinvention, of the thermometer.

(iii) Mention of controlled experiment should not be taken to imply that the experimental method was widely practised from the beginning of the sixteenth century. On the contrary, it is the comparative rarity of clear cases in the first half at any rate of the century which makes it necessary to draw attention to it as something which was just beginning to be understood. Now, it is clear that experiment, in the sense of deliberately contrived experiment, is inseparable from the use of tentative hypotheses. It is true that one might devise an experiment simply to see what happens; but in actual practice controlled experiment is devised as a means of verifying a hypothesis. To perform an experiment is to put a question to Nature, and asking that particular question normally presupposes some hypothesis. One would not drop balls of different weight from a tower in order to see whether they do or do not hit the ground at the same time, unless one wished to confirm a preconceived hypothesis or unless one envisaged two possible hypotheses and desired to discover which was correct. It would be wrong to suppose that all Renaissance scientists had a clear conception of the hypothetical character of their theories: but that they used hypotheses is clear enough. It is most obvious in the case of astronomy, to which I now turn.

Nicholas Copernicus (1473–1543), the famous and learned Polish ecclesiastic, was by no means the first to realize that the apparent movement of the sun from east to west is no conclusive proof that it does actually move in this way. As we have seen, this fact had been clearly realized in the fourteenth century. But whereas the fourteenth-century physicists had confined themselves to developing the hypothesis of the earth's daily rotation on its axis, Copernicus argued on behalf of the hypothesis that the rotating earth also rotates round a stationary sun. He thus substituted the heliocentric for the geocentric hypothesis. This is not to say, of course, that he discarded the Ptolemaic system entirely. In particular, he retained the old notion that the planets move in circular orbits, though he supposed that these were 'eccentric'. In order to make his heliocentric hypothesis square with the appearances, he then had to add a number of epicycles. He postulated less than half the number of circles postulated by the Ptolemaic system of his time, and he thus simplified it; but he went about matters in much the same way as his predecessors had done. That is to say, he made speculative additions in order to 'save the appearances'.

There can be little doubt that Copernicus was convinced of the truth of the heliocentric hypothesis. But a Lutheran clergyman called Andreas Osiander (1498–1552), to whom the manuscript of Copernicus' *De revolutionibus orbium cœlestium* had been entrusted by Georg Joachim Rheticus of Wittenberg, took it upon himself to substitute a new preface for that written by Copernicus. In this new preface Osiander made Copernicus propose the heliocentric theory as a mere hypothesis or mathematical fiction. In addition he omitted the references to Aristarchus which Copernicus had made; and this omission brought upon Copernicus charges of dishonest plagiarism. Luther and Melanchthon thoroughly disapproved of the new hypothesis; but it did not excite any pronounced opposition on the part of the Catholic authorities. Osiander's preface may have contributed to this, though it must also be remembered that Copernicus had circulated privately his *De hypothesibus motuum coelestium commentariolus* without arousing hostility. It is true that the *De revolutionibus*, which was dedicated to Pope Paul III, was put on the Index in 1616 (*donec corrigatur*), as objections were raised against some sentences which represented the heliocentric hypothesis as a certainty. But this does not alter the fact that the work did not arouse opposition on the part of Catholic ecclesiastical circles when it was first published. In 1758 it was omitted from the revised Index.

Copernicus' hypothesis did not immediately find enthusiastic adherents, however, apart from the Wittenberg mathematicians, Reinhold and Rheticus. Tycho Brahe (1546–1601) opposed the hypothesis and invented one of his own, according to which the sun circles round the earth, as in the Ptolemaic system, while Mercury, Venus, Mars, Jupiter and Saturn circle round the sun in epicycles. The first real improvement on Copernicus' theory was made by John Kepler (1571–1630). Kepler, who was a Protestant, had been convinced by Michael Mästlin of Tübingen that the Copernican hypothesis was true, and he defended it in his *Prodromus dissertationum cosmographicarum seu mysterium cosmographicum.* The work contained, however, Pythagorean speculations concerning the geometrical plan of the world, and Tycho Brahe characteristically suggested that the young Kepler should give more attention to sound observation before indulging in speculation. But he took Kepler as his assistant, and after his patron's death Kepler published the works in which he enunciated his famous three laws. These works were the *Astronomia nova* (1609), the *Epitome astronomiae copernicanae* (1618) and the *Harmonices mundi* (1619). The planets, said Kepler, move in ellipses having the sun as one focus. The radius sector of the ellipse sweeps out equal areas in equal times. Moreover, we can compare mathematically the times required by the various planets to complete their respective orbits by the use of the formula that the square of the time taken by any planet to complete its orbit is proportional to the cube of its distance from the sun. In order to explain the movement of the planets Kepler postulated a motive force (or *anima motrix*) in the sun which emits rays of force, rotating with the sun. Sir Isaac Newton (1642–1727) later showed that this hypothesis was unnecessary, for in 1666 he discovered the law of the inverse square, that the sun's gravitational pull on a planet which is n times the earth's distance from the sun is $1/n^2$ times the pull at the earth's distance, and in 1685 he at last found himself in a position to work out the mathematical calculations which agreed with the demands of observation. But though Newton showed that the movements of the planets can be explained without postulating Kepler's *anima motrix*, the latter had made a most important contribution to the advance of astronomy by showing that the movements of all the then known planets could be accounted for by postulating a number of ellipses corresponding to the number of planets. The old paraphernalia of circles and epicycles could thus be dispensed with. The heliocentric hypothesis was thus greatly simplified.

On the observational side the advance of astronomy was greatly promoted by the invention of the telescope. The credit for the practical invention of the telescope must be given, it seems, to one of two Dutchmen in the first decade of the seventeenth century. Galileo, hearing of the invention, made an instrument for himself. (A Jesuit, Father Scheiner, constructed an improved instrument by embodying a suggestion made by Kepler, and Huygens introduced further improvements.) By using the telescope Galileo was enabled to observe the moon, which revealed itself as having mountains; and from this he concluded that the moon consists of the same sort of material as the earth. He was also able to observe the phases of Venus and the satellites of Jupiter, his observations fitting in very well with the heliocentric, but not with the geocentric, hypothesis. Furthermore, he observed the existence of sunspots, which were also seen by Scheiner. The existence of varying sunspots showed that the sun consisted of changeable matter, and this fact further discredited the Aristotelian cosmology. In general the telescopic observations made by Galileo and others provided empirical confirmation of the Copernican hypothesis. Indeed, observation of the phases of Venus showed clearly the superiority of the heliocentric to the geocentric hypothesis, since they were inexplicable in terms of the Ptolemaic scheme.

Perhaps one should say something at this point about the deplorable clash between Galileo and the Inquisition. Its importance as evidence of the Church's supposed hostility towards science has often been greatly exaggerated. Indeed, the fact that it is to this particular case that appeal is almost always made (the case of Bruno was quite different) by those who wish to show that the Church is the enemy of science should by itself be sufficient to cast doubt on the validity of the universal conclusion which is sometimes drawn from it. The action of the ecclesiastical authorities does not, it is true, reflect credit on them. One could wish that they had all realized more clearly the truth, suggested by Galileo himself in a letter of 1615, envisaged by Bellarmine and others at the time, and clearly affirmed by Pope Leo XIII in his encyclical letter *Providentissimus Deus,* that a Biblical passage like *Josue* 10, 12–13 can be taken as an accommodation to the ordinary way of speaking and not as an assertion of a scientific fact. We all speak of the sun as moving, and there is no reason why the Bible should not employ the same way of speaking, without one's being entitled to draw therefrom the conclusion that the sun rotates round a stationary earth. Moreover, even though Galileo had not proved the truth of the Copernican hypothesis beyond question, he had certainly shown its superiority to the geocentric hypothesis. This fact is not altered by his having laid particular stress on an argument based on a mistaken theory about the ebb and flow of the tides in his *Dialogo sopra i due massimi sistemi del mondo,* the work which precipitated a serious clash with the Inquisition. On the other hand, Galileo obstinately refused to recognize the hypothetical character of his theory. Given his naïvely realist view of the status of scientific hypotheses, it might perhaps have been difficult for him to recognize it; but Bellarmine pointed out that the empirical verification of a hypothesis does not necessarily prove its absolute truth, and if Galileo had been ready to recognize this fact, which is familiar enough today, the whole unfortunate episode with the Inquisition could have been avoided. However, Galileo not only persisted in maintaining the non-hypothetical character of the Copernican hypothesis but was also needlessly provocative into the bargain. Indeed, the clash of personalities played a not unimportant part in the affair. In fine, Galileo was a great scientist, and his opponents were not great scientists. Galileo made some sensible remarks about the interpretation of the Scriptures, the truth of which is recognized today and might well have been recognized more clearly by the theologians involved in the case. But the fault was by no means all on one side. In regard to the status of scientific theories Bellarmine's judgment was better than Galileo's, even though the latter was a great scientist and the former was not. If Galileo had had a better understanding of the nature of scientific hypotheses, and if the theologians in general had not taken up the attitude which they did in regard to the interpretation of isolated Biblical texts, the clash would not have occurred. It did occur, of course, and in regard to the superiority of the heliocentric over the geocentric hypothesis Galileo was undoubtedly right. But no universal conclusion can legitimately be drawn from this case about the Church's attitude to science.

(iv) It is clear that in the astronomy of the Renaissance hypothesis as well as observation played an indispensable rôle. But the fruitful combination of hypothesis and verification, both in astronomy and in mechanics, would not have been possible without the aid of mathematics. In the sixteenth and seventeenth centuries mathematics made considerable progress. A notable step forward was taken when John Napier (1550–1617) conceived the idea of logarithms. He communicated his idea to Tycho Brahe in 1594, and in 1614 he published a description of the general principle in his *Mirifici logarithmorum canonis descriptio*. Shortly afterwards the practical application of the principle was facilitated by the work of Henry Briggs (1561–1630). In 1638 Descartes published an account of the general principles of analytic geometry, while in 1635 Cavalieri, an Italian mathematician, published a statement of the 'method of indivisibles', which had already been used in a primitive form by Kepler. This was, in essence, the first statement of the calculus of infinitesimals. In 1665–6 Newton discovered the binomial theorem, though he did not publish his discovery until 1704. This hesitation in publishing results led to the celebrated dispute between Newton and Leibniz and their respective supporters about priority in discovering the differential and integral calculi. The two men discovered the calculus independently, but although Newton had written a sketch of his ideas in 1669 he did not actually publish anything on the matter until 1704, whereas Leibniz began publication in 1684. These elaborations of the calculus were, of course, much too late to be utilized by the great scientists of the Renaissance, and a man like Galileo had to rely on older and clumsier mathematical methods. But the point is that his ideal was that of developing a scientific view of the world in terms of mathematical formulae. He may be said to have combined the outlook of a mathematical physicist with that of a philosopher. As a physicist he tried to express the foundations of physics and the observed regularities of Nature in terms of mathematical propositions, so far as this was possible. As a philosopher he drew from the success of the mathematical method in physics the conclusion that mathematics is the key to the actual structure of reality. Though partly influenced by the nominalist conception of causality and the nominalist substitution of the study of the behaviour of things for the traditional search for essences, Galileo was also strongly influenced by the mathematical ideas of Platonism and Pythagoreanism; and this influence predisposed him to believe that the objective world is the world of the mathematician. In a well-known passage of his work *Il saggiatore* (6) he declared that philosophy is written in the book of the universe but that 'it cannot be read until we have learnt the language and understood the characters in which it is written. It is written in mathematical language, and its characters are triangles, circles and other geometrical figures, without which it is impossible to understand a single word.'

(v) This aspect of Galileo's idea of Nature expressed itself in a mechanistic view of the world. Thus he believed in atoms and explained change on the basis of an atomist theory. Again, he maintained that qualities like colour and warmth exist as qualities only in the sensing subject: they are 'subjective' in character. Objectively they exist only in the form of the motion of atoms; and they can thus be explained mechanically and mathematically. This mechanistic conception of Nature, based on an atomist theory, was also maintained by Pierre Gassendi, as we saw earlier. It was further developed by

Robert Boyle (1627–91), who believed that matter consists of solid particles, each possessing its own shape, which combine with one another to form what are now termed 'molecules'. Finally Newton argued that if we knew the forces which act upon bodies, we could deduce the motions of those bodies mathematically, and he suggested that the ultimate atoms or particles are themselves centres of force. He was concerned immediately only with the movements of certain bodies; but in the preface to his *Philosophiae naturalis principia mathematica* he put forward the idea that the movements of all bodies could be explained in terms of mechanical principles and that the reason why natural philosophers had been unable to achieve this explanation was their ignorance of the active forces in nature. But he took care to explain that it was his purpose to give only 'a mathematical notion of those forces, without considering their physical causes or seats'. Hence when he showed that 'the force' of gravity which causes an apple to fall to the ground is identical with 'the force' which causes the elliptical movements of the planets, what he was doing was to show that the movements of planets and falling apples conform to the same mathematical law. Newton's scientific work enjoyed such a complete success that it reigned supreme, in its general principles that is to say, for some two hundred years, the period of the Newtonian physics.

3. The rise of modern science or, better, of the classical science of the Renaissance and post-Renaissance periods naturally had a profound effect on men's minds, opening up to them new vistas of knowledge and directing them to new interests. No sensible man would wish to deny that the scientific advance of the sixteenth and seventeenth centuries was one of the most important and influential events in history. But it is possible to exaggerate its effect on the European mind. In particular, it is, I think, an exaggeration to imply that the success of the Copernican hypothesis had the effect of upsetting belief about man's relation to God, on the ground that the earth could no longer be regarded as the geographical centre of the universe. That it did have this effect is not infrequently implied, and one writer repeats what another has said on the subject; but any necessary connection between the revolution in astronomy and a revolu-

tion in religious belief has yet to be demonstrated. Further, it is a mistake to suppose that the mechanical view of the universe either was or ought logically to have been a bar to religious belief. Galileo, who considered that the application of mathematics to the world is objectively ensured, believed that it was ensured by God's creation of the world as a mathematically intelligible system. It was divine creation which guaranteed the parallelisms between mathematical deduction and the actual system of Nature. Robert Boyle also was convinced of divine creation. And that Newton was a man of firm piety is well known. He even conceived absolute space as the instrument by which God is omnipresent in the world and embraces all things in His immanent activity. It is true, of course, that the mechanistic view of the world tended to promote deism, which brings in God simply as an explanation of the origin of the mechanical system. But it must be remembered that even the old astronomy, for example, can be regarded as a mechanical system in a sense: it is a mistake to suppose that the scientific advance of the Renaissance suddenly cut away, as it were, the link between the world and God. The mechanical-mathematical view naturally involved the elimination from physics of the consideration of final causes; but, whatever the psychological effect of this change on many minds may have been, the elimination of final causes from physics did not necessarily involve a denial of final causality. It was a consequence of the advance in scientific method in a particular field of knowledge; but this does not mean that men like Galileo and Newton regarded physical science as the sole source of knowledge.

I want to turn, however, to the influence of the new science on philosophy, though I shall confine myself to indicating two or three lines of thought without attempting at this stage to develop them. As a preliminary, one may remind oneself of the two elements of scientific method, namely the observational and inductive side and the deductive and mathematical side.

The first aspect of scientific method, namely observation of the empirical data as a basis for induction, for discovering causes, was stressed by Francis Bacon. But as his philosophy will form the subject of the next chapter I shall say no more about him here. What I want to do at the moment is to draw attention to the connection between the emphasis laid by Francis Bacon on observation and induction in scientific method and the classical British empiricism. It would certainly be quite wrong to regard classical empiricism as being simply the philosophical reflection of the place occupied by observation and experiment in Renaissance and post-Renaissance science. When Locke asserted that all our ideas are based on sense-perception and introspection he was asserting a psychological and epistemological thesis, the antecedents of which can be seen in mediaeval Aristotelianism. But it can legitimately be said, I think, that a powerful impetus was given to philosophical empiricism by the conviction that the contemporary scientific advances were based on actual observation of the empirical data. The scientific insistence on going to the observable 'facts' as a necessary basis for explanatory theory found its correlative and its theoretical justification in the empiricist thesis that our factual knowledge is ultimately based on perception. The use of observation and experiment in science, and indeed the triumphant advance of science in general, would naturally tend, in the minds of many thinkers, to stimulate and confirm the theory that all our knowledge is based on perception, on direct acquaintance with external and internal events.

It was, however, the other aspect of scientific method, namely the deductive and mathematical aspect, which most influenced the continental 'rationalist' philosophy of the post-Renaissance period. The success of mathematics in the solution of scientific problems naturally enhanced its prestige. Not only was mathematics clear and exact in itself, but in its application to scientific problems it also made clear what had formerly been obscure. It appeared as the highroad to knowledge. It is understandable that the certainty and exactitude of mathematics suggested to Descartes, himself a talented mathematician and the chief pioneer in the field of analytic geometry, that an examination of the essential characteristics of the mathematical method would reveal the right method for use in philosophy also. It is understandable also that under the influence of mathematics as a model several of the leading philosophers on the Continent believed that they could reconstruct the world, as it were, in an *a priori* deductive manner with the aid of certain fundamental ideas analogous to the definitions and axioms of mathematics. Thus a mathematical model provided the framework of Spinoza's *Ethica more geometrico demonstrata*, though it scarcely provided its content.

We have seen how the development of astronomy and of mechanics at the time of the Renaissance promoted the growth of a mechanical view of the world. This outlook was reflected in the field of philosophy. Descartes, for example, considered that the material world and its changes can be explained simply in terms of matter, identified with geometrical extension, and motion. At creation God placed, as it were, a certain amount of motion or energy in the world, which is transmitted from body to body according to the laws of mechanics. Animals can be considered as machines. Descartes himself did not apply these mechanistic analogies to the human being as a whole, but some later French thinkers did. In England Thomas Hobbes, who objected against Descartes that thought is an activity of bodies and that the activity of bodies is motion, believed that just as the behaviour of inanimate bodies can be deduced from certain fundamental ideas and laws so the behaviour of human societies, which are simply organizations of bodies, can be deduced from the properties of these organized groupings of bodies. Mechanics thus furnished a partial model for Descartes and a more complete model for Hobbes.

The foregoing remarks are intentionally brief and summary: they are designed only to indicate some of the lines on which the development of science influenced philosophic thought. Names of philosophers have been introduced who will be treated of in the next volume; and it would be out of place to say more about them here. It may be as well, however, to point out in conclusion that the philosophic ideas which have been mentioned reacted in turn on science. For example, Descartes' conception of organic bodies may have been crude and inadequate, but it probably helped to encourage scientists to investigate the processes and behaviour of organic bodies in a scientific manner. A hypothesis need not be completely true in order to bear fruit in some particular direction.

Chapter Nineteen

FRANCIS BACON

English philosophy of the Renaissance – Bacon's life and writings – The classification of the sciences – Induction and 'the idols'.

1. The first outstanding philosopher of the post-mediaeval period in England was Francis Bacon: it is his name which is for ever associated with the philosophy of the Renaissance in Great Britain. With the exception of St. Thomas More and Richard Hooker, whose political ideas will be briefly considered in the next chapter, the other British philosophers of the Renaissance merit little more than bare mention. It should, however, be emphasized that the general tone of philosophical thinking in the English universities at the time of the Renaissance was conservative. The Aristotelian-Scholastic logical tradition persisted for many years, especially at Oxford, and it formed the background of John Locke's university education in the seventeenth century. Latin works of logic, like the *Institutionum dialecticarum libri IV* of John Sanderson (1587–1602) or the *Logicae libri* V *de praedicabilibus* of Richard Crakanthorpe (1569–1624), began to give place to works in the vernacular like *The rule of reason, containing the arte of logique* (1552) by Thomas Wilson or *The philosopher's game* (1563) and the *Arte of reason rightly termed Witcraft* (1573) of Ralph Lever; but such works contained nothing much in the nature of novelty. Sir William Temple (1533–1626) defended the Ramist logic; but he was attacked by Everard Digby (1550–92), who wrote a refutation of Ramism in the name of Aristotelianism. Sir Kenelm Digby (1603–65), who became a Catholic in Paris,

where he was acquainted with Descartes, endeavoured to combine the Aristotelian metaphysics with the corpuscular theory of matter. Everard Digby, though an Aristotelian in logic, was influenced by the neo-Platonic ideas of Reuchlin. Similarly, Robert Greville, Lord Brooke (1608–43), was influenced by the Platonic Academy of Florence; and in *The Nature of Truth* he maintained a doctrine of the divine light which helped to prepare the way for the group of Cambridge Platonists. Ideas of Cardinal Nicholas of Cusa and of Paracelsus were represented by Robert Fludd (1574–1637), who travelled extensively on the Continent and was influenced by the continental Renaissance. In his *Philosophia Mosaica* he depicted God as the synthesis in identity of opposites. In Himself God is incomprehensible darkness; but considered in another aspect He is the light and wisdom which manifests itself in the world, which is the *explicatio Dei*. The world manifests in itself the twofold aspect of God, for the divine light is manifested in, or is the cause of, warmth, rarefaction, light, love, goodness and beauty, while the divine darkness is the origin of cold, condensation, hate and unloveliness. Man is a microcosm of the universe, uniting in himself the two aspects of God which are revealed in the universe. There is in man a constant strife between light and darkness.

2. The leading figure of the philosophy of the Renaissance in England was, however, a thinker who turned consciously against Aristotelianism and who did so not in favour of Platonism or of theosophy but in the name of scientific and technical advancement in the service of man. The value and justification of knowledge, according to Francis Bacon, consists above all in its practical application and utility; its true function is to extend the dominion of the human race, the reign of man over nature. In the *Novum Organum*[1] Bacon calls attention to the practical effects of the invention of printing, gunpowder and the magnet, which 'have changed the face of things and the state of the world; the first in literature, the second in warfare; the third in navigation'. But inventions such as these did not come from the traditional Aristotelian physics; they came from direct acquaintance with nature herself. Bacon certainly represents 'humanism' in the sense that he was a great writer; but his emphasis on man's dominion over nature by means of science distin-

guishes him sharply from the Italian humanists, who were more concerned with the development of the human personality, while his insistence on going direct to nature, on the inductive method, and his mistrust of speculation distinguish him from the neo-Platonists and the theosophists. Though he did not make positive contributions to science himself and though he was far more influenced by Aristotelianism than he realized, Bacon divined in a remarkable way the technical progress which was to come, a technical progress which, he was confident, would serve man and human culture. This vision was present, in a limited sense, to the minds of the alchemists; but Bacon saw that it was a scientific knowledge of nature, not alchemy or magic or fantastic speculation, which was to open up to man the path of dominion over nature. Bacon stood not only chronologically but also, in part at least, mentally on the threshold of a new world revealed by geographical discovery, the finding of fresh sources of wealth and, above all, by the advance in natural science, the establishment of physics on an experimental and inductive basis. It must be added, however, that Bacon had, as we shall see, an insufficient grasp and appreciation of the new scientific method. That is why I stated that he belonged mentally 'in part at least' to the new era. However, the fact remains that he did look forward to the new era of scientific and technical achievement: his claim to be a herald or *buccinator* of that era was justified, even if he over-estimated his power of vision.

Francis Bacon was born in 1561 in London. After studying at Cambridge he spent two years in France with the British ambassador and then took up the practice of law. In 1584 he entered Parliament and enjoyed a successful career which culminated in his appointment as Lord Chancellor in 1618 and the reception of the title Baron Verulam. He was created Viscount of St. Albans in 1621; but in the same year he was accused of accepting bribes in his judicial capacity. Found guilty he was sentenced to deprivation of his offices and of his seat in Parliament, a large fine and imprisonment in the Tower. In actual fact, however, he was released from the Tower after a few days and payment of the fine was not exacted. Bacon admitted that he had accepted presents from litigants, though he claimed that his judicial decisions had not been influenced thereby. His claim may or may not be valid; one cannot know the truth about this matter; but in any case it would be an anachronism to expect of a judge in the reigns of Elizabeth and James I precisely the same standard of behaviour which is demanded today. This is not to defend Bacon's behaviour, of course; and the fact that he was brought to trial bears witness to contemporary realization of the fact that his behaviour was improper. But it must be added at the same time that his fall was not brought about simply by a disinterested desire for pure justice on the part of his opponents: partly at least he was the victim of political intrigue and jealousy. In other words, though it is true that Bacon was not a man of profound moral integrity, he was not a wicked man or an iniquitous judge. His reception of presents, as also his behaviour towards Essex, has sometimes been presented in a grossly exaggerated light. It is quite incorrect to regard him as an example of a sort of 'split personality', a man who combined in himself the two irreconcilable characters of the disinterested philosopher and the egoistic politician who cared nothing for the demands of morality. He was by no means a saint like Thomas More; but neither was he an instance of Jekyll and Hyde. His death occurred on April 9th, 1626.

The Advancement of Learning appeared in 1606 and the *De sapientia veterum* in 1609. Bacon planned a great work, the *Instauratio magna*, of which the first part, the *De dignitate et augmentis scientiarum*, appeared in 1623. This was a revision and extension of *The Advancement of Learning*. The second part, the *Novum organum*, had appeared in 1620. This had its origin in the *Cogitata et visa* (1607); but it was never completed, a fate which overtook most of Bacon's literary plans. In 1622 and 1623 he published parts of his projected *Historia naturalis et experimentalis ad condendam philosophiam: sive phenomena universi*. The *Sylva sylvarum* and the *New Atlantis* were published posthumously. Numerous other writings include essays and a history of Henry VII.

3. According to Bacon[2] 'that division of human learning is most true which is derived from the threefold faculty of the rational soul'. Taking memory, imagination and reason to be the three faculties of the rational soul, he assigns history

to memory, poetry to imagination and philosophy to reasoning. History, however, comprises not only 'civil history', but also 'natural history', and Bacon remarks that 'literary history' should be attended to.[3] Philosophy falls into three main divisions; the first being concerned with God (*de Numine*), the second with nature and the third with man. The first division, that concerned with God, is natural or rational theology; it does not comprise 'inspired or sacred theology', which is the result of God's revelation rather than of man's reasoning. Revealed theology is, indeed, 'the haven and sabbath of all human contemplations',[4] and it is a province of knowledge (*scientia*), but it stands outside philosophy. Philosophy is the work of the human reason, nature being known directly (*radio directo*), God indirectly by means of creatures (*radio refracto*), and man by reflection (*radio reflexo*). Bacon's division of human learning or knowledge according to the faculties of the rational soul is unhappy and artificial; but when he comes to determine the main divisions of philosophy he divides them according to objects: God, nature and man.

The divisions of philosophy, he says,[5] are like the branches of a tree which are united in a common trunk. This means that there is 'one universal science, which is the mother of the rest' and is known as 'first philosophy'. This comprises both fundamental axioms, like *quae in eodem tertio conveniunt, et inter se conveniunt*, and fundamental notions like 'possible' and 'impossible', 'being' and 'not-being', etc. Natural theology, which is the knowledge of God that can be obtained 'by the light of nature and the contemplation of created things'[6] treats of God's existence and of His nature, but only so far as this is manifested in creatures; and it has as its appendix *doctrina de angelis et spiritibus*. The philosophy of nature Bacon divides into speculative and operative natural philosophy. Speculative natural philosophy is subdivided into *physics* (*physica specialis*) and metaphysics. Metaphysics, as part of natural philosophy, must be distinguished, Bacon says,[7] from first philosophy and natural theology, to neither of which does he give the name 'metaphysics'. What, then, is the difference between physics and metaphysics? It is to be found in the types of causes with which they are respectively concerned. Physics treats of efficient and material causes, metaphysics of formal and final causes. But Bacon presently declares that 'inquiry into final causes is sterile and, like a virgin consecrated to God, produces nothing'.[8] One can say, then, that metaphysics, according to him, is concerned with formal causes. This was the position he adopted in the *Novum organum*.

One is naturally tempted to interpret all this in Aristotelian terms and to think that Bacon was simply continuing the Aristotelian doctrine of causes. This would be a mistake, however, and Bacon himself said that his readers should not suppose that because he used a traditional term he was employing it in the traditional sense. By 'forms', the object of metaphysics, he meant what he called 'fixed laws'. The form of heat is the law of heat. Actually there is no radical division between physics and metaphysics. Physics started with examining specific types of matter or bodies in a restricted field of causality and activity; but it goes on to consider more general laws. Thus it shades off into metaphysics, which is concerned with the highest or widest laws of nature. Bacon's use of Aristotelian terminology is misleading. Metaphysics is for him the most general part of what might otherwise be called physics. Moreover, it is not directed to contemplation but to action. We seek to learn the laws of nature with a view to increasing human control over bodies.

Speculative natural philosophy consisting, then, of physics and metaphysics, what is operative natural philosophy? It is the application of the former; and it falls into two parts, mechanics (by which Bacon means the science of mechanics) and magic. Mechanics is the application of physics in practice, while magic is applied metaphysics. Here again Bacon's terminology is apt to mislead. By 'magic' he does not mean, he tells us, the superstitious and frivolous magic which is as different from true magic as the chronicles about King Arthur are different from Caesar's commentaries: he means the practical application of the science of 'hidden forms' or laws. It is improbable that youth could be suddenly and magically restored to an old man; but it is probable that a knowledge of the true natures of assimilation, bodily 'spirits', etc., could prolong life or even partly restore youth 'by means of diets, baths, unctions, the right medicines, suitable exercises and the like'.[9]

The 'appendix' of natural philosophy is mathematics.[10]

Pure mathematics comprises geometry, which treats of continuous abstract quantity, and arithmetic, which treats of discrete abstract quantity. 'Mixed mathematics' comprises perspective, music, astronomy, cosmography, architecture, etc. Elsewhere,[11] however, Bacon remarks that astronomy is rather the noblest part of physics than a part of mathematics. When astronomers pay exclusive attention to mathematics they produce false hypotheses. Even if Bacon did not reject outright the heliocentric hypothesis of Copernicus and Galileo, he certainly did not embrace it. Apologists for Bacon point out that he was convinced that the appearances could be saved either on the heliocentric or on the geocentric hypothesis and that the dispute could not be settled by mathematical and abstract reasoning. Doubtless he did think this; but that does not alter the fact that he failed to discern the superiority of the heliocentric hypothesis.

The third main part of philosophy is the part dealing with man. It comprises *philosophia humanitatis* or anthropology and *philosophia civilis* or political philosophy. The former treats first of the human body and is subdivided into medicine, cosmetics, athletics and *ars voluptuaria*, including, for example, music considered from a certain point of view. Secondly it treats of the human soul, though the nature of the rational, divinely created and immortal soul (*spiraculum*) as distinct from the sensitive soul is a subject which belongs to theology rather than to philosophy. The latter is, however, able to establish the fact that man possesses faculties which transcend the power of matter. Psychology thus leads on to a consideration of logic, *doctrina circa intellectum*, and ethics, *doctrina circa voluntatem*.[12] The parts of logic are the *artes inveniendi, judicandi, retinendi et tradendi*. The most important subdivision of the *ars inveniendi* is what Bacon calls 'the interpretation of nature', which proceeds *ab experimentis ad axiomata, quae et ipsa nova experimenta designent*.[13] This is the *novum organum*. The art of judging is divided into induction, which belongs to the *novum organum*, and the syllogism. Bacon's doctrine concerning the *novum organum* will be considered presently, as also his theory of the 'idols' which forms one of the topics comprised under the heading of the doctrine of the syllogism. In passing it may be mentioned that apropos of pedagogy, which is an 'appendix' of the *ars tradendi*, Bacon observes, 'Consult the schools of the Jesuits: for nothing that has been practised is better than these.'[14] Ethics deals with the nature of human good (*doctrina de exemplari*), not only private but also common, and with the cultivation of the soul with a view to attaining the good (*doctrina de georgica animi*). The part dealing with the common good does not treat of the actual union of men in the State but with the factors which render men apt for social life.[15] Finally *philosophia civilis*[16] is divided into three parts, each of which considers a good which accrues to man from civil society. *Doctrina de conversatione* considers the good which comes to man from association with his fellows (*solamen contra solitudinem*); *doctrina de negotiis* considers the help man receives from society in his practical affairs; and the *doctrina de imperio sive republica* considers the protection from injury which he obtains through government. Or one can say that the three parts consider the three types of prudence; *prudentia in conversando*, *prudentia in negotiando* and *prudentia in gubernando*. Bacon adds[17] that there are two *desiderata* in the part dealing with government, namely a theory concerning the extension of rule or empire and a science of universal justice, the *de justitia universali sive de fontibus iuris*.

In the ninth and last book of the *De augmentis scientiarum* Bacon touches briefly on revealed theology. Just as we are bound to obey the divine law, he says, even when the will resists; so we are obliged to put faith in the divine word even when reason struggles against it. 'For, if we believe only those things which are agreeable to our reason, we assent to things, not to their Author' (that is to say, our belief is based on the evident character of the propositions in question, not on the authority of God revealing). And he adds that 'the more improbable (*absonum*, discordant) and incredible a divine mystery is, so much the more honour is paid to God through believing, and so much the nobler is the victory of faith'. This is not to say, however, that reason has no part to play in Christian theology. It is used both in the attempt to understand the mysteries of faith, so far as this is possible, and in drawing conclusions from them.

Bacon's outline of philosophy in the *De augmentis scientiarum* is on the grand scale and comprises a very extensive programme. He was undoubtedly influenced by traditional philosophy, probably to a greater extent than he realized; but I have already pointed out that the use of Aristotelian terms by Bacon is no sure guide to the meaning he gave them. And in general one can see a new philosophical outlook taking shape in his writings. In the first place, he eliminated from physics consideration of final causality, on the ground that the search for final causes leads thinkers to be content with assigning specious and unreal causes to events when they ought to be looking for the real physical causes, knowledge of which alone is of value for extending human power. In this respect, says Bacon,[18] the natural philosophy of Democritus was more solid and profound than the philosophies of Plato and Aristotle, who were constantly introducing final causes. It is not that there is no such thing as final causality; and it would be absurd to attribute the origin of the world to the fortuitous collision of atoms, after the manner of Democritus and Epicurus. But this does not mean that final causality has any place in physics. Furthermore, Bacon did not assign to metaphysics a consideration of final causality in the Aristotelian sense. Metaphysics was for him neither the study of being as being nor a contemplation of unmoving final causes: it is rather the study of the most general principles or laws or 'forms' of the material world, and this study is undertaken in view of a practical end. His conception of philosophy was to all intents and purposes naturalistic and materialistic. This does not mean that Bacon affirmed atheism or that he denied that man possesses a spiritual and immortal soul. It does mean, however, that he excluded from philosophy any consideration of spiritual being. The philosopher may be able to show that a first Cause exists; but he cannot say anything about God's nature, the consideration of which belongs to theology. Similarly, the subject of immortality is not one which can be treated philosophically. Bacon thus made a sharp division between theology and philosophy, not simply in the sense that he made a formal distinction between them but also in the sense that he accorded full liberty to a materialistic and mechanistic interpretation of Nature. The philosopher is concerned with what is material and with what can be considered from the mechanistic and naturalistic point of view. Bacon may have spoken on occasion in more or less traditional terms about natural theology, for example, but it is clear that the real direction of his thought was to relegate the immaterial to the sphere of faith. Moreover, in spite of his retention of the Aristotelian term 'first philosophy', he did not understand by it precisely what the Aristotelians had understood by it: for him first philosophy was the study of the axioms which are common to the different sciences and of various 'transcendental' concepts considered in their relations to the physical sciences. In a broad sense, Bacon's conception of philosophy was positivistic in character, provided that this is not taken to imply a rejection of theology as a source of knowledge.

4. I turn now to the second part of the *Instauratio magna*, which is represented by the *Novum organum sive indicia vera de interpretatione naturae*. In this work Bacon's philosophical attitude is most clearly revealed. 'Knowledge and human power come to the same thing', for 'nature cannot be conquered except by obeying her'.[19] The purpose of science is the extension of the dominion of the human race over nature; but this can be achieved only by a real knowledge of nature; we cannot obtain effects without an accurate knowledge of causes. The sciences which man now possesses, says Bacon,[20] are useless for obtaining practical effects (*ad inventionem operum*) and our present logic is useless for the purpose of establishing sciences. 'The logic in use is of more value for establishing and rendering permanent the errors which are based on vulgar conceptions than for finding out the truth; so that it is more harmful than useful.'[21] The syllogism consists of propositions; and propositions consist of words; and words express concepts. Thus, if the concepts are confused and if they are the result of over-hasty abstraction, nothing which is built upon them is secure. Our only hope lies in true *induction*.[22] There are two ways of seeking and finding the truth.[23] First, the mind may proceed from sense and from the perception of particulars to the most general axioms and from these deduce the less general propositions. Secondly it may proceed from sense and the perception of particulars to immediately attainable axioms and thence, gradually and patiently, to more general axioms. The first way is known and employed; but it is unsatisfactory, because particulars are not examined with sufficient accuracy, care and comprehensive-

ness and because the mind jumps from an insufficient basis to general conclusions and axioms. It produced *anticipationes naturae*, rash and premature generalizations. The second way, which has not yet been tried, is the true way. The mind proceeds from a careful and patient examination of particulars to the *interpretatio naturae*.

Bacon does not deny, then, that some sort of induction had been previously known and employed; what he objected to was rash and hasty generalization, resting on no firm basis in experience. Induction starts with the operation of the senses; but it requires the co-operation of mind, though the mind's activity must be controlled by observation. Bacon may have lacked an adequate notion of the place and importance of hypothesis in scientific method; but he saw clearly that the value of conclusions based on observation depend on the character of that observation. This led him to say that it is useless to attempt to graft the new on to the old; we must start again from the beginning.[24] He does not accuse the Aristotelians and Scholastics of neglecting induction entirely but rather of being in too much of a hurry to generalize and to draw conclusions. He thought of them as being more concerned with logical consistency, with ensuring that their conclusions followed in due form from their premisses, than with giving a sure foundation to the premisses on the truth of which the conclusions depended. Of the logicians he says[25] that 'they seem to have given scarcely any serious consideration to induction; they pass it over with a brief mention and hurry on to the formulas of disputation'. He, on the other hand, rejects the syllogism on the ground that induction must take its rise in the observation of things, of particular facts or events, and must stick to them as closely as possible. The logicians wing their way at once to the most general principles and deduce conclusions syllogistically. This procedure is admittedly very useful for purposes of disputation; but it is useless for purposes of natural and practical science. 'And so the order of demonstration is reversed';[26] in induction we proceed in the opposite direction to that in which we proceed in deduction.

It might appear that Bacon's insistence on the practical ends of inductive science would itself tend to encourage the drawing of over-hasty conclusions. This was not his intention at least. He condemns[27] the 'unreasonable and puerile' desire to snatch at results which, 'as an Atlanta's apple, hinders the race'. In other words, the establishment of scientific laws by the patient employment of the inductive method will bring greater light to the mind and will prove of more utility in the long run than unco-ordinated particular truths, however immediately practical the latter may seem to be.

But to attain a certain knowledge of nature is not so easy or simple as it may sound at first hearing, for the human mind is influenced by preconceptions and prejudices which bear upon our interpretation of experience and distort our judgments. It is necessary, then, to draw attention to 'the idols and false notions' which inevitably influence the human mind and render science difficult of attainment unless one is aware of them and warned against them. Hence Bacon's famous doctrine of 'the idols'.[28] There are four main types, the idols of the tribe, the idols of the cave or den, the idols of the market-place and the idols of the theatre. 'The doctrines of the idols stands to the interpretation of nature as the doctrine of sophistical arguments stands to common logic.'[29] Just as it is useful for the syllogistic dialectician to be aware of the nature of sophistical arguments, so it is useful for the scientist or natural philosopher to be aware of the nature of the idols of the human mind, that he may be on his guard against their influence.

The 'idols of the tribe' (*idola tribus*) are those errors, the tendency to which is inherent in human nature and which hinder objective judgment. For example, man is prone to rest content with that aspect of things which strikes the senses. Apart from the fact that this tendency is responsible for the neglect of investigation into the nature of those things which, like air or the 'animal spirits', are not directly observable, 'sense is in itself weak and misleading'. For the scientific interpretation of nature it is not enough to rely on the senses, not even when they are supplemented by the use of instruments; suitable experiments are also necessary. Then, again, the human mind is prone to rest in those ideas which have once been received and believed or which are pleasing to it and to pass over or reject instances which run counter to received or cherished beliefs. The human mind is not immune from the influence of the will and affections: 'for what a man would like to be true, to that he tends to give credence'. Further, the human mind is prone to indulge in abstractions; and it tends to conceive as constant what is really changing or in flux. Bacon thus draws attention to the danger of relying on appearances, on the untested and uncriticized data of the senses; to the phenomenon of 'wishful thinking'; and to the mind's tendency to mistake abstractions for things. He also draws attention to man's tendency to interpret nature anthropomorphically. Man easily reads into nature final causes 'which proceed from the nature of man rather than from that of the universe'. On this matter one may recall what he says in his work *The Advancement of Learning* (2) concerning the introduction of final causes into physics. 'For to say that the hairs of the eyelids are for a quickset and fence about the sight; or that the firmness of the skins and hides of living creatures is to defend them from the extremities of heat or cold; or that the clouds are for watering of the earth' is 'impertinent' in physics. Such considerations 'stay and slug the ship from farther sailing, and have brought this to pass, that the search of the physical causes hath been neglected and passed in silence'. Although Bacon says, as we have seen, that final causality 'is well inquired and collected in metaphysics', it is pretty clear that he regarded notions like the above as instances of man's tendency to interpret natural activity on an analogy with human purposeful activity.

The 'idols of the den' (*idola specus* are the errors peculiar to each individual, arising from his temperament, education, reading and the special influences which have weighed with him as an individual. These factors lead him to interpret phenomena according to the viewpoint of his own den or cave. 'For each one has (in addition to the aberrations of human nature in general) a certain individual cave or cavern of his own, which breaks and distorts the light of nature.' Bacon's language designedly recalls Plato's parable of the cave in the *Republic*.

The 'idols of the market-place' (*idola fori*) are errors due to the influence of language. The words used in common language describe things as commonly conceived; and when an acute mind sees that the commonly accepted analysis of things is inadequate, language may stand in the way of the expression of a more adequate analysis. Sometimes words are employed when there are no corresponding things. Bacon gives examples like *fortuna* and *primum mobile*. Sometimes words are employed without any clear concept of what is denoted or without any commonly recognized meaning. Bacon takes as an example the word 'humid', *humidum*, which may refer to various sorts of things or qualities or actions.

The 'idols of the theatre' (*idola theatri*) are the philosophical systems of the past, which are nothing better than stage-plays representing unreal worlds of man's own creation. In general there are three types of false philosophy. First there is 'sophistical' philosophy, the chief representative of which is Aristotle, who corrupted natural philosophy with his dialectic. Secondly, there is 'empirical' philosophy, based on a few narrow and obscure observations. The chemists are the chief offenders here: Bacon mentions the philosophy of William Gilbert, author of *De magnete* (1600). Thirdly there is 'superstitious' philosophy, characterized by the introduction of theological considerations. The Pythagoreans indulged in this sort of thing, and, more subtly and dangerously, Plato and the Platonists.

Bad demonstrations are the allies and support of the 'idols': 'by far the best demonstration is experience'.[30] But it is necessary to make a distinction. Mere experience is not enough; it may be compared to a man groping his way in the dark and clutching at anything which offers, in the hope that he will eventually take the right direction. True experience is planned: it may be compared to the activity of a man who first lights a lamp and sees the way clearly.[31] It is not a question of simply multiplying experiments, but of proceeding by an orderly and methodically inductive process.[32] Nor is true induction the same thing as *inductio per enumerationem simplicem*, which is 'puerile' and leads to precarious conclusions which are arrived at without sufficient examination and often with a total neglect of negative instances.[33] Bacon seems to have thought, wrongly, that the only form of induction known to the Aristotelians was perfect induction or induction 'by simple enumeration', in which no serious attempt was made to discover a real causal connection. But it is undeniable that insufficient consideration had been paid to the subject of inductive method.

What, then, is true induction, positively considered? Human power is directed to or consists in being able to generate a new form in a given nature. From this it follows that human science is directed to the discovery of the forms of things.[34] 'Form' does not here refer to the final cause: the form or formal cause of a given nature is such that, 'given the form, the nature infallibly follows'.[35] It is the law which constitutes a nature. 'And so the form of heat or the form of light is the same thing as the law of heat or the law of light.'[36] Wherever heat manifests itself it is fundamentally the same reality which manifests itself, even if the things in which heat manifests itself are heterogeneous; and to discover the law governing this manifestation of heat is to discover the form of heat. The discovery of these laws or forms would increase human power. For example, gold is a combination of various qualities or natures, and whoever knew the forms or laws of these various qualities or natures could produce them in another body; and this would infallibly result in the transformation of that body into gold.[37]

The discovery of forms in this sense, that is, of the eternal and unchangeable forms or laws, belongs, however, to metaphysics, to which, as has already been mentioned, the consideration of 'formal causes' properly belongs. Physics are concerned with efficient causes or with the investigation of concrete bodies in their natural operation rather than with the possible transformation of one body into another through a knowledge of the forms of simple natures. The physicist will investigate 'concrete bodies as they are found in the ordinary course of nature'.[38] He will investigate what Bacon calls the *latens processus,* the process of change which is not immediately observable but needs to be discovered. 'For example, in every generation and transformation of bodies inquiry must be made as to what is lost and flies away, what remains and what is added; what is dilated and what is contracted; what is united and what is separated; what is continued and what is cut off; what impels and what hinders; what dominates and what succumbs; and much else besides. Nor are these things to be investigated only in the generation and transformation of bodies but also in all other alterations and motions . . .'[39] The process of natural change depends on factors which are not immediately observed by the senses. The physicist will also investigate what Bacon calls the *latens schematismus,* the inner structure of bodies.[40] 'But the thing will not on that account be reduced to the atom, which presupposes the vacuum and unchanging matter (both of which are false) but to true particles, as they may be found to be.'[41]

We have thus the investigation of the eternal and changeless forms of simple natures, which constitutes metaphysics, and the investigation of the efficient and material causes and of the *latens processus* and *latens schematismus* (all of which relate to 'the common and ordinary course of nature, not to the fundamental and eternal laws'), which constitutes physics.[42] The purpose of both is, however, increase of man's power over nature; and this cannot be fully attained without a knowledge of the ultimate forms.

The problem of induction is, therefore, the problem of the discovery of forms. There are two distinct stages. First, there is the 'eduction' of axioms from experience; and, secondly, there is the deduction or derivation of new experiments from the axioms. In more modern language we should say that a hypothesis must first be formed on the basis of the facts of experience, and then observations which will test the value of the hypothesis must be deduced from the hypothesis. This means, says Bacon, that the primary task is to prepare a 'sufficient and good natural and experimental history', based on the facts.[43] Suppose that one desires to discover the form of heat. First of all one must construct a list of cases in which heat is present (*instantiae convenientes in natura calidi*); for example, the rays of the sun, the striking of sparks from flint, the interior of animals, or nasturtium when chewed. Then we shall have a *tabula essentiae et praesentiae.*[44] After this a list should be made of cases which are as much as possible alike to the first but in which heat is nevertheless absent. For example, 'the rays of the moon and of the stars and of comets are not found to be warm to the sense of touch'.[45] In this way *a tabula declinationis sive absentiae in proximo* will be constructed. Finally what Bacon calls a *tabula graduum* or *tabula comparativae* must be made of cases in which the nature whose form is being investigated is present in varying degrees.[46] For example, the heat of animals is increased by exercise and by fever. These tables having been constructed, the work of induction really begins. By comparing the instances we must discover what is always present when a given nature (heat, for example) is present; what is always absent when it is absent; and what varies in correspondence with the variations of that 'nature'.[47] First of all, we shall be able to exclude (as the form of a given nature) what is not present in some instance in which that nature is present or which is present in an instance in which the nature is absent or which does not vary in correspondence with the variations of that nature. This is the process of *rejectio* or *exclusio*.[48] But it simply lays the foundations of true induction, which is not completed until a positive affirmation is arrived at.[49] A provisional positive affirmation is arrived at by comparing the positive 'tables'; and Bacon calls this provisional affirmation a *permissio intellectus* or *interpretatio inchoata* or *vindemiatio prima*.[50] Taking heat as an example, he finds the form of heat in motion or, more exactly, in *motus expansivus, cohibitus, et nitens per partes minores*, expanding and restrained motion which makes its way through the smaller parts.

However, in order to render the provisional affirmation certain further means have to be employed; and the rest of the *Novum organum*[51] is devoted to the first of these, which Bacon calls the way of *praerogativae instantiarum*, privileged cases or instances. One class of privileged case is that of unique cases, *instantiae solitariae*. These are cases in which the nature under investigation is found in things which have nothing in common save their participation in that nature. The plan of the *Novum organum* demands that after treating of the *praerogativae instantiarum* Bacon should go on to treat first of seven other 'helps to the intellect' in true and perfect induction and then of the *latentes processus* and *latentes schematismi* in nature; but in actual fact he gets no further than the completion of his treatment of the *praerogativae instantiarum*.

In the *Nova Atlantis*, which also is an unfinished work, Bacon pictures an island in which is situated Solomon's House, an institute devoted to the study and contemplation 'of the works and creatures of God'. Bacon is informed that 'the purpose of our foundation is the knowledge of the causes and motions and inner virtues in nature and the furthest possible extension of the limits of human dominion'. He is then told of their researches and inventions, among which figure submarines and aeroplanes. All this illustrates Bacon's conviction concerning the practical function of science. But though he performed experiments himself he cannot be said to have contributed much personally to the practical realization of his dreams. He certainly exerted himself to find a patron able and willing to endow a scientific institute of the type of which he dreamed, but he met with no success. This lack of immediate success should not, however, be taken as an indication that Bacon's ideas were unimportant, still less that they were silly. The Scholastic, and in general the metaphysician, will lay much more emphasis on and attach much more value to 'contemplation' (in the Aristotelian sense) than Bacon did; but the latter's insistence on the practical function of science, or of what he called 'experimental philosophy', heralded a movement which has culminated in modern technical civilization, rendered possible by those laboratories and institutes of research and applied science which Bacon envisaged. He vehemently attacked the English universities, for which, in his opinion, science meant at the best mere learning and at the worst mere play with words and obscure terms, and he looked on himself, with his idea of fruitful knowledge, as the herald of a new era. So indeed he was. There has been a strong tendency to depreciate Francis Bacon and to minimize his importance; but the influence of his writings was considerable, and the outlook which he represented has entered profoundly into the western mind. Perhaps it is only fitting, if one can say so without being misunderstood, that the most recent systematic and appreciative study of his philosophy is the work of an American. For my own part I find Bacon's outlook inadequate, if it is considered as a comprehensive philosophy; but I do not see how one can legitimately deny its importance and significance. If one looks upon him as a metaphysician or as an epistemologist, he scarcely bears favourable comparison with the leading philosophers of the classical modern period; but if one looks upon him as the herald of the scientific age he stands in a place by himself.

One of the reasons why Bacon has been depreciated is, of course, his failure to attribute to mathematics that importance in physics which it actually possessed. And it would be difficult, I think, even for his most ardent admirer to maintain successfully that Bacon had a proper understanding of the sort of work which was being accomplished by the leading scientists of his day. Furthermore, he implies that right use of the inductive method would put all intellects more or less on the same level, as though 'not much is left to acuteness and strength of talent'.[52] It is difficult, he says, to draw a perfect circle without a pair of compasses, but with it anyone can do so. A practical understanding of the true inductive method serves a function analogous to that of the pair of compasses. It was a weakness in Bacon that he did not fully realize that there is such a thing as scientific genius and that its rôle cannot be adequately supplied by the use of a quasi-mechanical method. No doubt he distrusted the illegitimate employment of imagination and fantasy in science, and rightly so; but there is considerable difference between the great scientist who divines a fruitful hypothesis and the man who is capable of making experiments and observations when he has been told on what lines to work.

On the other hand, Bacon was by no means blind to the use of hypothesis in science, even if he did not attach sufficient importance to scientific deduction. In any case the deficiencies in Bacon's conception of method ought not to prevent one giving him full credit for realizing the fact that a 'new organ' was required, namely a developed logic of inductive method. Not only did he realize the need and make a sustained attempt to supply it, but he also anticipated a great deal of what his successor in this matter was to say in the nineteenth century. There are, of course, considerable differences between Bacon's philosophy and that of J. S. Mill. Bacon was not an empiricist in the sense in which Mill was an empiricist, for he believed in 'natures' and in fixed natural laws; but his suggestions as to inductive method contain essentially the canons later formulated by Mill. Bacon may not have made any profound study of the presuppositions of induction. But, then, if induction requires a 'justification', it was certainly not supplied by Mill. Bacon obviously did not solve all problems of induction, nor did he give a final and adequate logical systematization of scientific method; but it would be absurd to expect or to demand that he should have done so. With all his shortcomings the author of the *Novum organum* occupies one of the most important positions in the history of inductive logic and of the philosophy of science.

Chapter Twenty

POLITICAL PHILOSOPHY

General remarks – Niccolò Machiavelli – St. Thomas More – Richard Hooker – Jean Bodin – Joannes Althusius – Hugo Grotius.

1. We have seen that political thought at the close of the Middle Ages still moved, to a great extent, within the general framework of mediaeval political theory. In the political philosophy of Marsilius of Padua we can certainly discern a strong tendency to the exaltation of the self-sufficiency of the State and to the subordination of Church to State; but the general outlook of Marsilius, as of kindred thinkers, lay under the influence of the common mediaeval dislike of absolutism. The conciliar movement aimed at the constitutionalization of ecclesiastical government; and neither Ockham nor Marsilius had advocated monarchic absolutism within the State. But in the fifteenth and sixteenth centuries we witness the growth of political absolutism; and this historical change was naturally reflected in political theory. In England we witness the rise of the Tudor absolutism, which began with the reign of King Henry VII (1485–1509), who was able to establish centralized monarchic power at the close of the Wars of the Roses. In Spain the marriage of Ferdinand and Isabella (1469) united the kingdoms of Aragon and Castile and laid the foundation for the rise of the Spanish absolutism which reached its culmination, so far as imperialistic glory was concerned, in the reign of Charles V (1516–56), who was crowned emperor in 1520 and abdicated in 1556 in favour of Philip II (d. 1598). In France the Hun-

dred Years War constituted a set-back to the growth of national unity and the consolidation of the central power; but when in 1439 the Estates agreed to direct taxation by the sovereign for the purpose of supporting a permanent army, the foundation of monarchic absolutism was laid. When France emerged from the Hundred Years War in 1453, the way was open for the establishment of the absolute monarchy which lasted until the time of the Revolution. Both in England, where absolutism was comparatively short-lived, and in France, where it enjoyed a long life, the rising class of merchants favoured the centralization of power at the expense of the feudal nobility. The rise of absolutism meant the decay of the feudal society. It meant also the inauguration of a period of transition between mediaeval and 'modern' conceptions of the State and of sovereignty. However, later developments can be left out of account here; it is with the Renaissance that we are concerned; and the Renaissance period was the period in which monarchic absolutism arose in an obvious manner.

This does not mean, of course, that the political theories of the Renaissance period were all theories of monarchic despotism. Catholics and Protestants were at one in regarding the exercise of sovereign power as divinely limited. For example, the famous Anglican writer, Richard Hooker, was strongly influenced by the mediaeval idea of law as divided into eternal, natural and positive law, while a Catholic theorist like Suárez insisted strongly on the unchangeable character of natural law and the indefeasibility of natural rights. The theory of the divine right of kings, as put forward by William Barclay in his *De regno et regali potestate* (1600), by James I in his *Trew Law of Free Monarchies* and by Sir Robert Filmer in his *Patriarcha* (1680), was not so much a theoretical reflection of practical absolutism as an attempt to support a challenged and passing absolutism. This is especially true of Filmer's work, which was largely directed against both Catholic and Protestant opponents of royal absolutism. The theory of the divine right of kings was not really a philosophical theory at all. Philosophers like the Calvinist Althusius and the Catholic Suárez did not regard monarchy as the sole legitimate form of government. Indeed, the theory of the divine right of kings was a passing phenomenon, and it was eminently exposed to the type of ridicule with which John Locke treated it.

But though the consolidation of centralized power and the growth of royal absolutism did not necessarily involve the acceptance of absolutism on the plane of political theory, they were themselves the expression of the felt need for unity in the changing economic and historical circumstances; and this need for unity was indeed reflected in political theory. It was reflected notably in the political and social philosophy of Machiavelli who, living in the divided and disunited Italy of the Renaissance, was peculiarly sensible to the need for unity. If this led him, in one aspect of his philosophy, to emphasize monarchic absolutism, the emphasis was due, not to any illusions about the divine right of kings, but to his conviction that a strong and stable political unity could be secured only in this way. Similarly, when at a later date Hobbes supported centralized absolutism in the form of monarchic government he did not do so out of any belief in the divine right of monarchs or in the divine character of the principle of legitimacy, but because he believed that the cohesion of society and national unity could be best secured in this way. Moreover, both Machiavelli and Hobbes believed in the fundamental egoism of individuals; and a natural consequence of this belief is the conviction that only a strong and unfettered central power is capable of restraining and overcoming the centrifugal forces which tend to the dissolution of society. In the case of Hobbes, whose philosophy will be considered in the next volume of this history, the influence of his system in general on his political theory in particular has also to be taken into account.

The growth of royal absolutism in Europe was also, of course, a symptom of, and a stimulant to, the growth of national consciousness. The rise of the nation-States naturally produced more prolonged reflection on the nature and basis of political society than had been given to this subject during the Middle Ages. With Althusius we find a use of the idea of contract, which was to play so prominent a part in later political theory. All societies, according to Althusius, depend on contract, at least in the form of tacit agreement, and the State is one of the types of society. Again, government rests on agreement or contract, and the sovereign has a trust to fulfil. This contract theory was accepted also by Grotius, and it played a part in the political philosophies of the Jesuits Mariana and Suárez. The theory may be employed, of course, in different ways and with different purposes. Thus Hobbes used it to defend absolutism whereas Althusius employed it in defence of the conviction that political sovereignty is, of necessity, limited. But in itself the theory involves no particular view as to the form of government, though the idea of promise or agreement or contract as the basis of organized political society and of government might seem to stress the moral basis and the moral limitations of government.

The rise of absolutism naturally led to further reflection on the natural law and on natural rights. On this matter Catholic and Protestant thinkers were at one in continuing more or less the typical mediaeval attitude. They believed that an unchangeable natural law exists which binds all sovereigns and all societies and that this law is the foundation of certain natural rights. Thus the appeal to natural rights was allied with a belief in the limitation of sovereign power. Even Bodin, who wrote his *Six livres de la république* with a view to strengthening the royal power, which he considered to be necessary in the historical circumstances, had nevertheless a firm belief in natural law and in natural rights, particularly in the rights of private property. For the matter of that, not even the upholders of the divine right of kings imagined that the monarch was entitled to disregard the natural law: indeed, it would have constituted a contradiction had they done so. The theory of natural law and natural rights could not be asserted without a limitation on the exercise of political power being at the same time implied; but it did not involve an acceptance of democracy.

The Reformation naturally raised new issues in the sphere of political theory, or at least it set these issues in a fresh light and rendered them in certain respects more acute. The salient issues were, of course, the relation of Church to State and the right of resistance to the sovereign. The right of resistance to a tyrant was recognized by mediaeval philosophers, who had a strong sense of law; and it was only natural to find this view perpetuated in the political theory of a Catholic theologian and philosopher like Suárez. But the concrete circumstances in those countries which were affected by the Reformation set the problem in a new light. Similarly, the problem of the relation of Church to State took a new form in the minds of those who did not understand by 'Church' the super-national body the head of which is the pope as Vicar of Christ. One cannot conclude, however, that there was, for example, one clearly defined Protestant view on the right of resistance or one clearly defined Protestant view of the relation of Church to State. The situation was much too complicated to allow of such clearly defined views. Owing to the actual course taken by religious history we find different groups and bodies of Protestants adopting different attitudes to these problems. Moreover, the course of events sometimes led members of the same confession to adopt divergent attitudes at different times or in different places.

Both Luther and Calvin condemned resistance to the sovereign; but the attitude of passive obedience and submission came to be associated with Lutheranism, not with Calvinism. The reason for this was that in Scotland and in France Calvinists were at odds with the government. In Scotland John Knox stoutly defended resistance to the sovereign in the name of religious reform, while in France the Calvinists produced a series of works with the same theme. The best known of these, the *Vindiciae contra tyrannos* (1579), the authorship of which is uncertain, represented the view that there are two contracts or covenants, the one between people and sovereign, the other between the people together with the sovereign and God. The first contract creates the State; the second makes the community a religious body or Church. The point of bringing in this second contract was to enable the author to maintain the people's right not only of resistance to a ruler who tries to enforce a false religion but also of bringing pressure to bear on a 'heretical' ruler.

Owing to historical circumstances, then, some groups of Protestants seemed to those who favoured the idea of submission to the ruler in religious matters to be akin to the Catholics, that is to say, to be maintaining not only the distinction of Church and State but also the superiority of the former to the latter. And to a certain extent this was indeed the case. When ecclesiastical power was combined with secular power, as when Calvin ruled at Geneva, it was a simple matter to preach obedience to the sovereign in religious matters; but in Scotland and France a different situation obtained. John Knox found himself compelled to depart from the attitude of Calvin himself, and in Scotland the Calvinist body by no means considered itself obliged to submit to a 'heretical' sovereign. When, in France, the author of the *Vindiciae contra tyrannos* introduced the idea of the contract, he did so in order to find a ground for corporate Huguenot resistance and, ultimately, for bringing pressure to bear on ungodly rulers; he did not do so in order to support 'private judgment' or individualism or toleration. The Calvinists, in spite of their bitter hostility to the Catholic religion, accepted not only the idea of revelation but also that of invoking the aid of the civil power in establishing the religion in which they believed.

The Reformation thus led to the appearance of the perennial problem of the relation of Church and State in a new historical setting; but, as far as the Calvinists were concerned, there was some similarity at least between the solution they gave to the problem and the solution given by Catholic thinkers. Erastianism or the subordination of Church to State, was indeed a different solution; but neither Calvinists nor Erastians believed in the dissociation of religion from politics. Moreover, it would be a mistake to confuse either the limitations placed by Calvinists on the civil power or the Erastian subordination of Church to State with an assertion of 'democracy'. One could scarcely call the Scottish Presbyterians or the French Huguenots 'democrats', in spite of their attacks on their respective monarchs, while Erastianism could be combined with a belief in royal absolutism. It is true, of course, that religious movements and sects arose which did favour what may be called democratic liberalism; but I am speaking of the two most important of the Reformers, Luther and Calvin, and of the more immediate effects of the movements they inaugurated. Luther was by no means always consistent in his attitude or teaching; but his doctrine of submission tended to strengthen the power of the State. Calvin's teaching would have had the same effect but for historical circumstances which led to a modification of Calvin's attitude by his followers and to a forcing of Calvinists in certain countries into opposition to the royal power.

2. Niccoló Machiavelli (1469–1527) is celebrated for his

attitude of indifference towards the morality or immorality of the means employed by the ruler in the pursuit of his political purpose, which is the preservation and increase of power. In *The Prince* (1513), which he addressed to Lorenzo, Duke of Urbino, he mentions such good qualities as keeping faith and showing integrity and then observes that 'it is not necessary for a prince to have all the good qualities I have enumerated, but it is very necessary that he should appear to have them'.[1] If, says Machiavelli, the prince possesses and invariably practises all these good qualities, they prove injurious, though the appearance of possessing these qualities is useful. It is a good thing to appear to be merciful, faithful, humane, religious and upright, and it is a good thing to be so in reality; but at the same time the prince ought to be so disposed that he is able to act in a contrary way when circumstances require. In fine, in the actions of all men, and especially of princes, it is results which count and by which people judge. If the prince is successful in establishing and maintaining his authority, the means he employs will always be deemed honourable and will be approved by all.

It has been said that in *The Prince* Machiavelli was concerned simply to give the mechanics of government, that he prescinded from moral questions and wished simply to state the means by which political power may be established and maintained. No doubt this is true; but the fact remains that he obviously considered the ruler entitled to use immoral means in the consolidation and preservation of power. In the *Discourses* he makes it quite clear that in his opinion it is legitimate in the sphere of politics to use an immoral means in order to attain a good end. It is true that the end which Machiavelli has in mind is the security and welfare of the State; but, quite apart from the immoral character of the implied principle that the end justifies the means, the obvious difficulty arises that conceptions of what is a good end may differ. If morality is to be subordinated to political considerations, there is nothing but the actual possession of power to prevent political anarchy.

This does not mean that Machiavelli had any intention of counselling widespread immorality. He was perfectly well aware that a morally degraded and decadent nation is doomed to destruction; he lamented the moral condition of

Italy as he saw it and he had a sincere admiration for the civic virtues of the ancient world. Nor do I think that one is entitled to state without any qualification that he explicitly rejected the Christian conception of virtue for a pagan conception. It is perfectly true that he says in the *Discourses*[2] that the Christian exaltation of humility and contempt of the world has rendered Christians weak and effeminate; but he goes on to say that the interpretation of the Christian religion as a religion of humility and love of suffering is an erroneous interpretation. Still, one must admit that a statement of this kind, when taken in connection with Machiavelli's general outlook, approaches very nearly to an explicit repudiation of the Christian ethic. And if one also takes into account his doctrine of the amoral prince, a doctrine which is at variance with the Christian conscience, whether Catholic or Protestant, one can hardly refrain from allowing that Nietzsche's reading of Machiavelli's mind was not without foundation. When, in *The Prince*,[3] Machiavelli remarks that many men have thought that the world's affairs are irresistibly governed by fortune and God, and when he goes on to say that, although he is sometimes inclined to that opinion, he considers that fortune can be resisted, implying that virtue consists in resisting the power which governs the world, it is difficult to avoid the impression that 'virtue' meant for him something different from what it means for the Christian. He admired strength of character and power to achieve one's ends: in the prince he admired ability to win power and keep it: but he did not admire humility and he had no use for any universal application of what Nietzsche would call the 'herd morality'. He took it for granted that human nature is fundamentally egoistic; and he pointed out to the prince where his best interests lay and how he could realize them. The fact of the matter is that Machiavelli admired the unscrupulous though able potentate as he observed him in contemporary political or ecclesiastical life or in historical examples; he idealized the type. It was only through such men, he thought, that good government could be assured in a corrupt and decadent society.

The last sentence gives the key to the problem of the apparent discrepancy between Machiavelli's admiration for the Roman Republic, as manifested in the *Discourses on the*

First Ten Books of Titus Livius and the monarchical doctrine of *The Prince*. In a corrupt and decadent society in which man's natural badness and egoism have more or less free scope, where uprightness, devotion to the common good, and the religious spirit are either dead or submerged by license, lawlessness and faithlessness, it is only an absolute ruler who is able to hold together the centrifugal forces and create a strong and unified society. Machiavelli was at one with the political theorists of the ancient world in thinking that civic virtue is dependent on law; and he considered that in a corrupt society reformation is possible only through the agency of an all-powerful lawgiver. 'This is to be taken for a general rule that it happens rarely, or not at all, that any republic or kingdom is either well-ordered at the beginning or completely reformed in regard to its old institutions, if this is not done by one man. It is thus necessary that there should be one man alone who settles the method and on whose mind any such organization depends.'[4] An absolute legislator is necessary, therefore, for the founding of a State and for the reform of a State; and in saying this Machiavelli was thinking primarily of contemporary Italian States and of the political divisions of Italy. It is law which gives birth to that civic morality or virtue which is required for a strong and unified State, and the promulgation of law requires a legislator. From this Machiavelli drew the conclusion that the monarchic legislator may use any prudent means to secure this end and that, being the cause of law and of civic morality, he is independent of both so far as is required for the fulfilment of his political function. The moral cynicism expressed in *The Prince* by no means constitutes the whole of Machiavelli's doctrine; it is subordinate to the final purpose of creating or of reforming what he regarded as the true State.

But, though Machiavelli regarded the absolute monarch or legislator as necessary for the foundation or reformation of the State, absolute monarchy was not his ideal of government. In the *Discourses*[5] he roundly asserts that, in respect of prudence and constancy, the people have the advantage and are 'more prudent, more steady and of better judgment than princes'.[6] The free republic, which was conceived by Machiavelli on the model of the Roman Republic, is superior to the absolute monarchy. If constitutional law is maintained and the people have some share in the government, the State is more stable than if it is ruled by hereditary and absolute princes. The general good, which consists, according to Machiavelli, in the increase of power and empire and in the preservation of the liberties of the people,[7] is regarded nowhere but in republics; the absolute monarch generally has regard simply for his private interests.[8]

Machiavelli's theory of government may be somewhat patchwork and unsatisfactory in character, combining, as it does, an admiration for the free republic with a doctrine of monarchic despotism; but the principles are clear. A State, when once well-ordered, will hardly be healthy and stable unless it is a republic; this is the ideal; but in order that a well-ordered State should be founded or in order that a disordered State should be reformed, a monarchic legislator is necessary in practice. Another reason for this necessity is the need for curbing the power of the nobles, for whom Machiavelli, contemplating the Italian political scene, had a particular dislike. They are idle and corrupt, and they are always enemies of civil government and order;[9] they maintain bands of mercenaries and ruin the country. Machiavelli also looked forward to a prince who would liberate and unify Italy, who would 'heal her wounds and put an end to the ravaging and plundering of Lombardy, to the swindling and taxing of the kingdom of Naples and of Tuscany'.[10] In his view the papacy, not having sufficient strength to master the whole of Italy but being strong enough to prevent any other Power from doing so, was responsible for the division of Italy into principalities, with the result that the weak and disunited country was a prey for the barbarians and for anyone who thought fit to invade it.[11]

Machiavelli, as historians have remarked, showed his 'modernity' in the emphasis he laid on the State as a sovereign body which maintains its vigour and unity by power-politics and an imperialistic policy. In this sense he divined the course of historical development in Europe. On the other hand he did not work out any systematic political theory; nor was he really concerned to do so. He was intensely interested in the contemporary Italian scene; he was an ardent patriot; and his writings are coloured through and through by this interest; they are not the writings of a detached philosopher. He also over-estimated the part played in historical development by politics in a narrow sense; and he failed to discern the importance of other factors, religious and social. He is chiefly known, of course, for his amoral advice to the prince, for his 'Machiavellianism'; but there can be little doubt that the principles of statecraft he laid down have not infrequently, even if regrettably, been those actually operative in the minds of rulers and statesmen. But historical development is not conditioned entirely by the intentions and deeds of those who occupy the limelight on the political stage. Machiavelli was clever and brilliant; but he can scarcely be called a profound political philosopher.

On the other hand, one must remember that Machiavelli was concerned with actual political life as he saw it and with what is actually done rather than with what ought to be done from the moral point of view. He expressly disclaims any intention of depicting ideal States[12] and he remarks that if a man lives up consistently to the highest moral principles in political life, he is likely to come to ruin and, if he is a ruler, to fail to preserve the security and welfare of the State. In the preface to the first book of the *Discourses*, he speaks of his new 'way', which, he claims, has been hitherto left untrodden. His method was one of historical induction. From a comparative examination of cause-effect sequences in history, ancient and recent, with due allowance for negative instances, he sought to establish certain practical rules in a generalized form. Given a certain purpose to be achieved, history shows that a certain line of action will or will not lead to the achievement of that purpose. He was thus immediately concerned with political mechanics; but his outlook implied a certain philosophy of history. It implied, for example, that there is repetition in history and that history is of such a nature that it affords a basis for induction. Machiavelli's method was not, of course, altogether new. Aristotle, for example, certainly based his political ideas on an examination of actual constitutions and he considered not only the ways in which States are destroyed but also the virtues which the ruler should pretend to have if he is to be successful.[13] But Aristotle was much more concerned than Machiavelli with abstract theory. He was also primarily interested in political organizations as the setting for moral and intellectual education, whereas Machiavelli was much more interested in the actual nature and course of concrete political life.

3. A very different type of thinker was St. Thomas More (1478–1535), Lord Chancellor of England, who was beheaded by Henry VIII for refusing to acknowledge the latter as supreme head of the Church in England. In his *De optimo reipublicae statu deque nova insula Utopia* (1516) he wrote, under the influence of Plato's *Republic*, a kind of philosophical novel describing an ideal State on the island of Utopia. It is a curious work, combining a sharp criticism of contemporary social and economic conditions with an idealization of the simple moral life, which was scarcely in harmony with the more worldly spirit of the time. More was unacquainted with *The Prince*; but his book was in part directed against the idea of statecraft represented in Machiavelli's work. It was also directed against the growing spirit of commercial exploitation. In these respects it was a 'conservative' book. On the other hand More anticipated some ideas which reappear in the development of modern socialism.

In the first book of his *Utopia* More attacks the destruction of the old agricultural system through the enclosure of land by wealthy and wealth-seeking proprietors. Desire of gain and wealth leads to the conversion of arable land into pasture, in order that sheep may be reared on a wide scale and their wool sold in foreign markets. All this greed for gain and the accompanying centralization of wealth in the hands of a few leads to the rise of a dispossessed and indigent class. Then, with a view to keeping this class in due subjection, heavy and fearful punishments are decreed for theft. But the increased severity of the criminal law is useless. It would be much better to provide the means of livelihood for the indigent, since it is precisely want which drives these people to crime. The government, however, does nothing: it is busily engaged in diplomacy and wars of conquest. War necessitates extortionate taxation, and, when war is over, the soldiers are thrown into a community which is already unable to support itself. Power-politics thus aggravates the economic and social evils.

In contrast with an acquisitive society More presents an agricultural society, in which the family is the unit. Private property is abolished, and money is no longer used as a means of exchange. But More did not depict his Utopia as a republic of uneducated peasants. The means of livelihood are assured to all, and the working hours are reduced to six hours a day, in order that the citizens may have leisure for cultural pursuits. For the same reason a slave class sees to the harder and more burdensome work, the slaves consisting partly of condemned criminals, partly of captives of war.

It is sometimes said that More was the first to proclaim the ideal of religious toleration. It must be remembered, however, that in sketching his Utopia he prescinded from the Christian revelation and envisaged simply natural religion. Divergent views and convictions were to be tolerated for the most part, and theological strife was to be avoided; but those who denied God's existence and providence, the immortality of the soul and sanctions in the future life would be deprived of capacity to hold any public office and accounted as less than men. The truths of natural religion and of natural morality might not be called in question, whatever a man might think privately, for the health of the State and of society depended on their acceptance. There can be little doubt that More would have regarded the Wars of Religion with horror; but he was certainly not the type of man who asserts that it is a matter of indifference what one believes.

More had no use at all for the dissociation of morals from politics, and he speaks very sharply of statesmen who rant about the public good when all the time they are seeking their own advantage. Some of his ideas, those concerning the criminal code, for example, are extremely sensible, and in his ideals of security for all and of reasonable toleration he was far ahead of his time. But though his political ideal was in many respects enlightened and practical, in some other respects it can be regarded as an idealization of a past cooperative society. The forces and tendencies against which he protested were not to be stayed in their development by any Utopia. The great Christian humanist stood on the threshold of a capitalistic development which was to run its course. Yet in due time some at any rate of his ideals were to be fulfilled.

4. More died before the Reformation in England had taken a definite form. In *The Laws of Ecclesiastical Polity* by Richard Hooker (1553–1600) the problem of Church and State finds its expression in the form dictated by religious

conditions in England after the Reformation. Hooker's work, which had its influence on John Locke, was written in refutation of the Puritan attack on the established Church of England; but its scope is far wider than that of the ordinary controversial writing of the time. The author treats first of law in general, and on this matter he adheres to the mediaeval idea of law, particularly to that of St. Thomas. He distinguishes the eternal law, 'that order which God before all ages hath set down with Himself for Himself to do all things by',[14] from the natural law. He then proceeds to distinguish the natural law as operative in non-free agents, which he calls 'natural agents', from the natural law as perceived by the human reason and as freely obeyed by man.[15] 'The rule of voluntary agents on earth is the sentence that reason giveth concerning the goodness of those things which they are to do.'[16] 'The main principles of reason are in themselves apparent';[17] that is to say, there are certain general moral principles the obligatory character of which is immediately apparent and evident. A sign of this is the general consent of mankind. 'The general and perpetual voice of men is as the sentence of God Himself. For that which all men have at all times learned Nature herself must needs have taught; and God being the author of Nature, her voice is but His instrument.'[18] Other more particular principles are deduced by reason.

In addition to the eternal law and the natural law there is human positive law. The natural law binds men as men and it does not depend on the State;[19] but human positive law comes into being when men unite in society and form a government. Owing to the fact that we are not self-sufficient as individuals 'we are naturally induced to seek communion and fellowship with others'.[20] But societies cannot exist without government, and government cannot be carried on without law; 'a distinct kind of law from that which hath been already declared'.[21] Hooker teaches that there are two foundations of society; the natural inclination of man to live in society, and 'an order expressly or secretly agreed upon, touching the manner of their union in living together. The latter is that which we call the law of a common weal, the very soul of a politic body, the parts whereof are by law animated, held together, and set on work in such actions as the common good requireth.'[22]

The establishment of civil government thus rests upon consent, 'without which consent there were no reason that one man should take upon him to be lord or judge over another'.[23] Government is necessary; but Nature has not settled the kind of government or the precise character of laws, provided that the laws enacted are for the common good and in conformity with the natural law. If the ruler enforces laws without explicit authority from God or without authority derived in the first instance from the consent of the governed, he is a mere tyrant. 'Laws they are not therefore which public approbation hath not made so', at least through 'Parliaments, Councils, and the like assemblies'.[24] How, then, does it come about that whole multitudes are obliged to respect laws in the framing of which they had no share at all? The reason is that 'corporations are immortal: we were then alive in our predecessors, and they in their successors do live still'.[25]

Finally there are 'the laws that concern supernatural duties',[26] 'the law which God Himself hath supernaturally revealed'.[27] Thus Hooker's theory of law in general follows the theory of St. Thomas, with the same theological setting or, rather, with a like reference of law to its divine foundation, God. Nor does he add anything particularly new in his theory of the origin of political society. He introduces the idea of contract or agreement; but he does not represent the State as a purely artificial construction; on the contrary, he speaks explicitly of man's natural inclination to society, and he does not explain the State and government simply in terms of a remedy for unbridled egoism.

When he comes to treat of the Church, Hooker distinguishes between truths of faith and Church government, which is 'a plain matter of action'.[28] The point he tries to develop and defend is that the ecclesiastical law of the Church of England is in no way contrary to the Christian religion or to reason. It ought, therefore, to be obeyed by Englishmen, for Englishmen are Christians and, as Christians, they belong to the Church of England. The assumption is that Church and State are not distinct societies, at least not when the State is Christian. Hooker did not, of course, deny that Catholics and Calvinists were Christians; but he assumed in a rather naïve fashion that the Christian faith as a whole requires no universal institution. He also assumed that ecclesiastical government was more or less a matter of indifference, a view which would commend itself, for different reasons, neither to Catholics nor to Calvinists.

Hooker is remarkable principally for his continuation of the mediaeval theory and divisions of law. In his political theory he was obviously not an upholder of the divine right of kings or of monarchic despotism. On the other hand, he did not propose his doctrine of consent or contract in order to justify rebellion against the sovereign. Even if he had considered rebellion justified, he would hardly have laboured such a point in a book designed to show that all good Englishmen should conform to the national Church. In conclusion one may remark that Hooker writes for the most part with remarkable moderation of tone, if, that is to say, one bears in mind the prevailing atmosphere of contemporary religious controversy. He was essentially a man of the *via media* and no fanatic.

5. Jean Bodin (1530–96), who had studied law at the university of Toulouse, endeavoured to make a close alliance between the study of universal law and the study of history in his *Methodus ad facilem historiarum cognitionem* (1566). After dividing history into three types he says: 'Let us for the moment abandon the divine to the theologians, the natural to the philosophers, while we concentrate long and intently upon human actions and the rules governing them'.[29] His leading interest is revealed by the following statement in his *Dedication*. 'Indeed, in history the best part of universal law lies hidden; and what is of great weight and importance for the best appraisal of legislation–the custom of the peoples, and the beginnings, growth, conditions, changes and decline of all States–are obtained from it. The chief subject matter of this *Method* consists of these facts, since no rewards of history are more ample than those usually gathered about the governmental form of states.' The *Method* is remarkable for its strongly marked tendency to the naturalistic interpretation of history. For example, he treats of the effects of geographical situation on the physiological constitution, and so on the habits, of peoples. 'We shall explain the nature of peoples who dwell to the north and to the south, then of those who

live to the east and to the west.'[30] This sort of idea reappears later in the writings of philosophers like Montesquieu. Bodin also evolved a cyclical theory of the rise and fall of States. But the chief importance of Bodin consists in his analysis of sovereignty. Originally sketched in chapter 6 of the *Methodus,* it is treated at greater length in the *Six livres de la république* (1576).[31]

The natural social unit, from which the State arises, is the family. In the family Bodin included not simply father, mother and children, but also servants. In other words he had the Roman conception of the family, with power residing in the *paterfamilias.* The State is a secondary or derived society, in the sense that it is 'a lawful government of several households, and of their common possessions, with sovereign power'; but it is a different kind of society. The right of property is an inviolable right of the family; but it is not a right of the ruler or the State, considered, that is to say, as ruler. The ruler possesses sovereignty; but sovereignty is not the same thing as proprietorship. It is clear, then, that for Bodin, as he says in the *Methodus,*[32] 'the State is nothing else than a group of families or fraternities subjected to one and the same rule'. From this definition it follows that 'Ragusa or Geneva, whose rule is comprised almost within its walls, ought to be called a State' and that 'what Aristotle said is absurd—that too great a group of men, such as Babylon was, is a race, not a State'.[33] It is also clear that for Bodin sovereignty is essentially different from the power of the head of a family and that a State cannot exist without sovereignty. Sovereignty is defined as 'supreme power over citizens and subjects, unrestrained by law'.[34] It involves the power to create magistrates and define their offices; the power to legislate and to annul laws; the power to declare war and make peace; the right of receiving appeals; and the power of life and death. But, though it is clear that sovereignty is distinct from the power of the head of a family, it is not at all clear how sovereignty comes into being, what ultimately gives the sovereign his title to exercise sovereignty and what is the foundation of the citizen's duty of obedience. Bodin apparently thought that most States come into existence through the exercise of force; but he did not consider that force justifies itself or that the possession of physical power *ipso facto* confers sovereignty on its possessor. What does confer legitimate sovereignty is, however, left obscure.

Sovereignty is inalienable and indivisible. Executive functions and powers can, of course, be delegated, but sovereignty itself, the possession of supreme power, cannot be parcelled out, as it were. The sovereign is unrestrained by law, and he cannot limit his sovereignty by law, so long as he remains sovereign, for law is the creation of the sovereign. This does not mean, of course, that the sovereign is entitled to disregard the divine authority or the natural law; he cannot, for instance, expropriate all families. Bodin was insistent on the natural right of property, and the communistic theories of Plato and More drew sharp criticism from his pen. But the sovereign is the supreme fount of law and has ultimate and full control over legislation.

This theory of sovereignty must give the impression that Bodin believed simply in royal absolutism, especially if one speaks of the sovereign as 'he'. But though he certainly wished to strengthen the position of the French monarch, since he felt that this was necessary in the historical circumstances, his theory of sovereignty is not in itself bound up with monarchic absolutism. An assembly, for example, can be the seat of sovereignty. Forms of government may differ in different States; but the nature of sovereignty remains the same in all those States, if they are well-ordered States. Moreover, there is no reason why a monarch should not delegate a great deal of his power and govern 'constitutionally', provided that it is recognized that this governmental arrangement depends on the will of the monarch, if, that is to say, sovereignty rests with the monarch. For it does not necessarily follow that because a State happens to have a king, the latter is sovereign. If the king is really dependent on an assembly or parliament, he cannot be called a sovereign in the strict sense.

As historians have pointed out, however, Bodin was by no means always consistent. It was his intention to increase the prestige and insist on the supreme power of the French monarch; and it followed from his theory of sovereignty that the French monarch should be unrestricted by law. But it followed from his theory of natural law that there might be cases when the subject would be not only justified in disobeying a law promulgated by the sovereign but also morally obliged to do so. Moreover, he even went so far as to state that taxation, as it involves an interference with property, requires the assent of the Estates, though the latter, according to the theory of sovereignty, depend for their existence on the sovereign. Again, he recognized certain *leges imperii* or constitutional limitations on the power of the king. In other words, his desire to emphasize the monarch's supreme and sovereign power was at variance with his inclination towards constitutionalism and led him into contradictory positions.

Bodin emphasized the philosophical study of history and he certainly made a sustained attempt to understand history; but he was not altogether free from the prejudices and superstitions of his time. Though he rejected astrological determinism, he nevertheless believed in the influence of the heavenly bodies on human affairs and he indulged in speculations concerning numbers and their relations to governments and States.

In conclusion it may be mentioned that in his *Colloquium heptaplomeres*, a dialogue, Bodin pictures people of different religions living together in harmony. In the midst of historical events which were not favourable to peace among the members of different confessions he supported the principle of mutual toleration.

6. Bodin had given no very clear account of the origin and foundation of the State; but in the philosophy of the Calvinist writer Joannes Althusius (1557–1638) we find a clear statement of the contract theory. In Althusius' opinion a contract lies at the basis of every association or community of men. He distinguishes various types of community; the family, the *collegium* or corporation, the local community, the province and the State. Each of these communities corresponds to a natural need in man; but the formation of any definite community rests upon an agreement or contract whereby human beings agree to form an association or community for their common good in respect of specified purposes. In this way they become *symbiotici*, living together as sharers in a common good. The family, for instance, corresponds to a natural need in man; but the foundation of any definite family rests on a contract. So it is with the State. But a community, in order to attain its purpose, must have a

common authority. So we can distinguish a second contract between the community and the administrative authority, a contract which is the foundation of the duties pertaining to either party.

There is a further important point to be made. As each type of community corresponds to a definite human need, the constitution of a wider or more extensive community does not annul or abolish the narrower community: rather is the wider community constituted by the agreement of a number of narrower communities, which themselves remain in existence. The local community, for example, does not annul the families or the corporations composing it; it owes its existence to their agreement and its purpose is distinct from theirs. They are not, therefore, swallowed up by the wider community. Again, the State is immediately constituted by the agreement of provinces rather than directly by a contract between individuals, and it does not render the provinces superfluous or useless. From this a certain federation logically follows. Althusius was far from considering the State as resting on a contract whereby individuals handed over their rights to a government. A number of associations, which, of course, ultimately represent individuals, agree together to form the State and agree on a constitution or law regulating the attainment of the common purpose or good for which the State is formed.

But, if the State is one among a number of communities or associations, what is its distinguishing and peculiar mark? As in Bodin's political theory it is sovereignty (*ius maiestatis*); but, unlike Bodin, Althusius declared that sovereignty rests always, necessarily and inalienably, with the people. This does not mean, of course, that he envisaged direct government by the people; through the law of the State, a law itself resting on agreement, power is delegated to the administrative officers or magistrates of the State. Althusius contemplated a supreme magistrate, who might, of course, though not necessarily, be a king, and 'ephors' who would see that the constitution was observed. But the theory does involve a clear assertion of popular sovereignty. It also involves the right of resistance, since the power of the ruler rests on a contract, and if he is faithless to his trust or breaks the contract, power reverts to the people. When this happens, the people may appoint another ruler, though this will be done in a constitutional manner.

Althusius assumed, of course, the sanctity of contracts, resting on the natural law; and the natural law itself he regarded, in the traditional manner, as resting on divine authority. It was Grotius, rather than Althusius, who re-examined the idea of natural law. But Althusius' political theory is remarkable for its assertion of popular sovereignty and the use made of the idea of contract. As a Calvinist he insisted on the right of resistance to the ruler; but it must be added that he had no idea of religious freedom or of a State which would be officially indifferent to forms of religion. Such a notion was no more acceptable to the Calvinist than to the Catholic.

7. The chief work of Hugo Grotius or Huig de Groot (1583–1645) is his famous *De iure belli ac pacis* (1625). In the *Prolegomena* to that work[35] he represents Carneades as holding that there is no such thing as a universally obligatory natural law, 'because all creatures, men as well as animals, are impelled by nature towards ends advantageous to themselves'. Each man seeks his own advantage; human laws are dictated simply by consideration of expediency; they are not based upon or related to a natural law, for the latter does not exist. To this Grotius replies that 'man is, to be sure, an animal, but an animal of a superior kind', and 'among the traits characteristic of man is an impelling desire for society, that is, for the social life, not of any and every sort, but peaceful and organized according to the measure of his intelligence. . . . Stated as a universal truth, therefore, the assertion that every animal is impelled by nature to seek only its own good cannot be conceded.'[36] There is a natural social order, and it is the maintenance of this social order which is the source of law. 'To this sphere of law belong the abstaining from that which is another's . . . the obligation to fulfil promises . . .'[37] Furthermore, man is possessed of the power of judging 'what things are agreeable or harmful (as to both things present and things to come) and what can lead to either alternative'; and 'whatever is clearly at variance with such judgment is understood to be contrary also to the law of nature, that is, to the nature of man'.[38]

The nature of man is thus the foundation of law. 'For the very nature of man, which even if we had no lack of anything would lead us into the mutual relations of society, is the mother of the law of nature.'[39] The natural law enjoins the keeping of promises; and as the obligation of observing the positive laws of States arises from mutual consent and promise, 'nature may be considered, so to say, the great-grandmother of municipal law'. In point of fact, of course, individuals are by no means self-sufficient; and expediency has a part to play in the institution of positive law and subjection to authority. 'But just as the laws of each State have in view the advantage of that State, so by mutual consent it has become possible that certain laws should originate as between all States or a great many States; and it is apparent that the laws thus originating had in view the advantage, not of particular States, but of the great society of States. And this is what is called the law of nations, whenever we distinguish that term from the law of nature.'[40] But it is not simply a question of expediency: it is also a question of natural justice. 'Many hold, in fact, that the standard of justice which they insist upon in the case of individuals within the State is inapplicable to a nation or the ruler of a nation.'[41] But, 'if no association of men can be maintained without law . . . surely also that association which binds together the human race, or binds many nations together, has need of law; this was perceived by him who said that shameful deeds ought not to be committed even for the sake of one's country'.[42] It follows that 'war ought not to be undertaken except for the enforcement of rights; when once undertaken, it should be carried on only within the bounds of law and good faith'.[43]

Grotius is convinced, then, that 'there is a common law among nations, which is valid alike in peace and war'.[44] We have, therefore, the natural law, the municipal law or positive law of States, and the law of nations. In addition, Grotius, a believing Protestant, admits the positive Christian law. 'This, however—contrary to the practice of most men—I have distinguished from the law of nature, considering it as certain that in that most holy law a greater degree of moral perfection is enjoined upon us than the law of nature, alone and by itself, would require.'[45]

Historians generally attribute to Grotius an important rôle in the 'freeing' of the idea of natural law from theological foundations and presuppositions and in naturalizing it. In this respect, it is said, he was much closer than were the Schoolmen to Aristotle, for whom he had a great admiration. It is certainly true to some extent that Grotius separated the idea of natural law from the idea of God. 'What we have been saying would have a degree of validity even if we should concede that which cannot be conceded without the utmost wickedness, that there is no God, or that the affairs of men are of no concern to Him.'[46] But he proceeds to say that the law of nature, 'proceeding as it does from the essential traits implanted in man, can nevertheless rightly be attributed to God, because of His having willed that such traits exist in us'.[47] And he quotes Chrysippus and St. John Chrysostom in support. Moreover he defines the law of nature as follows. 'The law of nature is a dictate of right reason which points out that an act, according as it is or is not in conformity with rational nature, has in it a quality of moral baseness or moral necessity; and that, in consequence, such an act is either forbidden or enjoined by the author of nature, God.'[48] Among his references on this matter he refers to Thomas Aquinas and Duns Scotus, whose remarks, he says, are by no means to be slighted. While, then, it may be true to say that, as a historical fact, Grotius' treatment of the idea of natural law contributed to the 'naturalization' of the idea inasmuch as he was treating law, not as a theologian, but as a lawyer and philosopher of law, it is wrong to suggest that Grotius made any radical break with the position of, say, St. Thomas. What seems to impress some historians is his insistence on the fact that an act enjoined or forbidden by the natural law is enjoined or forbidden by God because it is, in itself, obligatory or wrong. The natural law is unchangeable, even by God.[49] It is not right or wrong because of God's decision that it should be right or wrong. But the notion that the moral quality of acts permitted, enjoined or forbidden by the natural law depends on God's arbitrary *fiat* was certainly not that of St. Thomas. It represents, more or less, the Ockhamist view; but it is in no way necessarily bound up with the attribution of an ultimate metaphysical and 'theological' foundation to the natural law. When Grotius points out[50] the difference between the natural law and 'volitional divine law', he is making a statement with which St. Thomas would have agreed. It seems to me that it is Grotius' 'modernity', his careful and systematic treatment of law from the standpoint of a lay lawyer and philosopher, which is responsible for the impression that he made a bigger break with the past than he actually did.

In his *Prolegomena*[51] Grotius says, 'I have made it my concern to refer the proofs of things touching the law of nature to certain fundamental conceptions which are beyond question, so that no one can deny them without doing violence to himself'. In the first book[52] he asserts that *a priori* proof, which 'consists in demonstrating the necessary agreement or disagreement of anything with a rational and social nature', is 'more subtle' than *a posteriori* proof, though the latter is 'more familiar'. But later in his work,[53] when treating of the causes of doubt in moral questions, he remarks that 'what Aristotle wrote is perfectly true, that certainty is not to be found in moral questions in the same degree as in mathematical science'. To this statement Samuel Pufendorf took exception.[54] I do not think, therefore, that one ought to lay great stress on Grotius' place in the movement of philosophical thought which was characterized by emphasis on deduction, an emphasis due to the influence of the success of mathematical science. No doubt he did not escape this influence; but the doctrine that there are self-evident principles of natural morality was by no means new.

'The State', says Grotius,[55] 'is a complete association of free men, joined together for the enjoyment of rights and for their common interests.' The State itself is the 'common subject' of sovereignty, sovereignty being the power 'whose actions are not subject to the legal control of another, so that they cannot be rendered void by the operation of another human will'.[56] The 'special subject is one or more persons, according to the laws and customs of each nation'.[57] Grotius proceeds to deny the opinion of Althusius (who is not named, however) that sovereignty always and necessarily resides in the people. He asks why it should be supposed that the people should be incapable of transferring sovereignty.[58] Though sovereignty is in itself indivisible, in the sense that it means something definite, the actual exercise of sovereign power can be divided. 'It may happen that a people, when choosing a king, may reserve to itself certain powers but may confer the others on the king absolutely.'[59] Divided sovereignty may have its disadvantages, but so has every form of government; 'and a legal provision is to be judged not by what this or that man considers best, but by what accords with the will of him with whom the provision originated'.[60]

As to resistance or rebellion against rulers, Grotius argues that it is quite incompatible with the nature and purpose of the State that the right of resistance should be without limitation. 'Among good men one principle at any rate is established beyond controversy, that if the authorities issue any order that is contrary to the law of nature or to the commandments of God, the order should not be carried out';[61] but rebellion is a different matter. However, if in the conferring of authority the right of resistance was retained or if the king openly shows himself the enemy of the whole people or if he alienates the kingdom, rebellion, that is, resistance by force, is justified.

Grotius teaches that a just war is permissible; but he insists that 'no other just cause for undertaking war can there be excepting injury received'.[62] It is permissible for a State to wage war against another State which has attacked it, or in order to recover what has been stolen from it, or to 'punish' another State, that is, if the other State is obviously infringing the natural or divine law. But preventive war may not be waged unless there is moral certainty that the other State intends attack;[63] nor may it be waged simply for advantage's sake,[64] nor to obtain better land,[65] nor out of a desire to rule others under the pretext that it is for their good.[66] War should not be waged in cases of doubt as to its justice,[67] and, even for just causes, it should not be undertaken rashly:[68] it should only be undertaken in cases of necessity,[69] and peace should always be kept in view.[70] In the actual conduct of war what is permissible can be viewed either absolutely, in relation to the law of nature, or in relation to a previous promise, in relation, that is, to the law of nations.[71] Discussion of the permissible in war with reference to a previous promise is discussion concerning good faith among enemies; and Grotius insists that good faith is always to be kept, because 'those who are enemies do not in fact cease to be men'.[72] For example, treaties should be scrupulously observed. The law of nature binds, of course, all men as men: the law of nations 'is the law which has received its obligatory force from the will of all nations, or of many nations'.[73] It is distinct, therefore, from the law of nature and rests on promise and on custom. 'The law of nations, in fact,' as Dio Chrysostom well observes, 'is the creation of time and custom. And for the study of it the illustrious writers of history are of the greatest value to us.'[74] In other words, custom, consent and contract between States give rise to an obligation just as promises between individuals give rise to an obligation. In the absence of any international authority or tribunal or court of arbitration war between States necessarily takes the place of litigation between individuals; but war should not be waged if it can be avoided by arbitration or conferences (or even lot, says Grotius); and if it cannot be avoided, if, that is to say, it proves to be necessary for the enforcement of rights, it should be waged only within the bounds of good faith and with a scrupulous attention to proper procedure analogous to that observed in judicial processes. It is obvious that Grotius considered 'public war' not as a justifiable instrument of policy, imperialistic ambition or territorial greed, but as something which cannot be avoided in the absence of an international tribunal capable of rendering war as unnecessary as law-courts have rendered 'private war'. Nevertheless, just as individuals enjoy the right of self-defence, so do States. There can be a just war; but it does not follow that every means is legitimate even in a just war. The 'law of nations' must be observed.

Grotius was a humanist, a humanitarian and a learned man; he was also a convinced Christian. He desired the healing of the rifts between Christians; and he defended toleration in regard to the different confessions. His great work, *De iure belli ac pacis*, is remarkable, not only for its systematic and its humanitarian character, but also for its dispassionate freedom from bigotry. Its spirit is well expressed in a remark he makes about the Schoolmen. The latter, he says, 'furnish a praiseworthy example of moderation; they contend with one another by means of arguments—not, in accordance with the practice which has lately begun to disgrace the calling of letters, with personal abuse, base offspring of a spirit lacking self-mastery'.[75]

In this chapter I have avoided discussion of treatises on political theory by Scholastic writers, since I propose to treat of Renaissance Scholasticism in the next part of this work. But it may be as well to draw attention here to the fact that Scholastic authors formed an important channel whereby the mediaeval philosophy of law was transmitted to men like Grotius. This is particularly true of Suárez. In addition, the treatments of the 'law of nations' and of war by Vitoria and Suárez were not without influence on non-Scholastic writers of the Renaissance and post-Renaissance periods. One does not wish to depreciate the importance of a man like Grotius, but it is as well to realize the continuity which existed between mediaeval thought and the political and legal theories of the Renaissance period. Moreover, an understanding of the Scholastic philosophies of law helps one to avoid attributing to Grotius and kindred thinkers a degree of 'secularization' of thought which is not, in my opinion, present in their writings. The notion that the Scholastics in general made the natural law dependent on the arbitrary divine will naturally inclines those who hold it to regard a man like Grotius as one who humanized and secularized the concept of natural law. But the notion is incorrect and is based either on ignorance of Scholasticism in general or on an assumption that the peculiar ideas of some of the nominalist school represented the common views of Scholastic philosophers.

Part Three

SCHOLASTICISM OF THE RENAISSANCE

Chapter Twenty-one

A GENERAL VIEW

The revival of Scholasticism – Dominican writers before the Council of Trent; Cajetan – Later Dominican writers and Jesuit writers – The controversy between Dominicans and Jesuits about grace and free will – The substitution of 'philosophical courses' for commentaries on Aristotle – Political and legal theory.

1. One might perhaps have expected that the life and vigour of Aristotelian Scholasticism would have been finally sapped by two factors, first the rise and spread of the nominalist movement in the fourteenth century and secondly the emergence of new lines of thought at the time of the Renaissance. Yet in the fifteenth and sixteenth centuries there occurred a remarkable revival of Scholasticism, and some of the greatest names in Scholasticism belong to the period of the Renaissance and the beginning of the modern era. The chief centre of this revival was Spain, in the sense that most, though not all, of the leading figures were Spaniards. Cajetan, the great commentator on the writings of St. Thomas, was an Italian but Francis of Vitoria, who exercised a profound influence on Scholastic thought, was a Spaniard, as were also Dominic Soto, Melchior Cano, Dominic Báñez, Gabriel Vásquez and Francis Suárez. Spain was comparatively untouched either by the ferment of Renaissance thought or by the religious dissensions of the Reformation; and it was only natural that a renewal of studies which was carried through predominantly, though not, of course, exclusively, by Spanish theolo-

gians should take the form of a revivification, prolongation and development of Scholasticism.

This renewal of Scholastic thought is associated with two religious Orders in particular. First in the field were the Dominicans, who produced noted commentators on St. Thomas like Cajetan and De Sylvestris and eminent theologians and philosophers like Francis of Vitoria, Dominic Soto, Melchior Cano and Dominic Báñez. Indeed, the first stage of the revival of Scholasticism, namely the stage which preceded the Council of Trent, was in a special degree the work of the Order of Preachers. The Council of Trent began in 1545, and it gave a powerful impulse to the renewal of Scholastic thought. The Council was primarily concerned, of course, with theological doctrines, questions and controversies, but the handling and discussion of these themes involved also a treatment of philosophical matters, in the sense at least that the theologians who assisted at the Council or who discussed the subjects which arose in the Council were necessarily involved to some extent in philosophical discussions. The work of the Dominicans in commenting on the works of St. Thomas and in elucidating and developing his thought was thus reinforced by the impulse contributed by the Council of Trent to the promotion of Scholastic studies. A further enrichment of life was given to Scholasticism by the Society of Jesus, which was founded in 1540 and which is especially associated with the work of the so-called Counter-Reformation, inaugurated by the Council. The Society of Jesus not only made a most important general contribution to the deepening and extension of intellectual life among Catholics through the foundation of numerous schools, colleges and universities but it also played a signal part in the theological and philosophical discussions and controversies of the time. Among the eminent Jesuits of the sixteenth century and the early part of the seventeenth we find names like Toletus, Molina, Vásquez, Lessius, St. Robert Bellarmine and, above all, Francis Suárez. I do not mean to imply that other Orders did not also play a part in the renewal of Scholasticism. There were well-known writers, like the Franciscan, Lychetus, who belonged to other Orders. But it remains true that the two bodies of men who did most for Scholastic thought at the time of the Renaissance were the Dominicans and the Jesuits.

2. Of the Scholastics who died before or shortly after the beginning of the Council of Trent one may mention, for example, Petrus Niger (d. 1477), author of *Clypeum thomistarum*, Barbus Paulus Soncinas (d. 1494), author of an *Epitome Capreoli*, and Dominic of Flanders (d. 1500), who published among other works *In XII libros metaphysicae Aristotelis quaestiones*. These three were all Dominicans. So also was Chrysostom Javelli (*c.* 1470–*c.* 1545) who was named Chrysostomus Casalensis after his birthplace. He lectured at Bologna and composed commentaries on the principal works of Aristotle; *Compendium logicae isagogicum, In universam naturalem philosophiam epitome, In libros XII metaphysicorum epitome, In X ethicorum libros epitome, In VIII politicorum libros epitome, Quaestiones super quartum meteorum, super librum de sensu et sensato, super librum de memoria et reminiscentia.* He also defended Aquinas's exposition of Aristotle in *Quaestiones acutissimae super VIII libros physices ad mentem S. Thomae, Aristotelis et Commentatoris decisae* and in *Quaestiones super III libros de anima, super XII libros metaphysicae.* In addition he wrote *In Platonis ethica et politica epitome* and a *Christiana philosophia seu ethica,* besides publishing a refutation of Pomponazzi's arguments to show that the human soul is naturally mortal. This last theme he took up again in his *Tractatus de animae humanae indeficientia in quadruplici via, sc. peripatetica, academica, naturali et christiana.* He also wrote on the thorny subject of predestination.

Mention should also be made of Francis Sylvester de Sylvestris (*c.* 1474–1528), known as Ferrariensis, who lectured at Bologna and published *Quaestiones* on Aristotle's *Physics* and *De anima, Annotationes* on the *Posterior Analytics* and a commentary on St. Thomas's *Summa contra Gentiles.* But a much more important writer was Cajetan.

Thomas de Vio (1468–1534), commonly known as Cajetan, was born at Gaeta and entered the Dominican Order at the age of sixteen. After studying at Naples, Bologna and Padua he lectured in the university of Padua; and it was there that he composed his treatise on Aquinas's *De ente et essentia.* Subsequently he lectured for a time at Pavia, after which he held various high offices in his Order. In 1508 he was elected Master-General, and in this post he gave constant attention to promoting higher studies among the Dominicans. He was created a cardinal in 1517, and from 1518 to 1519 he was papal legate in Germany. In 1519 he was appointed Bishop of Gaeta. His numerous works include commentaries on the *Summa theologica* of St. Thomas, on the *Categories, Posterior Analytics* and *De anima* of Aristotle, and on the *Praedicabilia* of Porphyry, as well as his writings *De nominum analogia, De subiecto naturalis philosophiae, De conceptu entis, De Dei infinitate* and the already-mentioned *De ente et essentia.* Although Cajetan took part in theological and philosophical controversy he wrote with admirable calm and moderation. He was, however, accused of obscurity by Melchior Cano, who was more influenced than Cajetan by contemporary humanism and care for literary style.

In his *De nominum analogia* Cajetan developed a view of analogy which has exercised a considerable influence among Thomists. After insisting[1] on the importance of the rôle which analogy plays in metaphysics he goes on to divide analogy into three main kinds. (i) The first kind of analogy, or of what is sometimes called analogy, is 'analogy of inequality'.[2] Sensitive or animal life, for example, is found in a higher degree of perfection in men than in brutes; and in this sense they are 'unequally' animals. But this does not alter the fact, says Cajetan, that animality is predicated univocally of men and brutes. Corporeity is nobler in a plant than in a metal; but plants and metals are bodily things in a univocal sense. This type of analogy is called 'analogy', therefore, only by a misuse of the term. (ii) The second kind of analogy is analogy of attribution,[3] though the only type of this kind of analogy which Cajetan recognized was analogy of extrinsic attribution. An animal, for example, is called healthy because it possesses health formally, while food and medicine are called healthy only because they preserve or restore health in something other than themselves, an animal, for instance. This example may, however, be misleading. Cajetan did not assert that finite things are good, for example, only in the sense in which food is called healthy: he was well aware that each finite thing has its own inherent goodness. But he insisted that if finite things are called good precisely because of their relationship to the divine goodness as their efficient, exemplary or final cause, they are being called good only by extrinsic denomination. And he thought that when an analogous term is predicated of A only because of a relationship which A has to B, of which alone the analogous term is formally predicated, the predication is called analogous only on sufferance, as it were. Analogy in the proper and full sense occurs only in the case of the third kind of analogy. (iii) This third kind of analogy is analogy of proportionality.[4]

Analogy of proportionality can be either metaphorical or nonmetaphorical. If we speak of a 'smiling meadow' this is an instance of metaphorical analogy; 'and sacred Scripture is full of this kind of analogy'.[5] But there is analogy of proportionality in the proper sense only when the common term is predicated of both analogates without the use of metaphor. If we say that there is an analogy between the relation of God's activity to His being and the relation of man's activity to his being, there is analogy of proportionality, since an imperfect similarity is asserted as holding between these two 'proportions' or relations; but activity is attributed formally and properly to both God and man. Again, we can predicate wisdom of God and man, meaning that an analogy holds between the relation of the divine wisdom to the divine being and the relation of man's wisdom to his being, and we do so without using the word 'wisdom' metaphorically.

According to Cajetan, this kind of analogy is the only kind which obtains between creatures and God; and he made a valiant effort[6] to show that it is capable of yielding a real knowledge of God. In particular, he tried to show that we can argue by analogy from creatures to God without committing the fallacy of equivocation. Suppose an argument like the following. Every pure perfection which is found in a creature exists also in God. But wisdom is found in human beings and it is a pure perfection. Therefore wisdom is found in God. If the word 'wisdom' in the minor premiss means human wisdom, the syllogism involves the fallacy of equivocation, because the word 'wisdom' in the conclusion does not mean human wisdom. In order to avoid this fallacy one must employ the word 'wisdom' neither univocally nor equivocally, that is, neither in one simple sense nor in two distinct senses, but in a sense which contains both uses *proportionaliter*. The conception 'father', for example, as predicated analogously of God and man contains both uses. It is true that we obtain a knowledge of wisdom, for instance, through an acquaintance with human wisdom and then apply it analogously to God; but, says Cajetan,[7] we should not confuse the psychological origin of a concept with its precise content when it is used analogously.

Apart from the obscurity of Cajetan's account of analogy, it is clear, I think, that to lay down rules for the term in order to avoid the fallacy of equivocation is not the same thing as to show that we are objectively justified in using the term in this way. It is one thing to say, for example, that if we assert that there is some similarity between the relation of the divine wisdom to the divine being and the relation of man's wisdom to his being we must not use the term 'wisdom' either univocally or equivocally; but it is another thing to show that we are entitled to speak at all of the divine wisdom. How could this possibly be shown if the only analogy which obtains between creatures and God is analogy of proportionality? It is difficult to see how this kind of analogy can be of any value at all in regard to our knowledge of God, unless the analogy of intrinsic attribution is presupposed. Cajetan had doubtless much of value to say on the wrong uses of analogy; but I venture to doubt whether his restriction of analogy, as applied to God and creatures, to analogy of proportionality represents the view of St. Thomas. And it is perhaps a little difficult to see how his position does not lead in the end to agnosticism.

Cajetan criticized Scotism on many occasions, though always politely and temperately. Still more did he criticize the 'Averroism' of his day. But it is worth noting that in his commentary on the *De anima* of Aristotle he allowed that the Greek philosopher had really held the opinion attributed to him by the Averroists, namely that there is only one intellectual and immortal soul in all men and that there is no individual or personal immortality. Cajetan certainly rejected both the Averroist thesis, that there is only one intellectual and immortal soul in all men, and the Alexandrist thesis, that the soul is naturally mortal. But he apparently came to think that the immortality of the human soul cannot be philosophically demonstrated though probable arguments can be adduced to show that it is immortal. In his commentary on the *Epistle to the Romans,*[8] he explicitly says that he has no philosophic or demonstrative knowledge (*nescio* is the word he uses) of the mystery of the Trinity, of the immortality of the soul, of the Incarnation 'and the like, all of which, however, I believe'. If he was ready to couple the immortality of the soul with the mystery of the Trinity in this way, he cannot have thought that the former is a philosophically demonstrable truth. Moreover, in his commentary on *Ecclesiastes*[9] he says explicitly that 'no philosopher has yet demonstrated that the soul of man is immortal: there does not appear to be a demonstrative argument; but we believe it by faith, and it is in agreement with probable arguments' (*rationibus probabilibus consonat*). One can understand, then, his objection to the proposed decree of the fifth Lateran Council (1513) calling upon professors of philosophy to justify the Christian doctrine in their lectures. In Cajetan's opinion this was the task of theologians and not of philosophers.

3. Among the later Dominican writers of the period one can mention first Francis of Vitoria (1480–1546), who lectured at Salamanca and composed commentaries on the *Pars prima* and on the *Secunda secundae* of Aquinas's *Summa theologica.* But he is best known for his political and juridical ideas, and these will be treated later. Dominic Soto (1494–1560), who also lectured at Salamanca, published, among other works, commentaries on Aristotle's logical writings and his *Physics* and *De anima,* as well as on the fourth book of the *Sentences* of Peter Lombard. Melchior Cano (1509–60) is justly celebrated for his *De locis theologicis,* in which he endeavoured to establish the sources of theological doctrine in a systematic and methodic manner. Bartholomew of Medina (1527–81), Dominic Báñez (1528–1604) and Raphael Ripa or Riva (d. 1611) were also outstanding Dominican theologians and philosophers.

Among the Jesuit writers an eminent name is that of Francis Toletus (1532–96), who was a pupil of Dominic Soto at Salamanca and afterwards lectured at Rome, where he was created cardinal. He published commentaries on the logical works of Aristotle and on his *Physics, De anima* and *De generatione et corruptione*, as well as on St. Thomas's *Summa theologica*. A set of learned commentaries on Aristotle were published by a group of Jesuit writers, known as the *Conimbricenses* from their connection with the university of Coimbra in Portugal. The chief member of this group was Peter de Fonseca (1548–99), who composed commentaries on the *Metaphysics*, as well as publishing *Institutiones dialecticae* and an *Isagoge philosophica* or introduction to philosophy. Among other Jesuit theologians and philosophers mention should be made of Gabriel Vásquez (*c.* 1551–1604), who lectured chiefly at Alcalá and Rome, and Gregory of Valentia (1551–1603). Both these men published commentaries on the *Summa theologica* of St. Thomas. Leonard Lessius (1554–1623), however, who lectured at Douai and Louvain, wrote independent works like his *De iustitia et iure ceterisque virtutibus cardinalibus* (1605), *De gratia efficaci, decretis, divinis libertate arbitrii et praescientia Dei conditionata disputatio apologetica* (1610), *De providentia Numinis et animae immortalitate* (1613), *De summo bono et aeterna beatitudine hominis* (1616) and *De perfectionibus moribusque divinis* (1620).

The Franciscan Lychetus (d. 1520) commented on the *Opus Oxoniense* and the *Quodlibeta* of Scotus. It was not until 1593, however, that the latter was declared the official Doctor of the Franciscan Order. Giles of Viterbo (d. 1532), an Augustinian, composed a commentary on part of the first book of the *Sentences* of Peter Lombard. And one must not omit to mention the group of professors associated with the university of Alcalá, founded by Cardinal Ximenes in 1489, who are known as the *Complutenses*. The leading member of the group was Gaspar Cardillo de Villalpando (1537–81), who edited commentaries on Aristotle in which he tried to establish critically the actual meaning of the text.

4. Perhaps this is the place to say a few words about the famous controversy which broke out in the sixteenth century between Dominican and Jesuit theologians concerning the relation between divine grace and human free will. I do not wish to say much on the subject, as the controversy was primarily of a theological character. But it ought to be mentioned, I think, as it has philosophical implications.

Leaving out of account preliminary stages of the controversy one can start by mentioning a famous work by Luis de Molina (1535–1600), a Jesuit theologian who lectured for many years at the university of Evora in Portugal. This work, entitled *Concordia liberi arbitrii cum gratiae donis, divina praescientia, providentia, praedestinatione et reprobatione*, was published at Lisbon in 1589. In it Molina affirmed that 'efficacious grace', which includes in its concept the free consent of the human will, is not intrinsically different in nature from merely 'sufficient grace'. Grace which is merely sufficient is grace which is sufficient to enable the human will to elicit a salutary act, if the will were to consent to it and co-operate with it. It becomes 'efficacious', if the will does in fact consent to it. Efficacious grace is thus the grace with which a human will does in fact freely co-operate. On the other hand, if God exercises universal and particular providence, He must have infallible knowledge of how any will would react to any grace in any set of circumstances; and how can He know this if an efficacious grace is efficacious in virtue of the will's free consent? In order to answer this question Molina introduced the concept of *scientia media*, the knowledge by which God knows infallibly how any human will, in any conceivable set of circumstances, would react to this or that grace.

It is quite clear that Molina and those who agreed with him were concerned to safeguard the freedom of the human will. Their point of view may perhaps be expressed by saying that we start from what is best known to us, namely human freedom, and that we must explain the divine foreknowledge and the action of grace in such a way that the freedom of the will is not explained away or tacitly denied. If it did not seem fanciful to introduce such considerations into a theological dispute, one might perhaps suggest that the general humanistic movement of the Renaissance was reflected to some extent in Molinism. In the course of the controversy Molinism was modified by Jesuit theologians like Bellarmine and Suárez, who introduced the idea of 'congruism'. 'Congruous' grace is a grace which is congruous with or suited to the circumstances of the case and obtains the free consent of the will. It is opposed to 'incongruous' grace, which for some reason or other is not suited to the circumstances of the case, in that it does not obtain the free consent of the will, though in itself it is 'sufficient' to enable the will to make a salutary act. In virtue of the *scientia media* God knows from eternity what graces would be 'congruous' in regard to any will in any circumstances.

Molina's adversaries, of whom the most important was the Dominican theologian Báñez, started from the principle that God is the cause of all salutary acts and that God's knowledge and activity must be prior to and independent of the human will's free act. They accused Molina of making the power of divine grace subordinate to the human will. According to Báñez, efficacious grace is intrinsically different from merely sufficient grace, and it obtains its effect by reason of its own intrinsic nature. As for Molina's *scientia media* or 'intermediate knowledge', this is a mere term without any corresponding reality. God knows the future free acts of men, even conditional future free acts, in virtue of His predetermining decrees, by which He decides to give the 'physical premotion' which is necessary for any human act. In the case of a salutary act this physical premotion will take the form of efficacious grace.

Báñez and the theologians who agreed with him thus began with metaphysical principles. God, as first cause and prime mover, must be the cause of human acts in so far as they have being. Báñez, it must be emphasized, did not deny freedom. His view was that God moves non-free agents to act necessarily and free agents, when they act as free agents, to act freely. In other words God moves every contingent agent to act in a manner conformable to its nature. According to the Bannezian view, one must begin with assured metaphysical principles and draw the logical conclusions. The Molinist view, according to the Bannezians, was unfaithful to the principles of metaphysics. According to the Molinists on the other hand, it was very difficult to see how the Bannezians could retain human freedom in anything except in name. Moreover, if the idea of a divine concurrence which is logically prior to the free act and which infallibly brings about a certain act was admitted, it was very difficult to see how one is to avoid making God responsible for sin. The Molinists did not think that the distinctions introduced by their opponents in order to avoid the conclusion that God is responsible for sin were of any substantial use for this purpose. *Scientia media* was admittedly a hypothesis; but it was preferable to make this hypothesis rather than to suppose that God knows the future free acts of men in virtue of His predetermining decrees.

The dispute between the Dominicans and the Jesuits induced Pope Clement VIII to set up a special Congregation in Rome to examine the points at issue. The Congregation was known as the *Congregatio de auxiliis* (1598–1607). Both parties had full opportunity to state their respective cases; but the end of the matter was that both opinions were permitted. At the same time the Jesuits were forbidden to call the Dominicans Calvinists, while the Dominicans were told that they must not call the Jesuits Pelagians. In other words, the different parties could continue to propound their own ways of reconciling God's foreknowledge, predestination and saving activity with human freedom, provided that they did not call each other heretics.

5. Cajetan was the first to take Aquinas's *Summa theologica* as a theological text-book instead of the *Sentences* of Peter Lombard; and both Dominicans and Jesuits looked on St. Thomas as their Doctor. Aristotle was still regarded as 'the Philosopher'; and we have seen that Renaissance Scholastics continued to publish commentaries on his works. At the same time there was gradually effected a separation of philosophy from theology more systematic and methodic than that which had generally obtained in the mediaeval Schools. This was due partly to the formal distinction between the two branches of study which had already been made in the Middle Ages and partly, no doubt, to the rise of philosophies which owed nothing, professedly at least, to dogmatic theology. We find, then, the gradual substitution of philosophical courses for commentaries on Aristotle. Already with Suárez (d. 1617) we find an elaborate discussion of philosophical problems in separation from theology; and the order of treating metaphysical themes and problems which had been adopted by Suárez in his *Disputationes metaphysicae* exercised an influence on later Scholastic method. In the freer style of philosophical writing which was inaugurated by Suárez one can doubtless see the influence of Renaissance humanism. I said earlier in this chapter that Spanish Scholasticism was comparatively unaffected by the Renaissance. But one must make an exception, I think, in regard to literary

style. Suárez was, it must be admitted, a diffuse writer; but his work on metaphysics did a great deal to break through the former tradition of writing philosophy in the form of commentaries on Aristotle.

The eminent Dominican theologian and philosopher John of St. Thomas (1589–1644) published his *Cursus philosophicus* before his *Cursus theologicus*, and, to take another Dominican example, Alexander Piny issued a *Cursus philosophicus thomisticus* in 1670. The Carmelite Fathers of Alcalá published a *Cursus artium* in 1624, which was revised and added to in later editions. Among the Jesuits, Cardinal John de Lugo (1583–1660) left an unpublished *Disputationes metaphysicae*, while Peter de Hurtado de Mendoza published *Disputationes de universa philosophia* at Lyons in 1617 and Thomas Compton-Carleton a *Philosophia universa* at Antwerp in 1649. Similarly, both Rodrigo de Arriaga and Francis de Oviedo published philosophical courses, the former at Antwerp in 1632 and the latter at Lyons in 1640. A *Cursus philosophicus* by Francis Soares appeared at Coimbra in 1651, and a *Philosophia peripatetica* by John-Baptist de Benedictis at Naples in 1688. Similar philosophical courses were written by Scotists. Thus John Poncius and Bartholomew Mastrius published respectively a *Cursus philosophicus ad mentem Scoti* (1643) and a *Philosophiae ad mentem Scoti cursus integer* (1678). Among writers belonging to other religious Orders Nicholas of St. John the Baptist, a Hermit of St. Augustine, published his *Philosophia augustiniana, sive integer cursus philosophicus iuxta doctrinam sancti Patris Augustini* at Geneva in 1687, while Celestino Sfondrati, a Benedictine, published a *Cursus philosophicus sangallensis* (1695–9).

In the course of the seventeenth century, then, *Cursus philosophici* tended to take the place of the former commentaries on Aristotle. This is not to say, however, that the former custom was abandoned. Sylvester Maurus (1619–87), for example, a Jesuit theologian and philosopher, published a commentary on Aristotle in 1668. Nor is one entitled to conclude from the change in the method of philosophic writing that the Scholastics of the Renaissance and of the seventeenth century were profoundly influenced by the new scientific ideas of the time. The Franciscan Emmanuel Maignan, who published a *Cursus philosophicus* at Toulouse in 1652, complained that the Scholastics of his time devoted themselves to metaphysical abstractions and subtleties and that some of them, when their opinions on physics were challenged in the name of experience and experiment, replied by denying the testimony of experience. Maignan himself was considerably influenced by Cartesianism and atomism. Honoré Fabri (*c.* 1607–88), a Jesuit writer, laid particular emphasis on mathematics and physics; and there were, of course, other Scholastics who were alive to the ideas of their time. But if one takes the movement of the Renaissance and post-Renaissance philosophy as a whole, it is fairly obvious that Scholasticism lay somewhat apart from the main line of development and that its influence on non-Scholastic philosophers was restricted. This is not to say that it had no influence; but it is obvious that when we think of Renaissance and post-Renaissance philosophy we do not think primarily of Scholasticism. Generally speaking, the Scholastic philosophers of the period failed to give sufficient attention to the problems raised by, for example, the scientific discoveries of the time.

6. There was, however, at least one department of thought in which the Renaissance Scholastics were deeply influenced by contemporary problems and in which they exercised a considerable influence. This was the department of political theory. I shall say something more in detail later about Suárez' political theory; but I want to make some general remarks here concerning the political theory of the Scholastics of the Renaissance.

The problem of the relation between Church and State did not, as we have already seen, come to an end with the close of the Middle Ages. Indeed, it was in a sense intensified by the Reformation and by the claim of some rulers to possess jurisdiction even in matters of religion. As far as the Catholic Church was concerned a doctrine of full submission to the State was impossible: it was precluded by the position accorded to the Holy See and by the Catholic idea of the Church and her mission. The Catholic theologians and philosophers, therefore, felt called upon to lay down the principles by which the relations between Church and State should be governed. Thus Cardinal Robert Bellarmine maintained in his work on the papal power[10] that the pope, while not possessing a direct power over temporal affairs, possesses an indirect power. Temporal interests must give way to spiritual interests, if a clash arises. This theory of the pope's indirect power in temporal affairs did not mean that Bellarmine regarded the civil ruler as the pope's vicar–the theory excluded any such idea; it was simply the consequence of applying the theological doctrine that man's end is a supernatural end, namely the beatific vision of God. The theory was also maintained by Francis Suárez in his *Defensio fidei catholicae* (1613), written against King James I of England.

But though Bellarmine and Suárez rejected the idea that the civil ruler is a vicar of the pope, they did not accept the theory that he derives his sovereignty directly from God, as was asserted by the upholders of the theory of the divine right of kings. And the fact that Suárez argued against this theory in his *Defensio fidei catholicae* was one of the reasons why James I had the book burned. Both Bellarmine and Suárez maintained that the civil ruler receives his power immediately from the political community. They held, indeed, that the civil ruler receives his authority ultimately from God, since all legitimate authority comes ultimately from Him; but it is derived immediately from the community.

One might be perhaps tempted to think that this theory was inspired by the desire to minimize the royal power at a time when the centralized and powerful monarchies of the Renaissance were very much in evidence. What better way of taking the wind out of the sails of the royalists could be devised than that of maintaining that though the monarch's power does not come from the pope it does not come directly from God either, but from the people? What better way of exalting the spiritual power could be found than that of asserting that it is the pope alone who receives his authority directly from God? But it would be a great mistake to regard the Bellarmine-Suárez theory of sovereignty as being primarily a piece of ecclesiastical propaganda or politics. The idea that political sovereignty is derived from the people had been put forward as early as the eleventh century by Manegold of Lautenbach; and the conviction that the civil ruler has a trust to fulfil and that if he habitually abuses his position he may be deposed was expressed by John of Salisbury in the twelfth, Aquinas in the thirteenth, and Ockham in the fourteenth century. Writers like Bellarmine and Suárez simply inherited the general outlook of the earlier Scholastic theologians and philosophers, though the fact that they gave a more formal and explicit statement of the theory that political sovereignty derives from the people was doubtless largely due to reflection on the concrete historical data of their time. When Mariana (d. 1624), the Spanish Jesuit, made his unfortunate statements about the use of tyrannicide as a remedy for political oppression (some of his remarks were interpreted as a defence of the murder of Henry III of France, and this caused his *De rege et regis institutione*, 1599, to be burned by the French Parliament) his principle was simply the principle of the legitimacy of resistance against oppression, which had been commonly accepted in the Middle Ages, though Mariana's conclusions were misguided.[11]

The Renaissance Scholastics were not, however, concerned simply with the position of the civil ruler in regard to the Church on the one hand and the political community on the other: they were concerned also with the origin and nature of political society. As far as Suárez is concerned, it is clear that he regarded political society as resting essentially on consent or agreement. Mariana, who derived the power of the monarch from a pact with the people, regarded the origin of political society as following a state of nature which preceded government; and the main step on the road to organized States and governments he found in the institution of private property. Suárez cannot be said to have followed Mariana in the latter hypothesis of a state of nature. But he found the origin of the State in voluntary consent, on the part of heads of families at least, though he evidently thought that such associations between men had occurred from the beginning.

Suárez may, then, be said to have held a double-contract theory, one contract being between the heads of families, the other between the society so formed and its ruler or rulers. But if one says this, one must realize that the contract theory as held by Suárez did not imply the artificial and conventional character either of political society or of government. His political theory, as we shall see more clearly later, was subordinate to his philosophy of law, in which he maintained the natural character of political society and political government. If we want to know Suárez' political theory, we have to turn primarily to his great treatise *De legibus,* which is above all things a philosophy of law. The idea of natural law, which goes back to the ancient world and which was given a metaphysical foundation by the philosophers of the Middle Ages, is essential to that philosophy and forms the background of his political theory. Political society is natural to man, and government is necessary for society; and as God is the Creator of human nature both society and government are willed by God. They are not, therefore, purely arbitrary or conventional human contrivances. On the other hand, though Nature requires political society, the formation of determinate political communities normally depends on human agreement. Again, though Nature demands that any society should have some governing principle, Nature has not fixed any particular form of government or designated any particular individual as ruler. In certain instances God has directly designated a ruler (Saul, for instance, or David); but normally it rests with the community to determine the form of government.

The theory that political society rests on some sort of agreement was not altogether new, and one can find anticipations of it even in the ancient world. In the Middle Ages John of Paris, in his *Tractatus de potestate regia et papali* (*c.* 1303), presupposed a state of nature and held that though primitive men probably did not make any definite contract they were persuaded by their more rational fellows to live together under common law. And Giles of Rome in the thirteenth century had put forward a contract theory as one of the possible explanations of the foundation of political society. With Mariana in the sixteenth century the theory became explicit. In the same century the Dominican Francis of Vitoria implied a contract theory, and he was followed by the Jesuit Molina, though neither made any very explicit statement of the theory. Thus there was a growing tradition of the social contract theory; and Suárez' statement of it must be seen in the light of that tradition. In the course of time, however, the theory became divorced from the mediaeval philosophy of law. This philosophy was taken over, as we have seen, by Richard Hooker, and from him it passed, in a watered-down form, to Locke. But in Hobbes, Spinoza and Rousseau it is conspicuous by its absence, even if the old terms were sometimes retained. There is, then, a very great difference between the contract theory of Suárez and that of Rousseau, for example. And for this reason it may be misleading to speak of a contract theory in Suárez, if, that is to say, one understands by the term the sort of theory held by Rousseau. There was some historical continuity, of course; but the setting, atmosphere and the interpretation of the theory had undergone a fundamental change in the intervening period.

Another problem with which some of the Renaissance Scholastics concerned themselves was that of the relations between individual States. Already at the beginning of the seventh century St. Isidore of Seville in his curious encyclopaedic work, the *Etymologies*, had spoken of the *ius gentium* and of its application to war, making use of texts of Roman lawyers. Again, in the thirteenth century St. Raymund of Peñafort examined the topic of the right of war in his *Summa poenitentiae*, while in the second half of the fourteenth century there appeared works like the *De bello* of John of Legnano, a professor of the university of Bologna. Far better known, however, is Francis of Vitoria (1480–1546). It was very largely to him that the revival of theology in Spain was due, as was testified by pupils like Melchior Cano and Dominic Soto, while the Spanish humanist, Vivés, writing to Erasmus, praised Vitoria highly and spoke of his admiration for Erasmus and his defence of him against his critics. But it is for his studies on international law that Vitoria is known to the world at large.

Vitoria looked on different States as forming in some sense one human community, and he regarded the 'law of nations' as being not merely an agreed code of behaviour but as having the force of law, 'having been established by the authority of the whole world'.[12] His position seems to have been more or less as follows. Society could not hold together without laws the infringement of which renders transgressors liable to punishment. That such laws should exist is a demand of the natural law. There have therefore grown up a number of principles of conduct, for example the inviolability of ambassadors, on which society as a whole is agreed, since it is realized that principles of this kind are rational and for the common good. They are derivable in some way from the natural law and they must be reckoned to have the force of law. The *ius gentium* consists of prescriptions for the common good in the widest sense, which either belong directly to the natural law or are derivable in some way from it. 'What natural reason has established among all nations is called the *ius gentium*.'[13] According to Vitoria, the law of nations confers rights and creates obligations. Sanctions, however, can be applied only through the instrumentality of princes. But it is clear that his conception of international law leads to the idea of an international authority, though Vitoria does not say so.

Applying his ideas to war and to the rights of the Indians in regard to the Spaniards, Vitoria in the *De Indis* makes it clear that in his opinion physical power by itself confers no right to annex the property of others and that Christian missionary zeal confers no title to make war on the heathen. As regards slavery he adopted the usual position of theologians of the time, namely that slavery is legitimate as a penal measure (corresponding to modern penal servitude). But this concession must not be taken to imply that the Scholastic theologians and philosophers simply accepted the contemporary customs in regard to slavery. The example of the Jesuit Molina is interesting in this matter. Not content with theorizing in his study he went down to the port at Lisbon and questioned the slave-traders. As a result of these frank conversations he declared that the slave-trade was simply a commercial affair and that all the talk about exalted motives, like that of converting the slaves to Christianity, was nonsense.[14] But though he condemned the slave-trade, he admitted the legitimacy of slavery as a penal measure, when, for example, criminals were sent to the galleys in accordance with the penal customs of the time.

Suárez developed the idea of the 'law of nations'. He pointed out that it is necessary to make a distinction between the law of nations and the natural law. The former prohibits certain acts for a just and sufficient reason, and so it can be said to render certain acts wrong, but the natural law does not make acts wrong but prohibits certain acts because they are wrong. That treaties should be observed, for example, is a precept of the natural law rather than of the law of nations. The latter consists of customs established by all, or practically all, nations; but it is unwritten law, and this fact distinguishes it from civil law. Although, for instance, the obligation to observe a treaty once it has been made proceeds from the natural law, the precept that an offer of a treaty, when made for a reasonable cause, should be accepted is not a matter of strict obligation proceeding from the natural law; nor is there any written law about the matter. The precept is an unwritten custom which is in harmony with reason, and it belongs to the 'law of nations'.

The rational basis of the *ius gentium* is, according to Suárez, the fact that the human race preserves a certain unity in spite of the division of mankind into separate nations and States. Suárez did not consider a world-State to be practicable or desirable; but at the same time he saw that individual States are not self-sufficing in a complete sense. They need some system of law to regulate their relations with one another. Natural law does not provide sufficiently for this need. But the conduct of nations has introduced certain customs or laws which are in accord with the natural law, even though they are not strictly deducible from it. And these customs or laws form the *ius gentium*.

It has been said, not unreasonably, that Vitoria's idea of all nations as forming in some sense a world-community and of the *ius gentium* as law established by the authority of the whole world looked forward to the possible creation of a world-government, whereas Suárez' idea of the *ius gentium* looked forward rather to establishment of an international tribunal which would interpret international law and give concrete decisions without being itself a world-government, which Suárez did not regard as practicable.[15] However this may be, it is clear that in much of their political and legal philosophy the Renaissance Scholastics showed a grasp of concrete problems and a readiness to handle them in a 'modern' way. Men like Vitoria, Bellarmine and Suárez all maintained that political sovereignty is in some sense derived from the people; and they maintained the right of resistance to a ruler who acts tyrannically. Although they naturally thought in terms of contemporary forms of government, they did not consider that the actual form of government is a matter of prime importance. At the same time the fact that their conception of political society and of law was founded on a clear acceptance of the natural moral law constituted its great strength. They systematized and developed mediaeval legal and political philosophy and transmitted it to the seventeenth century. Grotius, for example, was certainly indebted to the Scholastics. Some people would maintain, I suppose, that the legal and political theory of the Renaissance Scholastics constituted a stage in the development from a predominantly theological outlook to a positivist outlook; and as a historical judgment this may be true. But it does not follow that the later secularization of the idea of natural law and its subsequent abandonment to all intents and purposes constituted a philosophical advance in any but a chronological sense.

Chapter Twenty-two

FRANCIS SUÁREZ (1)

Life and works – The structure and divisions of the Disputationes metaphysicae – *Metaphysics as the science of being – The concept of being – The attributes of being – Individuation – Analogy – God's existence – The divine nature – Essence and existence – Substance and accident – Modes – Quantity – Relations –* Entia rationis – *General remarks – Étienne Gilson on Suárez.*

1. Francis Suárez (1548–1617), known as *Doctor eximius*, was born at Granada and studied canon law at Salamanca. He entered the Society of Jesus in 1564 and in due course began his professional career by teaching philosophy at Segovia. Afterwards he taught theology at Avila, Segovia, Valladolid, Rome, Alcalá, Salamanca and Coimbra. Suárez, who was an exemplary and holy priest and religious, was also very much the student, scholar and professor; and his whole adult life was devoted to lecturing, study and writing. He was an indefatigable writer, and his works fill twenty-three volumes in the earlier editions and twenty-eight volumes in the Paris edition of 1856–78. A large number of these works were, of course, concerned with theological questions; and for present purposes his most important writings are the two volumes of *Disputationes metaphysicae* (1597) and his great work *De legibus* (1612). One may also mention his *De Deo uno et trino* (1606) and the *De opere sex dierum* (published posthumously in 1621).

Suárez was convinced that a theologian ought to possess a firm grasp and profound understanding of the metaphysical principles and foundations of speculation. He says explicitly that no one can become a perfect theologian unless he has first laid the firm foundations of metaphysics. Accordingly, in his *Disputationes metaphysicae* he set out to give a complete and systematic treatment of Scholastic metaphysics; and, indeed, the work was the first of its kind. It was incomplete in the sense that metaphysical psychology was omitted; but this was supplied in the *Tractatus de anima* (published posthumously in 1621). Suárez abandoned the order adopted by Aristotle in his *Metaphysics*[1] and divided the matter systematically into fifty-four disputations, subdivided into sections; though at the beginning he provided a table showing where the themes treated of in the successive chapters of Aristotle's *Metaphysics* were dealt with in his own work. In this work the author's astounding erudition is clearly expressed in his discussions of, or references and allusions to, Greek, Patristic, Jewish, Islamic and Scholastic authors and to Renaissance thinkers like Marsilius Ficinus and Pico della Mirandola. Needless to say, however, Suárez does not confine himself to the historical recital of opinions; his object is always the attainment of a positive and objective answer to the problems raised. He may be prolix, but he is certainly systematic. As an example of a competent non-Scholastic judgment of the work one may quote the following sentence. 'All the important Scholastic controversies are in this work lucidly brought together and critically examined and their results combined in the unity of a system.'[2]

In the present chapter I shall be concerned mainly with the *Disputationes metaphysicae*. In the next chapter I shall treat of the contents of the *Tractatus de legibus ac Deo legislatore in* X *libros distributus*. This last work summarized and systematized Scholastic legal theories, and in it the author presented his own development of Thomist legal and political theory. In this connection one must mention also Suárez' *Defensio fidei catholicae et apostolicae adversus Anglicanae sectae errores, cum responsione ad apologiam pro iure fidelitatis et praefationem monitoriam Serenissimi Jacobi Angliae Regis* (1613). In this book Suárez maintained Bellarmine's theory of the indirect power of the pope in temporal affairs and argued against the notion, dear to James I of England, that temporal monarchs receive their sovereignty immediately from God. As I remarked in the last chapter, James I had the book burned.

2. Before going on to outline some of Suárez' philosophical ideas I want to say something about the structure and arrangement of the *Disputationes metaphysicae*.

In the first disputation (or discussion) Suárez considers the nature of first philosophy or metaphysics, and he decides that it can be defined as the science which contemplates being as being. The second disputation deals with the concept of being, while disputations 3 to 11 inclusive treat of the *passiones entis* or transcendental attributes of being. Unity in general is the theme of the fourth disputation, while individual unity and the principle of individuation are dealt with in the fifth. The sixth disputation treats of universals, the seventh of distinctions. After considering unity Suárez passes to truth (disputation 8) and falsity (9), while in disputations 10 and 11 he treats of good and evil. Disputations 12 to 27 are concerned with causes; disputation 12 with causes in general, disputations 13 and 14 with the material cause, disputations 15 and 16 with the formal cause, disputations 17 to 22 with efficient causality, and disputations 23 and 24 with final causality, while exemplary causality is the subject of disputation 25. Finally, disputation 26 deals with the relations of causes to effects and disputation 27 with the mutual relations of the causes to one another.

The second volume begins with the division of being into infinite and finite being (disputation 28). Infinite or divine being is treated in the next two disputations, God's existence in disputation 29 and His essence and attributes in disputation 30. In disputation 31 Suárez goes on to consider finite created being in general, and in the following disputation he considers the distinction of substance and accidents in general. Disputations 33 to 36 contain Suárez' metaphysics of substance, and disputations 37 to 53 deal with the various categories of accidents. The last disputation of the work, 54, deals with *entia rationis*.

As has already been indicated, Suárez' *Disputationes metaphysicae* mark the transition from commentaries on Aristotle to independent treatises on metaphysics and to *Cursus philosophici* in general. It is true that one can discern among Suárez' predecessors, as for example with Fonseca, a growing tendency to shake off the bonds imposed by the commentary method; but it was Suárez who really originated the new form of treatment. After his time the *Cursus philosophici* and independent philosophical treatises became common, both inside and outside the Jesuit Order. Moreover, Suárez' decision not to include rational psychology in metaphysics but to treat it on its own and consider it as the highest part of 'natural philosophy'[3] had its influence on succeeding writers like Arriaga and Oviedo, who assigned the theory of the soul to physics rather than to metaphysics.[4]

One feature of Suárez' *Disputationes metaphysicae* which should be noticed is that no separation is made in this work between general and special metaphysics. The later distinction between ontology or general metaphysics on the one hand and special metaphysical disciplines like psychology, cosmology and natural theology on the other hand has commonly been ascribed to the influence of Christian Wolff (1679–1754), the disciple of Leibniz, who wrote separate treatises on ontology, cosmology, psychology, natural theology, etc. But further investigation into the history of Scholasticism in the second half of the seventeenth century has shown that the distinction between general and special metaphysics and the use of the word 'ontology' to describe the former, antedate the writings of Wolff. Jean-Baptiste Duhamel (1624–1706) used the word 'ontology' to describe general metaphysics in his *Philosophia vetus et nova* or *Philosophia universalis* or *Philosophia Burgundica* (1678). This is not to say, however, that Wolff's division of the philosophical disciplines was not of great influence or that the continued use of the word 'ontology' for general metaphysics is not to be ascribed primarily to him.

3. Metaphysics, says Suárez,[5] has as its *obiectum adequatum* being in so far as it is real being. But to say that the metaphysician is concerned with being as being is not the same thing as saying that he is concerned with being as being in complete abstraction from the ways in which being is concretely realized, that is to say, in complete abstraction from the most general kinds of being or *inferiora entis*. After all, the metaphysician is concerned with real being, with being as including in some way the *inferiora entis secundum proprias rationes*.[6] He is concerned, therefore, not only with the

concept of being as such but also with the transcendental attributes of being, with uncreated and created, infinite and finite being, with substance and accidents, and with the types of causes. But he is not concerned with material being as such: he is concerned with material things only in so far as knowledge of them is necessary in order to know the general divisions and categories of being.[7] The fact is that the concept of being is analogous, and so it cannot be properly known unless the different kinds of being are clearly distinguished.[8] For instance, the metaphysician is primarily concerned with immaterial, not with material substance; but he has to consider material substance in so far as knowledge of it is necessary in order to distinguish it from immaterial substance and in order to know the metaphysical predicates which belong to it precisely as material substance.[9]

With Suárez, then, as Suarezians at any rate would maintain, the fundamental metaphysical attitude of Thomism persists unchanged. The Aristotelian idea of 'first philosophy' as the study or science of being as being is maintained. But Suárez emphasizes the fact that by being he means real being; the metaphysician is not concerned simply with concepts. Again, though he is concerned primarily with immaterial reality, he is not so exclusively concerned with it that he has nothing to say of material reality. But he considers material reality only from the metaphysical point of view, not from the point of view of a physicist or of a mathematician; Suárez accepted the Aristotelian doctrine of the degrees of abstraction. Again, we may note that Suárez emphasized the analogical character of the concept of being; he would not allow that it is univocal. Lastly, as to the purpose of metaphysics, Suárez is convinced that it is the contemplation of truth for its own sake;[10] he remains in the serene atmosphere of the Aristotelian *Metaphysics* and of St. Thomas and is unaffected by the new attitude towards knowledge which manifested itself in a Francis Bacon.

4. In the second disputation Suárez treats of the concept of being; and he declares that 'the proper and adequate formal concept of being as such is one' and that 'it is different from the formal concepts of other things'.[11] As he goes on to say that this is the common opinion and reckons among its defenders 'Scotus and all his disciples', it might seem that

he is making the concept of being univocal and not analogical. It is necessary, then, to say something about Suárez' view on this matter.

In the first place the formal concept of being is one, in the sense that it does not signify immediately any particular nature or kind of thing: it does not signify a plurality of beings according as they differ from one another, but 'rather in so far as they agree with one another or are like to one another'.[12] The concept of being is really distinct from the concept of substance or the concept of accident: it abstracts from what is proper to each.[13] It will not do to say that there is a unity of word alone, for the concept precedes the word and its use.[14] Moreover, 'to the formal concept of being there corresponds an adequate and immediate objective concept, which does not expressly signify either substance or accident, either God or creature: it signifies them all in so far as they are in some way like to one another and agree in being.'[15] Does this mean that in a created substance, for instance, there is a form of being which is actually distinct from the form or forms which make it a created substance in particular? No, abstraction does not necessarily require a distinction of things or forms which actually precedes the abstraction: it is sufficient if the mind considers objects, not as each exists in itself, but according to its likeness to other things.[16] In the concept of being as such the mind considers only the likeness of things, not their differences from one another. It is true that a real being is such by its own being which is inseparable from it, that is to say, it is true that a thing's being is intrinsic to it; but this simply means that the concept of being as such does not include its 'inferiors'.

Suárez admits, then, that a concept of being can be formed which is strictly one; and on this matter he ranges himself with Scotus against Cajetan. But he emphasizes the fact that this concept is the work of the mind and that 'as it exists in the thing itself, it is not something actually distinct from the inferiors in which it exists. This is the common opinion of the whole School of St. Thomas.'[17] Why, then, does he insist that the concept of being represents reality? If it represents reality, in what does being as such consist and how does it belong to its inferiors? Does it not seem that if the concept of being as such represents reality, it must represent something in the inferiors, that is, in existent beings, which is distinct from that intrinsic entity or beingness which is peculiar to each? And, if this is not so, does it not follow that the concept of being as such does not represent reality?

Suárez distinguishes 'being' understood as a participle, that is to say, as signifying the act of existing, from 'being' understood as a noun, that is to say, as signifying what has a real essence, whether it actually exists or not. A 'real essence' is one which does not involve any contradiction and which is not a mere construction of the mind. Now, 'being' understood as a participle gives rise to one concept 'common to all actually existent beings, since they are like to one another and agree in actual existence' and this holds good both for the formal and for the objective concepts.[18] We can also have one concept of being understood as a noun, provided that the concept simply abstracts from, and does not exclude, actual existence.

It does not appear to me that the repetition of this statement of our ability to form one concept of being provides a very adequate answer to the difficulties which can be raised; but I wish now to indicate why Suárez does not call this concept a univocal concept.

In order that a concept should be univocal, it is not sufficient that it should be applicable in the same sense to a plurality of different inferiors which have an equal relationship to one another.[19] Suárez, therefore, demanded more for a univocal concept than that it should be one concept; he demanded that it should apply to its inferiors in the same way. We can, indeed, form a formal concept of being which is one and which says nothing about the differences of the inferiors; but no inferior is, so to speak, outside being. When the concept of being is narrowed down (*contrahitur*) to concepts of different kinds of being, what is done is that a thing is conceived more expressly,[20] according to its own mode of existence, than it is by means of the concept of being.[21] This does not mean, however, that something is added to the concept of being as though from outside. On the contrary, the concept of being is made more express or determinate. In order that the inferiors should be properly conceived as beings of a certain kind, the concept of being must indeed be contracted: but this means making more determinate what was already contained in the concept. The latter cannot, therefore, be univocal.

5. In the third disputation Suárez proceeds to discuss the *passiones entis in communi*, the attributes of being as such. There are only three such attributes, namely unity, truth and goodness.[22] These attributes do not, however, add anything positive to being. Unity signifies being as undivided; and this undividedness adds to being simply a denial of division, not anything positive.[23] Truth of knowledge (*veritas cognitionis*) does not add anything real to the act itself, but it connotes the object existing in the way that it is represented by the judgment as existing.[24] But truth of knowledge is found in the judgment or mental act and is not the same as *veritas transcendentalis*, which signifies the being of a thing with connotation of the knowledge or concept of the intellect, which represents, or can represent, the thing as it is.[25] This conformity of the thing to the mind must be understood primarily of a relation to the divine mind, and only secondarily of conformity to the human mind.[26] As to goodness, this means the perfection of a thing, though it also connotes in another thing an inclination to or capacity for the aforesaid perfection. This connotation, however, does not add to the thing which is called good anything absolute; nor is it, properly speaking, a relation.[27] None of the three transcendental attributes of being, then, adds anything positive to being.

6. In the fifth disputation Suárez considers the problem of individuation. All actually existing things—all things which can exist 'immediately'—are singular and individual.[28] The word 'immediately' is inserted in order to exclude the common attributes of being, which cannot exist immediately, that is to say, which can exist only in singular, individual beings. Suárez agrees with Scotus that individuality adds something real to the common nature; but he rejects Scotus' doctrine of the *haecceitas* 'formally' distinct from the specific nature.[29] What, then, does individuality add to the common nature? 'Individuality adds to the common nature something which is mentally distinct from that nature, which belongs to the same category, and which (together with the nature) constitutes the individual metaphysically, as an individual *differentia* contracting the species and constituting the individual.'[30] Suárez remarks that to say that what is

added is mentally distinct from the specific nature is not the same thing as saying that it is an *ens rationis;* he has already agreed with Scotus that it is *aliquid reale*. In answer, then, to the question whether a substance is individuated by itself Suárez replies that if the words 'by itself' refer to the specific nature as such, the answer is in the negative, but that, if the words 'by itself' mean 'by its own entity or being', the answer is in the affirmative. But it must be added that the thing's entity or being includes not only the *ratio specifica* but also the *differentia individualis,* the two being distinguished from one another by a mental distinction. Suárez emphasizes the fact that he is speaking of created things, not of the divine substance; but among created things he applies the same doctrine to both immaterial and material substances. From this it follows that he rejects the Thomist view of *materia signata* as the only principle of individuation.[31] In the case of a composite substance, composed, that is to say, of matter and form, 'the adequate principle of individuation is this matter and this form in union, the form being the chief principle and sufficient by itself for the composite, as an individual thing of a certain species, to be considered numerically one. This conclusion . . . agrees with the opinion of Durandus and Toletus; and Scotus, Henry of Ghent and the Nominalists do not hold anything substantially different' (*in re non dissentiunt*).[32] It is perfectly true that because our knowledge is founded on experience of sensible things, we often distinguish individuals according to their several 'matters' or according to the accidents, like quantity, which follow on the possession of matter; but if we are considering a material substance in itself, and not in relation simply to our mode of cognition, its individuality must be primarily ascribed to its principal constitutive element, namely the form.[33]

7. Having dealt at length with the doctrine of causes Suárez comes in disputation 28 to the division of being into infinite being and finite being. This division is fundamental; but it can be made 'under different names and concepts'.[34] For example, being can be divided into *ens a se* and *ens ab alio,* into necessary being and contingent being, or into being by essence and being by participation. But these and similar divisions are equivalent, in the sense that they are all divisions

of being into God and creatures and exhaust being, as it were.

The question then arises whether being is predicted equivocally, univocally or analogically of God and creatures. Suárez notes[35] that a doctrine of equivocation is wrongly attributed to Petrus Aureoli. The Scotist doctrine, that 'being signifies immediately one concept which is common to God and creatures and which is therefore predicated of them univocally, and not analogically',[36] Suárez rejects. But if being is predicated analogically of God and creatures, is the analogy in question the analogy of proportionality alone, as Cajetan taught, or the analogy of proportionality together with the analogy of attribution, as Fonseca, for example, considered? According to Suárez, the analogy in question cannot be the analogy of proportionality, for 'every true analogy of proportionality includes an element of metaphor', whereas 'in this analogy of being there is no metaphor'.[37] It must be, therefore, analogy of attribution, and, indeed, intrinsic attribution. 'Every creature is being in virtue of a relation to God, inasmuch as it participates in or in some way imitates the being (*esse*) of God, and, as having being, it depends essentially on God, much more than an accident depends on a substance.'[38]

8. In the following disputation (29) Suárez considers the question whether God's existence can be known by reason, apart from revelation. First of all he examines the 'physical argument', which is to all intents and purposes the argument from motion as found in Aristotle. Suárez' conclusion is that this argument is unable to demonstrate the existence of God. The principle on which the argument is founded, namely 'every thing which is moved is moved by another' (*omne quod movetur ab alio movetur*), he declares to be uncertain. Some things appear to move themselves, and it might be true of the motion of the heaven that the latter moves itself in virtue of its own form or of some innate power. 'How, then, can a true demonstration, proving God's existence, be obtained by the aid of uncertain principles?'[39] If the principle is rightly understood, it is more probable (*probabilius*) than its opposite, but all the same, 'by what necessary or evident argument can it be proved from this principle that there is an immaterial substance?'[40] Even if it can be shown that a mover is required, it does not follow that there is not a plural-

ity of movers, still less that the mover is immaterial pure act. Suárez' point is that one cannot prove the existence of God as immaterial uncreated substance and pure act by arguments drawn from 'physics'. In order to show that God exists it is necessary to have recourse to metaphysical arguments.

First of all it is necessary to substitute for the principle *omne quod movetur ab alio movetur* the metaphysical principle *omne quod fit, ab alio fit.*[41] The truth of the principle follows from the evident truth that nothing can produce itself. On the basis of this metaphysical principle one can argue as follows.[42] 'Every being is either made or not made (uncreated). But not all beings in the universe can be made. Therefore there is necessarily some being which is not made, but which is uncreated.' The truth of the major premiss can be made evident in this way. A made or produced being is produced by 'something else'. This 'something else' is itself either made or not made. If the latter, then we already have an uncreated being. If the former, then that on which the 'something else' depends for existence is itself either made or not made. In order to avoid an infinite regress or a 'circle' (which would obtain if one said that A was made by B, B by C, and C by A), it is necessary to postulate an uncreated being. In his discussion of the impossibility of an infinite regress[43] Suárez distinguishes *causae per se subordinatae* and *causae per accidens subordinatae;* but he makes it clear that he considers an infinite regress impossible even in the case of the latter. He adopts, then, a different opinion from that of St. Thomas. But he remarks that even if one accepts the possibility of an infinite regress in the series of *causae per accidens subordinatae,* this does not affect the main line of the argument, for the infinite series would be eternally dependent on a higher extrinsic cause. If it were not, there would be no causality or production at all.

This argument, however, does not immediately show that God exists: it has still to be shown that there is only one uncreated being. Suárez argues first of all that 'although individual effects, taken and considered separately, do not show that the maker of all things is one and the same, the beauty of the whole universe and of all things which are in it, their marvellous connection and order sufficiently show that there is one first being by which all things are governed and from which they derive their origin'.[44] Against the objection that there might be several governors of the universe Suárez argues that it can be shown that the whole sensible world proceeds from one efficient cause. The cause or causes of the universe must be intelligent; but several intelligent causes could not combine to produce and govern the one systematically united effect unless they were subordinated to a higher cause using them as organs or instruments.[45] There is, however, another possible objection. Might there not be another universe, made by another uncreated cause? Suárez allows that the creation of another universe would not be impossible, but he observes that there is no reason to suppose that there is another universe. Still, given the possibility, the argument from the universe to the unicity of God holds good, strictly speaking, only for those things which are capable of being known by human experience and reasoning. He concludes, therefore, that an *a priori* proof of the unicity of uncreated being must be given.

The *a priori* proof is not, Suárez notes, *a priori* in the strict sense: it is impossible to deduce God's existence from its cause, for it has no cause. 'Nor, even if it had, is God known by us so exactly and perfectly that we can apprehend Him by means of His own principles, so to speak.'[46] Nevertheless, if something about God has been already proved *a posteriori*, we may be in a position to argue *a priori* from one attribute to another.[47] 'When it has been proved *a posteriori* that God is a necessary self-existent being (*ens a se*), it can be proved *a priori* from this attribute that there cannot be any other necessary self-existent being, and consequently it can be proved that God exists.'[48] In other words, Suárez' argument is that it can be proved that there must be *a* necessary being and that it can then be shown conclusively that there cannot be more than *one* necessary being. How does he show that there can be only one necessary being? He argues that, in order that there may be a plurality of beings having a common nature, it is necessary that the individuality of each should be in some way (*aliquo modo*) outside the essence of the nature. For, if individuality was essential to the nature, the latter would not be multipliable. But in the case of uncreated being it is impossible for its individuality to be in any way distinct from its nature, for its nature is existence itself, and existence is always individual. The foregoing argument is the fourth which Suárez considers.[49] Later on[50] he remarks that 'although some of these arguments which have been considered do not perhaps, when taken separately, so convince the intellect that a froward or ill-disposed man cannot find ways of evading them, none the less all the arguments are most efficacious, and, especially if they are taken together, they abundantly prove the aforesaid truth'.

9. Suárez proceeds to consider the nature of God. He points out at the beginning of disputation 30 that the question of God's existence and the question of God's nature cannot be entirely isolated from one another. He also repeats his observation that, although our knowledge of God is *a posteriori*, we can in some cases argue *a priori* from one attribute to another. After these preliminary remarks he proceeds to argue that God is perfect being, possessing in Himself, as creator, all the perfections which He is capable of communicating. But He does not possess them all in the same way. Those perfections which do not of themselves contain any limitation or imperfection, God possesses 'formally' (*formaliter*). A perfection like wisdom, for example, though it exists in human beings in a finite or imperfect manner, does not include in its formal concept any limitation or imperfection, and it can be predicated formally of God, *salva analogia, quae inter Deum et creaturam semper intercedit.*[51] Perfections of this sort exist 'eminently' (*eminenter*) in God, for creaturely wisdom as such cannot be predicated of God; but there is, none the less, a formal analogous concept of wisdom which can be predicated formally, though analogously, of God. In the case, however, of perfections which involve inclusion of the being possessing them in a certain category these can be said to be present in God only *modo eminenti*, and not formally.

In succeeding sections Suárez argues that God is infinite,[52] pure act and without any composition,[53] omnipresent,[54] immutable and eternal, yet free,[55] one,[56] invisible,[57] incomprehensible,[58] ineffable,[59] living, intelligent and self-sufficient substance.[60] He then considers the divine knowledge[61] and the divine will[62] and the divine power.[63] In the section on the divine knowledge Suárez shows that God knows possible creatures and existent things and then remarks that the question of God's knowledge of conditional future contingent events cannot be properly treated without reference to theological sources, even though it is a metaphysical question, 'and so I entirely omit it'.[64] But he allows himself the remark that if statements like, 'if Peter had been here, he would have sinned' have a determinate truth, this truth cannot be unknown to God. That they have determinate truth is 'much more probable' (*multo probabilius*) than that they have not, in the sense that Peter in the example given would either have sinned or not have sinned and that, though we cannot know which would have happened, God can know it. However, as Suárez omits any further treatment of this matter in his metaphysical disputations, I too omit it.

10. Coming to the subject of finite being, Suárez treats first of the essence of finite being as such, of its existence, and of the distinction between essence and existence in finite being. He first outlines the arguments of those who hold the opinion that existence (*esse*) and essence are really distinct in creatures. 'This is thought to be St. Thomas's opinion, which, understood in this sense, has been followed by almost all the early Thomists.'[65] The second opinion mentioned by Suárez is that the creature's existence is 'formally' distinguished from its nature, as a mode of that nature. 'This opinion is attributed to Scotus.'[66] The third opinion is that essence and existence in the creature are distinguished only mentally (*tantum ratione*). This opinion, says Suárez,[67] was held by Alexander of Hales and others, including the nominalists. It is the opinion he himself defends, provided that 'existence' is understood to mean actual existence and 'essence' actually existing essence. 'And this opinion, if so explained, I think to be quite true.'[68] It is impossible, Suárez states, for anything to be intrinsically and formally constituted as a real and actual being by something distinct from it. From this it follows that existence cannot be distinguished from essence as a mode which is distinct from the essence or nature *ex natura rei*.[69] The right view is this.[70] If the terms 'existence' and 'essence' are understood to refer respectively to actual being (*ens in actu*) and potential or possible being (*ens in potentia*), then there is, of course, a real distinction; but this distinction is simply that between being and not-

being, since a possible is not a being and its potentiality for existence is simply logical potentiality, that is, the idea of it does not involve a contradiction. But if 'essence' and 'existence' are understood to mean, as they should be understood to mean in the present controversy, actual essence and actual existence, the distinction between them is a mental distinction with an objective foundation (*distinctio rationis cum fundamento in re*). We can think of the natures or essences of things in abstraction from their existence, and the objective foundation for our being able to do so is the fact that no creature exists necessarily. But the fact that no creature exists necessarily does not mean that when it exists its existence and essence are really distinct. Take away the existence, so to speak, and you cancel the thing altogether. On the other hand, a denial of the real distinction between essence and existence does not, Suárez argues, lead to the conclusion that the creature exists necessarily.

Existence and essence together form an *ens per se unum*; but this composition is a 'composition' in an analogical sense. For it is only really distinct elements that can together form a real composition. The union of essence and existence to form an *ens per se unum* is called a 'composition' only in a sense analogous to the sense in which the union of matter and form, two really distinct elements, is called a composition.[71] Moreover, the union of essence and existence differs from that of matter and form in this point also, that the former is found in all creatures, whereas the latter is confined to bodies. Composition out of matter and form is a physical composition and forms the basis of physical change, whereas composition out of essence and existence is a metaphysical composition. It belongs to the being of a creature, whether spiritual or material. The statement that it is a *compositio rationis* does not contradict the statement that it belongs to the being of a creature, for the reason why it belongs to the being of a creature is not the mental character of the distinction between essence and existence but rather the objective foundation of this mental distinction, namely the fact that the creature does not exist necessarily or of itself (*a se*).

Suárez considers the objection that it follows or seems to follow from his view that the existence of the creature is not received in a potential and limiting element and that consequently it is perfect and infinite existence. If, it is said, existence is not an act which is received in a potential element, it is unreceived, and consequently it is subsistent existence. But, says Suárez,[72] the existence of a creature is limited by itself, by its entity, and it does not need anything distinct from itself to limit it. Intrinsically it is limited by itself; extrinsically or *effective* it is limited by God. One can distinguish two kinds of limitation or contraction, namely metaphysical and physical. 'Metaphysical limitation (*contractio*) does not require an actual real distinction between the limited and limiting factors, but a distinction of concepts with some objective foundation is sufficient; and so we can admit (if we wish to use the language of many people) that essence is made finite and is limited with a view to existence and, conversely, that existence is rendered finite and limited by being the act of a particular essence.'[73] As to physical limitations, an angel does not need any intrinsic principle of limitation other than its simple substance, while a composite substance is limited by its intrinsic component factors or principles. This is equivalent to saying that a composite substance also is limited by itself, since it is not something distinct from those intrinsic component factors taken together in their actuality.

Suárez' view is, then, this. 'Because existence is nothing else than essence constituted in act, it follows that, just as actual essence is formally limited by itself, or by its own intrinsic principles, so also created existence has its limitation from the essence, not because essence is a potentiality in which existence is received, but because existence is in reality nothing else but the actual essence itself.'[74] A great deal has been written in Scholastic circles about the dispute between Suárez and his Thomist opponents on the subject of the distinction between essence and existence; but, whichever side is right, it should at least be clear that Suárez had no intention whatsoever of impairing, so to speak, the contingent character of the creature. The creature is created and contingent, but what is created is an actual essence, that is to say, an existent essence, and the distinction between the essence and its existence is only mental, though this mental distinction is grounded on and made possible by the creature's contingent character. Both Thomists and Suarezians agree, of course, about the creature's contingent character. Where they differ is in the analysis of what it means to be contingent. When the Thomists say that there is a real distinction between essence and existence in the creature, they do not mean that the two factors are separable in the sense that either or both of them could preserve actuality in isolation; and when the Suarezians say that the distinction is a *distinctio rationis cum fundamento in re*, they do not mean that the creature exists necessarily, in the sense that it cannot not exist. However, I do not propose to take sides in the controversy; nor shall I introduce reflections which, in the context of contemporary philosophy in Great Britain, might suggest themselves.

11. Passing to the subject of substance and accident, Suárez remarks[75] that the opinion that the division between substance and accident is a sufficient proximate division of created being is 'so common, that it has been received by all as if it were self-evident. Therefore it needs an explanation rather than a proof. That among creatures some things are substances and others accidents is clear from the constant change and alteration of things.' But being is not predicated univocally of substance and accidents: it is predicated analogically. Now, many people, like Cajetan, think that the analogy in question is the analogy of proportionality alone; 'but I think that the same must be said in this connection as has been said concerning being as common to God and to creatures, namely that there is here no analogy of proportionality, properly speaking, but only analogy of attribution'.[76]

In creatures primary substance (that is, existent substance, as distinguished from the universal or *substantia secunda*) is the same thing as a *suppositum*;[77] and a *suppositum* of rational nature is a person.[78] But Suárez discusses the question whether 'subsistence' (*subsistentia*), which makes a nature or essence a created *suppositum*, is something positive, distinct from the nature. According to one opinion existence and subsistence are the same; and that which being a *suppositum* adds to a nature is consequently existence. 'This opinion is now frequently met with among modern theologians.'[79] But Suárez cannot agree with this theory, as he does not believe that existence is really distinct from the actual nature or essence. 'Actual essence and its existence are not really distinct. Therefore, in so far as subsistence is distinct from actual essence, it must be distinct from the existence of that essence.'[80] Therefore being a *suppositum* or having subsistence, which makes a thing independent of any 'support' (that is, which makes a thing a substance) cannot, in so far as it is something added to an actual essence or nature, be the same thing as existence. What, if anything, does subsistence add to an actual essence or nature? Existence as such simply means having actual being: that a being exists does not, of itself, determine whether it exists as a substance or as an accident. 'But subsistence denotes a determinate mode of existing',[81] namely existing as a substance, not inhering in a substance as an accident inheres in a substance. Therefore subsistence does add something. But what it adds is a mode of existing, a way of existing, not existence itself; it determines the mode of existence and gives to the substance its completion *in ratione existendi*, on the level of existence. Having subsistence or being a *suppositum* adds, therefore, to an actual essence or nature a mode (*modus*), and *subsistentia* differs modally (*modaliter*) from the nature of which it is the subsistence as a thing's mode differs from the thing itself.[82] The composition between them is, then, the composition of a mode with the thing modified.[83] Created subsistence is thus 'a substantial mode, finally terminating the substantial nature and constituting a thing as *per se* subsistent and incommunicable'.[84]

12. Here we meet Suárez' idea of 'modes', of which he makes extensive use. For example, he says that probably 'the rational soul, even while joined to the body, has a positive mode of subsistence, and, when it is separated (from the body), it does not acquire a new positive mode of existence, but it is simply deprived of the positive mode of union with the body'.[85] In man, then, not only is there a 'mode' whereby soul and body are conjoined but the soul, even while in the body, also has its own mode of partial subsistence; and what happens at death is that the mode of union disappears, though the soul retains its own mode of subsistence. In purely material substances both form and matter have their own modes, in addition to the mode of union; but it is the 'partial mode' (*modus partialis*) of the matter alone which is conserved after separation of form and matter. The form of a purely

material substance does not, like the human soul, which is the form of the body, preserve any mode of subsistence after the corruption of the substance.[86] A material form has not got its own mode of existence or partial subsistence,[87] but matter has. It follows that God could conserve matter without any form.[88]

13. In his detailed treatment of the different kinds of accidents Suárez gives a good deal of attention to the subject of quantity. First of all, the opinion that quantity is really distinct from material substance must be accepted. 'For although it may not be possible to demonstrate its truth sufficiently by natural reason, it is nevertheless shown to be true by the principles of theology, especially on account of the mystery of the Eucharist. Indeed, the natural reason, enlightened by this mystery, understands that this truth is more in agreement and conformity with the natures themselves of things (than the opposite opinion). Therefore the first reason for this opinion is that in the mystery of the Eucharist God separated quantity from the substances of bread and wine . . .'[89] This distinction must be a real distinction, for, if the distinction were only modal, quantity could not exist in separation from that of which it is a mode.

Considerations taken from the theology of the Eucharist appear also in Suárez' treatment of the formal effect of quantity (*effectus formalis quantitatis*), which he finds in the quantitative extension of parts as apt to occupy place. 'In the body of Christ in the Eucharist besides the substantial distinction of parts of matter there is also a quantitative extension of parts. For, although the parts of that body are not actually extended in place, they are none the less so extended and ordered in relation to one another that, if they were not supernaturally prevented, they would have to possess actual extension in place. This (first) extension they receive from quantity, and it is impossible for them to be without it if they are not without quantity.'[90]

14. As to relations, Suárez maintains that there are in creatures real relations which constitute a special category.[91] But a real relation, although it signifies a real form, is not something actually distinct from every absolute form: it is in reality identified with an absolute form which is related to something else.[92] To take an example. In the case of two

white things the one thing has to the other a real relation of similarity. But that real relation is not something really distinct from the thing's whiteness: it is the whiteness itself (considered as an 'absolute form') as similar to the whiteness of another thing. This denial of a real distinction between the relation and its subject[93] does not, says Suárez, contradict the assertion that real relations belong to a category of their own, for 'the distinction between categories is sometimes only a *distinctio rationis cum aliquo fundamento in re*, as we shall say later in regard to action, passion and other categories'.[94]

It is only real relations which can belong to the category of relation; for mental relations (*relationes rationis*) are not real beings and cannot, therefore, belong to the category *ad aliquid*.[95] But it does not follow that all real relations belong to the category of relation. If there are two white things, the one is really like the other; but if one of them is destroyed or ceases to be white, the real relation of similarity also ceases. There are, however, says Suárez, some real relations which are inseparable from the essences of their subjects. For example, it belongs to the essence of an existent creature that it depends on the Creator: 'it does not seem that it can be conceived or exist without a transcendental relation to that on which it depends. It is in this relation that the potentiality and imperfection of a created being as such seem especially to consist.'[96] Again, 'matter and form have a true and real mutual relationship essentially included in their own being; and so the one is defined by its relation to the other'.[97] These relations, called by Suárez *relationes transcendentales*, are not mental relations; they are real; but they cannot disappear while the subject remains, as predicamental relations (that is, relations belonging to the category of relation) can disappear. A predicamental relation is an accident acquired by a thing which is already constituted in its essential being; but a transcendental relation is, as it were (*quasi*), a *differentia* constituting and completing the essence of that thing of which it is affirmed to be a relation.[98] The definition of a predicamental relation is 'an accident, the whole being of which is *ad aliud esse, seu ad aliud se habere, seu aliud respicere*'.[99] This definition might seem to cover also transcendental relations; but 'I think that transcendental relations are excluded by the phrase, *cuius totum esse est esse ad aliud,* if it is understood in the strict sense explained at the end of the preceding section. For those beings which include a transcendental relation are not so related to another thing that their whole being consists simply in a relation to that other thing.'[100] Suárez goes on to argue that a predicamental relation requires a subject, a foundation (for example, the whiteness of a white thing) and a term of the relation.[101] But a transcendental relation does not require these three conditions. For example, 'the transcendental relation of matter to form has no foundation, but it is intimately included in matter itself'.[102]

The two examples of transcendental relation given above, namely the relation of creature to Creator and of matter and form to one another, should not lead one to suppose that, for Suárez, there is a 'mutual' relation between the creature and the Creator. There is a real relation to the Creator on the part of the creature, but the Creator's relation to the creature is a *relatio rationis.*[103] The nominalists hold that[104] God acquires real relations in time, not in the sense that God acquires new perfections but in the sense, for example, that God is really Creator and, as creation took place in time, God becomes related to creatures in time. But Suárez rejects the opinion.[105] If the relation were real, God would acquire an accident in time which is an absurd idea; and it is useless to say that the relation would *assistere Deo,* and not *inesse Deo* (a distinction attributed to Gilbert de la Porrée), for the relation must be in a subject and, if it is not in the creature, it must be in God.

15. Suárez' final disputation (54) is devoted to the subject of *entia rationis.* He tells us that, although he has said in the first disputation that *entia rationis* are not included in the special subject-matter of metaphysics, he thinks that the general principles concerning this topic should be considered. The topic cannot be properly treated except by the metaphysician, even if it belongs to his subject-matter *quasi ex obliquo et concomitanter.*[106]

After distinguishing various possible meanings of the phrase *ens rationis,* Suárez says that, properly speaking, it signifies 'that which has being objectively only in the mind' or 'that which is thought of as being by the mind, although it has no being in itself'.[107] Blindness, for example, has no positive being of its own, though it is 'thought of' as if it were a being. When we say that a man is blind, we do not mean that there is anything positive in the man to which the word 'blindness' is given; we mean that he is deprived of vision. But we think of this deprivation as if it were a being, says Suárez. A purely mental relation is another example of an *ens rationis*. So is a chimera or purely imaginative construction, which cannot have being apart from the mind. Its being consists in being thought or imagined.

Three reasons can be assigned why we form these *entia rationis*. First of all, the human intellect tries to know negations and privations. These are nothing in themselves; but the mind, which has being as its object, cannot conceive that which is in itself nothing except *ad modum entis*, that is, as if it were being. Secondly, our intellect, being imperfect, has sometimes, in its endeavour to know something which it cannot know as it exists in itself, to introduce relations which are not real relations by comparing it to something else. The third reason is the mind's power to construct composite ideas which cannot have an objective counterpart outside the mind, though the ideas of the parts correspond to something extramental. For example, we can construct the idea of a horse's body with a man's head.

There can be no concept of being common to real beings and to *entia rationis*, for existence (*esse*) cannot be intrinsically participated in by the latter. To 'exist' only in the mind is not to exist (*esse*), but to be thought or mentally constructed. Therefore *entia rationis* cannot be said to possess essence. This distinguishes them from accidents. Nevertheless, an *ens rationis* is called *ens* in virtue of 'some analogy' to being, since it is founded in some way on being.[108]

Entia rationis are caused by the intellect conceiving that which has no real act of being as if it were a being.[109] The senses, appetite and will are not causes of *entia rationis*, though the imagination can be; and in this respect 'the human imagination shares in some way the power of the reason', and perhaps it never forms them save with the co-operation of reason.[110]

The three types of *entia rationis* are negations, privations and (purely mental) relations. A negation differs primarily from a privation in that, while a privation signifies the lack of a form in a subject naturally apt to possess that form, a negation signifies the lack of a form without there being any natural aptitude to possess that form.[111] For example, blindness is a privation; but a man's lack of wings is a negation. According to Suárez[112] imaginary space and imaginary time, conceived without any 'subject', are negations. The logical relations of, for example, genus and species, subject and predicate, antecedent and consequent, which are 'second intentions', are purely mental and so *entia rationis*, though they are not gratuitously formed but have some objective foundation.[113]

16. In the multitudinous pages of the *Disputationes metaphysicae* Suárez pursues the problems considered into their various ramifications, and he is careful to distinguish the different meanings of the terms employed. He shows himself to be an analytic thinker, in the sense that he is not content with broad generalizations, hasty impressions or universal conclusions based on an insufficient study of the different aspects of the problem at issue. He is thorough, painstaking, exhaustive. One cannot, of course, expect to find in his work an analysis which will satisfy all the demands made by modern analysts: the terms and ideas in which he thought were for the most part traditional in the Schools and were taken for granted. One might, indeed, take various points out of Suárez' writings and express them in the more fashionable terms of today. For example, his observations that to 'exist' only in the mind is not really to exist at all but to be thought or mentally constructed could be translated into a distinction between different types of sentences analysed in reference to their logical meaning as distinct from their grammatical form. One has, however, to take a past thinker in his historical setting, and if Suárez is seen in the light of the philosophical tradition to which he belonged, there can be no doubt that he possessed the gift of analysis in an eminent degree.

That Suárez possessed an analytic mind would hardly, I think, be denied. But it has been maintained that he lacked the power of synthesis. He became immersed in a succession of problems, it is sometimes said, and he gave such a careful consideration to the manifold ways in which these problems had been treated and solved in history that he was unable to see the wood for the trees. Moreover, his great erudition inclined him to eclecticism. He borrowed a view here and an opinion there, and the result was a patchwork rather than a system. His critics would not, I think, suggest that he was a superficial eclectic, since it needs no very close acquaintance with his writings to see that he was very far from being superficial; but they do suggest that he was an eclectic in a sense which is incompatible with possessing the gift of synthesis.

The accusation that a given philosopher was not a system-builder is not an accusation which is likely to carry much weight in contemporary philosophical circles. Provided that the accusation does not rest on the fact that the philosopher in question expounded a number of mutually incompatible theses, many modern philosophers would comment, 'so much the better'. However, leaving this aspect of the matter out of account one can ask whether the accusation is in fact true. And in the first place one can ask in what sense Suárez was an eclectic.

That Suárez was an eclectic in some sense seems to me undeniable. He had an extremely extensive knowledge of former philosophies, even if, as is only to be expected, he was sometimes mistaken in his assertions or interpretations. And he could hardly possess this knowledge without being influenced by the opinions of the philosophers he studied. But this does not mean that he accepted other people's opinions in an uncritical manner. If, for example, he accepted the opinion of Scotus and Ockham that there is a confused intellectual intuition of the individual thing, which logically precedes abstraction, he did so because he thought that it was true. And if he questioned the universal applicability of the principle *quidquid movetur ab alio movetur* he did not do so because he was a Scotist or an Ockhamist (he was neither) but because he considered that the principle, considered as a universal principle, is in fact questionable. Moreover, if Suárez was an eclectic, so was Aquinas. The latter did not simply accept Aristotelianism in its entirety; if he had done so, he would have occupied a far less important position in the development of mediaeval philosophy and would have shown himself to be devoid of any spirit of philosophical criticism. Aquinas borrowed from Augustine and other thinkers, as well as from Aristotle. And there is no cogent reason why Suárez should not have followed his example by utilizing what he considered valuable in philosophers who lived at a later date than Aquinas. Of course, if the accusation of eclecticism means simply that Suárez departed from the teaching of St. Thomas on a number of points, he was certainly an eclectic. But the relevant philosophical question would be not so much whether Suárez departed from Aquinas's teaching as whether he was objectively justified in doing so.

That Aquinas was also in some sense an eclectic would presumably be admitted by all. What philosopher is not in some sense an eclectic? But some would still maintain that there is this big difference between the philosophy of St. Thomas and that of Suárez. The former rethought all the positions which he adopted from others and developed them, welding these developments, together with his own original contributions, into a powerful synthesis with the aid of certain fundamental metaphysical principles. Suárez on the other hand juxtaposed various positions and did not create a synthesis.

The truth of this accusation is, however, extremely doubtful. In his preface (*Ad lectorem*) to the *Disputationes metaphysicae* Suárez says that he intends to play the part of philosopher in such a way as to have always before his eyes the truth that 'our philosophy ought to be Christian and the servant of divine theology' (*divinae Theologiae ministram*). And if one regards his philosophical ideas in this light, one can see a synthesis clearly emerging from the mass of his pages. For Aristotle, in the *Metaphysics* at least, God was simply the first unmoved mover: His existence was asserted in order to explain motion. The Christian philosophers, like St. Augustine, introduced the idea of creation, and St. Thomas attempted to weld together Aristotelianism and creationism. Beneath, as it were, the Aristotelian distinction of matter and form St. Thomas discerned the more fundamental distinction of essence and existence, which runs through all finite being. Act is limited by potentiality, and existence, which stands to essence as act to potentiality, is limited by essence. This explains the finitude of creatures. Suárez, however, was convinced that the utter dependence which logically precedes any distinction of essence and existence is itself the ultimate reason of finitude. There is absolute being, God, and there is participated being. Participation in this sense means total dependence on the Creator. This total dependence or contingency is the reason why the creature is limited or finite.[114] Suárez did not explain finitude and contingency in terms of the distinction between existence and essence: he explained this distinction, in the sense, that is, in which he accepted it, in terms of a finitude which is necessarily bound up with contingency.

It is sometimes said that Suarezianism is an 'essential' philosophy or a philosophy of essence rather than a philosophy of existence, like Thomism. But it would seem difficult to find a more 'existential' situation than the situation of utter dependence which Suárez finds to be the ultimate characteristic of every being other than God. Moreover, by refusing to admit a 'real' distinction between essence and existence in the creature Suárez avoided the danger of turning existence into a kind of essence. Cancel the creature's existence, and its essence is cancelled too. The Thomist would say the same, of course; but this fact suggests perhaps that there is not so great a difference between the Thomist 'real' distinction and the Suarezian conceptual distinction with an objective foundation as might be supposed. The difference lies perhaps rather in the fact that the Thomist appeals to the metaphysical principle of the limitation of act by potentiality, which suggests a view of existence that seems strange to many minds, whereas Suárez founds his distinction simply on creation. The view is at any rate arguable that he carried the 'purification' of Greek philosophy a stage further by bringing the concept of creation and of utter dependence which creation spells more into the centre of the picture. Again, whereas St. Thomas laid stress on the Aristotelian argument from motion in proving God's existence, Suárez, like Scotus, preferred a more metaphysical and less 'physical' line of thought, precisely because the existence of creatures is more fundamental than their movement and because God's creation of finite being is more fundamental than His concurrence in their activity.

There are, moreover, many other ideas in the philosophy of Suárez which follow in some way from, or are connected with, his fundamental idea of dependence or 'participation'.

Dependent being is necessarily finite, and as finite it is capable of acquiring further perfection. If it is a spiritual being it can do this freely. But as dependent it needs the divine concurrence even in the exercise of its freedom. And as utterly dependent on God it is subject to the divine moral law and is necessarily ordered to God. Again, as finite perfectible being the free creature is capable not only of acquiring perfection by its own activity, with the divine concurrence, but of receiving a perfection which lifts it above its natural life; as dependent spiritual being it is, as it were, malleable by God and possesses a *potentia obedientialis* for the reception of grace. Further, finite being is multipliable in diverse species and in a plurality of individuals in one species. And in order to explain the multipliability of individuals in a species it is not necessary to introduce the idea of matter as principle of individuation, with all the remnants of 'unpurified' Platonism attaching to that Aristotelian idea.

It has not been my intention in this last section of the present chapter to give my own views on the matters raised, and I do not wish to be understood in this sense. My intention has been rather that of showing that there is a Suarezian synthesis, that the key to it is the idea of 'participation' or dependence in being, and that it was this idea above all which must, Suárez was convinced, be the distinguishing mark of a Christian philosophy. To say this is not, of course, to suggest in any way that the idea is absent from Thomism. Suárez regarded himself as a follower of St. Thomas; and Suarezians do not set Suárez against St. Thomas. What they believe is that Suárez carried on and developed the work of St. Thomas in building up a metaphysical system in profound harmony with the Christian religion.

That the *Disputationes metaphysicae* exercised a wide influence in post-Renaissance Scholasticism scarcely needs saying. But they penetrated also into the Protestant universities of Germany, where they were studied by those who preferred Melanchthon's attitude towards philosophy to that of Luther. Indeed, the *Disputationes metaphysicae* served as a textbook of philosophy in a large number of German universities in the seventeenth century and part of the eighteenth. As for the leading post-Renaissance philosophers, Descartes mentions the work in his reply to the fourth set of objections, though apparently he did not know it at all well. But Leibniz tells us himself that he read the work as if it were a novel while he was still a youth. And Vico studied Suárez for a whole year. Again Suárez' idea of analogy is mentioned by Berkeley in his *Alciphron*.[115] At the present time the *Disputationes metaphysicae* are a living force primarily in Spain, where Suárez is considered one of the greatest, if not the greatest, of the national philosophers. To the modern world at large he is known rather for his *De legibus*, to which I shall turn in the next chapter.

17. Reference has been made in the preceding section to the contention that the metaphysics of Suárez is an essentialist, as contrasted with the existentialist, metaphysics. In *Being and Some Philosophers* Professor Étienne Gilson argues that Suárez, following Avicenna and Scotus but proceeding further in the same direction, lost sight of Aquinas's vision of being as the concrete act of existing and tended to reduce being to essence. And Suárez begot Christian Wolff who refers with approval to the Spanish Jesuit in his *Ontologia*. Finally Suárez' influence has corrupted large tracts of neo-Scholasticism. Modern existentialism has protested in the name of existence against the essentialist philosophy. Kierkegaard reacted strongly against the system of Hegel, who is to be numbered, so one gathers, among the spiritual descendants of Suárez. But modern existentialism has no true realization of existence. The consoling conclusion emerges, therefore, that St. Thomas Aquinas is the one true metaphysician.

That the position and character of the analysis of the concept of being which is found in many neo-Scholastic textbooks of metaphysics are very largely due to the influence of Suárez can hardly be denied. Nor can it well be denied, I think, that Suárez influenced Wolff and that a number of neo-Scholastic writers were influenced, indirectly at least, by Wolff. But the issues raised by Professor Gilson in his discussion of 'essentialist' metaphysics as contrasted with 'existentialist' metaphysics are so wide and far-reaching that they cannot, in my opinion, be properly treated in the form of a note to Suárez' philosophy. At the close of my *History of Philosophy* I hope to return to the subject in the course of considering the development of western philosophy as a whole. Meanwhile, it must suffice to have drawn the reader's attention to Gilson's estimate of Suárez' philosophy, which can be found in *L'être et l'essence* and *Being and Some Philosophers,* both of which books are listed in the Bibliography.

Chapter Twenty-three

FRANCIS SUÁREZ (2)

Philosophy of law and theology – The definition of law – Law (lex) *and right* (ius) *– The necessity of law – The eternal law – The natural law – The precepts of the natural law – Ignorance of natural law – The immutability of the natural law – The law of nations – Political society, sovereignty and government – The contract theory in Suárez – The deposition of tyrants – Penal laws – Cessation of human laws – Custom – Church and State – War.*

1. Suárez' philosophy of law was based on that of St. Thomas Aquinas; but it must, none the less, be judged an original creative development, if one bears in mind its amplitude, thoroughness and profundity. In the philosophy of law Suárez was the mediator between the mediaeval conception of law, as represented by Thomism, and the conditions prevailing at the time he wrote. In the light of those conditions he elaborated a legal philosophy and in connection therewith a political theory which in scope and completeness went beyond anything attained in the Middle Ages and which exercised a profound influence. There can be no doubt that Grotius was seriously indebted to Suárez, even if he did not acknowledge this indebtedness clearly. That he did not do so can be easily understood, if one bears in mind, on the one hand, Suárez' doctrine of political authority and of the right to resist, and on the other hand Grotius' dependence on the King of France at the time that he wrote his *De iure belli ac pacis*.

In his preface to the *De legibus ac Deo legislatore* (1612) Suárez observes that no one need be surprised to find a professional theologian embarking on a discussion of law. The theologian contemplates God, not only as He is in Himself, but also as man's last end. This means that he is concerned with the way of salvation. Now, salvation is attained by free acts and moral rectitude; and moral rectitude depends to a great extent on law considered as the rule of human acts. Theology, then, must comprise a study of law; and, being theology, it is necessarily concerned with God as lawgiver. It may be objected that the theologian, while legitimately giving his attention to divine law, should abstain from concerning himself with human law. But all law derives its authority ultimately from God; and the theologian is justified in treating all types of law, though he does so from a higher point of view than that of the moral philosopher. For example, the theologian considers natural law in its relation of subordination to the supernatural order, and he considers civil law or human positive law with a view to determining its rectitude in the light of higher principles or with a view to making clear the obligations bearing on the conscience in regard to civil law. And Suárez appeals, in the first place, to the example of St. Thomas.

2. Suárez begins by giving a definition of law (*lex*) taken from St. Thomas. 'Law is a certain rule and measure, according to which one is induced to act or is restrained from acting.'[1] He goes on, however, to observe that the definition is too broad. For example, as no mention of obligation is made, no distinction is drawn between law and counsel. It is only after a discussion of the various conditions requisite for law that Suárez finally gives his definition of it as 'a common, just and stable precept, which has been sufficiently promulgated'.[2] Law, as it exists in the legislator, is the act of a just and upright will binding an inferior to the performance of a particular act;[3] and it must be framed for a community. Natural law relates to the community of mankind;[4] but human laws may properly be enacted only for a 'perfect' community.[5] It is also inherent in the nature of law that it be enacted for the common good, though this must be understood in relation to the actual subject-matter of the law, not in relation to the subjective intentions of the legislator, which is a personal factor.[6] Furthermore, it is essential to law that it should prescribe what is just, that is, that it should pre-

scribe acts which can be justly performed by those whom the law affects. It follows from this that a law which is unjust or unrighteous is not, properly speaking, a law at all, and it possesses no binding force.[7] Indeed, an unrighteous law cannot be licitly obeyed, though in cases of doubt as to the righteousness of the law the presumption is in favour of the law. Suárez observes that in order for a law to be just three conditions must be observed.[8] First, it must be enacted, as already mentioned, for the common good, not for private advantage. Secondly, it must be enacted for those in regard to whom the legislator has authority to legislate, that is, for those who are his subjects. Thirdly, law must not proportion burdens unequally, in an inequitable manner. The three phases of justice which must characterize the law in regard to its form are, then, legal justice, commutative justice and distributive justice.[9] Law must also, of course, be practicable, in the sense that the acts it enjoins must be practicable.

3. What is the relation between law (*lex*) and right (*ius*)? Strictly speaking, *ius* denotes 'a certain moral power which every man has, either over his own property or with respect to what is due to him'.[10] Thus the owner of a thing has a *ius in re* in regard to that thing actually possessed, while a labourer, for example, has a right to his wages, *ius ad stipendium*. In this sense of the word *ius* is distinct from *lex*. But the term *ius* is often used, says Suárez, in the sense of 'law'.

4. Are laws necessary? Law is not necessary, if by 'necessity' is understood absolute necessity. God alone is a necessary being in an absolute sense, and God cannot be subject to law.[11] But, given the creation of rational creatures, law must be said to be necessary in order that the rational creature may live in a manner befitting his nature. A rational creature is capable of choosing well or ill, rightly or wrongly; and it is susceptible of moral government. In fact, moral government, which is effected through command, is connatural to the rational creature. Given, therefore, rational creatures, law is necessary. It is irrelevant, says Suárez,[12] to argue that a creature may receive the grace of impeccability; for the grace in question does not involve the creature's removal from the state of subjection to law but brings it about that the creature obeys the law without fail.

5. Suárez' treatment of the eternal law is contained in the

second book of the *De legibus*.[13] This law is not to be understood as a rule of right conduct imposed by God upon Himself:[14] it is a law of action in regard to the things governed. In regard to all things, irrational as well as rational? The answer depends on the degree of strictness in which the word 'law' is understood. It is true that all irrational creatures are subject to God and are governed by Him; but their subjection to God can be called 'obedience' only in a metaphorical sense, and the law by which God governs them is called a 'law' or 'precept' only metaphorically. In the strict sense, then, 'eternal law' has reference only to rational creatures.[15] It is the moral or human acts of rational creatures which form the proper subject-matter of the eternal law, 'whether the latter commands their performance, prescribes a particular mode of acting, or prohibits some other mode'.[16]

The eternal law is 'a frec decree of the will of God, who lays down the order to be observed; either generally, by the separate parts of the universe with respect to the common good . . . or else specifically, by intellectual creatures in their free actions'.[17] It follows that the eternal law, as a freely established law, is not absolutely necessary. This would be inconsistent with the eternity of the law only if nothing which is free could be eternal. The eternal law is eternal and immutable; but it is none the less free.[18] One can, however, distinguish law as it exists in the mind and will of the legislator from law as externally established and promulgated for the subjects. In the first phase the eternal law is truly eternal; but in the second phase it did not exist from eternity, because the subjects did not exist from eternity.[19] This being the case, one must conclude that actual promulgation to subjects is not the essence of eternal law. It is sufficient, for the eternal law to be called 'law', that it should have been made by the legislator to become effective at the proper time. In this respect the eternal law differs from other laws, which are not complete laws until they have been promulgated.[20]

Inasmuch as all created right reason partakes in 'the divine light which has been shed upon us', and inasmuch as all human power comes ultimately from God, all other law is a participation in the eternal law and an effect thereof.[21] It does not follow, however, that the binding force of human law is divine. Human law receives its force and efficacy directly from the will of a human legislator. It is true that the eternal law does not actually bind unless it is actually promulgated; and it is true that it is actually promulgated only through the medium of some other law, divine or human; but, in the case of human law, the obligation to observe it is caused proximately by this human law as enacted and promulgated by legitimate human authority, though fundamentally and mediately it proceeds from the eternal law.[22]

6. Turning to the subject of natural law, Suárez criticizes the opinion of his fellow-Jesuit, Father Vásquez, that rational nature and the natural law are the same. Suárez observes that, although rational nature is indeed the foundation of the objective goodness of the moral acts of human beings, it does not follow that it should be called 'law'. Rational nature may be called a 'standard'; but the term 'standard' is a term of wider extension than the term 'law'.[23] There is, however, a second opinion, according to which rational nature, considered as the basis of the conformity or nonconformity of human acts with itself, is the basis of natural rectitude, while natural reason, or the power of rational nature to discriminate between acts in harmony with itself and acts not in harmony with itself, is the law of nature.[24] So far as this opinion means that the dictates of right reason, considered as the immediate and intrinsic rule of human acts, is the natural law, it may be accepted. In the strictest sense, however, the natural law consists in the actual judgment of the mind; but the natural reason or the natural light of reason may also be called natural law, for we think of men as permanently retaining that law in their minds, even though they may not be engaged in any specific act of moral judgment. In other words, the question how natural law should be defined is partly a terminological question.[25]

As to the relation of the natural law to God, there are two extreme positions, which are opposed to one another. According to the first opinion, ascribed to Gregory of Rimini, the natural law is not a preceptive law in the proper sense; for it does not indicate the will of a superior but simply makes clear what should be done, as being intrinsically good, and what should be avoided, as being intrinsically evil. The natural law is thus a demonstrative law rather than a preceptive law; and it does not derive from God as legislator. It is, so to speak, independent of God, that is, of God considered as moral legislator. According to the second opinion, however, which is ascribed to William of Ockham, God's will constitutes the whole basis of good and evil. Actions are good or evil simply and solely in so far as they are ordered or prohibited by God.

Neither of these opinions is acceptable to Suárez. 'I hold that a middle course should be taken, this middle course being, in my judgment, the opinion held by St. Thomas and common to the theologians.'[26] In the first place, the natural law is a preceptive and not merely a demonstrative law; for it does not merely indicate what is good or evil, but it also commands and prohibits. But it does not follow from this that the divine volition is the total cause of the good or evil involved in the observance or transgression of the natural law. On the contrary, the divine volition presupposes the intrinsic moral character of certain acts. It is repugnant to reason to say, for example, that hatred of God is wrong simply and solely because it is prohibited by God. The divine volition presupposes a dictate of the divine reason concerning the intrinsic character of human acts. God is, indeed, the author of the natural law; for He is Creator and He wills to bind men to observe the dictates of right reason. But God is not the arbitrary author of the natural law; for He commands some acts because they are intrinsically good and prohibits other acts because they are intrinsically evil. Suárez does not, of course, mean to imply that God is, as it were, governed by a law which is external to His nature. What he means is that God (to speak anthropomorphically) could not help seeing that certain acts are in harmony with rational nature and that certain acts are morally incompatible with rational nature, and that God, seeing this, could not fail to command the performance of the former and prohibit the performance of the latter. It is true that the natural law, taken simply in itself, reveals what is intrinsically good and evil, without any explicit reference to God; but the natural light of reason none the less makes known to man the fact that actions contrary to the natural law are necessarily displeasing to the author and governor of nature. As to the promulgation of the natural law, 'the natural light is of itself a sufficient promulgation'.[27]

7. In the discussion of this matter in the *De legibus*, there is, I think, a certain prolixity and even a certain lack of clarity and exactitude. It is certainly clear that Suárez rejected the authoritarian ethical theory of William of Ockham and that, fundamentally, his own theory follows that of St. Thomas; but it does not seem to me to be made as clear as one could wish in what precise sense the term 'good' is being used. Suárez does, however, clarify the matter somewhat when he discusses the question what is the subject-matter dealt with by natural law.

He distinguishes various types of precepts which belong to the natural law.[28] First of all, there are general and primary principles of morality, such as 'one must do good and shun evil'. Secondly, there are principles which are more definite and specific, like 'God must be worshipped' and 'one must live temperately'. Both these types of ethical propositions are self-evident, according to Suárez. Thirdly, there are moral precepts which are not immediately self-evident but which are deduced from self-evident propositions and become known through rational reflection. In the case of some of these precepts, like 'adultery is wrong', their truth is easily recognized; but in the case of some other precepts, like 'usury is unjust' and 'lying can never be justified', more reflection is required in order to see their truth. Nevertheless, all these types of ethical propositions pertain to the natural law.

But if the natural law enjoins that good must be done, and if all righteous and licit acts are good acts, does it not seem to follow that the natural law enjoins the performance of all acts which are righteous and licit? Now, the act of contracting marriage is a good act. Is it, then, enjoined by the natural law? On the other hand, living according to the counsels of perfection is good. For example, it is good to embrace perpetual chastity. Is it, then, enjoined by the natural law? Certainly not; a counsel is not a precept. But why not? Suárez, developing a distinction made by St. Thomas, explains that, if virtuous acts are considered individually, not every such act falls under a natural precept. He mentions the counsels and contracting marriage.[29] One can also say[30] that all virtuous acts, in respect of the manner in which they should be performed, fall under the natural law, but that, in regard to their actual performance, they are not all absolutely prescribed by the natural law. It might, however, have been simpler to say that the natural law enjoins, not simply the doing of what is good, but the doing of good and the avoidance of evil, in the sense that what is prescribed absolutely is the doing of something good when its omission or the doing of something else would be evil. But the terms 'good' and 'evil' would still need some further clarificatory analysis. Some of the apparent confusion in Suárez' treatment of natural law seems to be due to his using the phrase 'natural law' both in a narrower sense, to mean the law based on human nature as such, and also in a wide sense, to include 'the law of grace'.[31] To embrace the evangelical counsels is certainly not made a matter of obligation by the essential propensities and requirements of human nature: but the life of the counsels is offered to the individual for a supernatural end, and it could become a matter of obligation only if God absolutely commanded an individual to embrace it or if he or she could achieve his or her last end only by embracing it.

Possibly the following may make Suárez' position a little clearer. An act is good if it is in accordance with right reason; and an act is evil if it is not in accordance with right reason. If doing a certain act averts a man from his last end, that act is evil and is not in accordance with right reason, which enjoins that the means necessary to the attainment of the last end shall be taken. Now, every concrete human act, that is, every concrete deliberate free act, is in the moral order and is either good or bad: it is either in accordance or not in accordance with right reason.[32] The natural law enjoins, therefore, that every concrete human act should be good and not evil. But to say this is not the same thing as to say that every possible good act should be done. This would scarcely be possible; and in any case omitting to do one good act does not necessarily involve doing a bad act. To take a rather trivial example. If taking some exercise is indispensable for my health and the proper fulfilment of my work, it is in accordance with right reason that I should take some exercise. But it does not follow that I ought to go for a walk; for I might also play golf or swim or do gymnastic exercises. Again, it might be a good thing for a man to become a friar; but it does not follow that he is doing evil if he does not become a friar. He might marry, for example; and to marry is to do a good act, even if, abstractly speaking at least, to become a friar is better. What the moral law enjoins is to do good *and* not to do evil: it does not always order which good act is to be done. The natural law prohibits all evil acts, since the avoidance of evil is necessary for morality; but it does not order all good acts, for to do a particular good act is not always necessary. From the obligation of never sinning there follows the positive obligation of acting well; but this positive obligation is conditional ('if a free act is to be done'), not simply absolute. 'It is a general obligation of doing good, when some act has to be done; and this obligation can be fulfilled by acts which are not absolutely enjoined. Therefore, it is not all good acts which, by virtue of the natural law, fall under a precept.'[33]

8. As to possible ignorance of the natural law, Suárez maintains that no one can be ignorant of the primary or most general principles of the natural law.[34] It is possible, however, to be ignorant of particular precepts, even of those which are self-evident or easily deducible from self-evident precepts. But it does not follow that such ignorance can be guiltless, not at least for any considerable length of time. The precepts of the Decalogue are of this character. Their binding force is so easily recognizable that no one can remain in ignorance of it for any considerable length of time without guilt. However, invincible ignorance is possible in regard to those precepts knowledge of which requires greater reflection.

9. Are the precepts of the natural law immutable? Before the question can be profitably discussed, it is necessary to make a distinction.[35] It is possible for a law to become intrinsically defective by becoming harmful instead of useful or irrational instead of rational. It is also possible for a law to be changed by a superior. Again, both intrinsic change and extrinsic change can affect either the law itself or some particular case or application. For instance, a superior might abolish the law as such or he might relax it or dispense from it in some particular case. Suárez first considers intrinsic change; and he maintains[36] that, properly speaking, the natural law cannot undergo any change, either in regard to its totality or in regard to particular precepts, so long as human nature endures, gifted with reason and free will. If rational

nature were abolished, natural law would also be abolished in regard to its concrete existence, since it exists in man or flows from human nature. As natural law flows from human nature, as it were, it cannot become injurious with the course of time; nor can it become irrational if it is grounded in self-evident principles. Apparent instances of intrinsic change in particular cases are due simply to the fact that the general terms in which a natural precept is customarily stated do not adequately express the natural precepts themselves. For instance, if a man has lent me a knife and demands it back, I ought to restore to him what is his property; but if he has become a homicidal maniac and I know that he wants to use the knife to murder someone, I ought not to restore it. This does not mean, however, that the precept that deposits should be restored on demand has undergone an intrinsic change in this case; it simply means that the precept, so stated, is an inadequate statement of what is contained in or involved by the precept itself. Similarly, the precept of the Decalogue, 'thou shalt not kill', really includes many conditions which are not explicitly mentioned; for example, 'thou shalt not kill on thine own authority and as an aggressor'.[37]

Can the natural law be changed by authority? Suárez maintains that 'no human power, even though it be the papal power, can abrogate any proper precept of the natural law' (that is, any precept properly belonging to the natural law), 'nor truly and essentially restrict such a precept, nor grant a dispensation from it'.[38] A difficulty may seem to arise in regard to property. According to Suárez,[39] nature has conferred on men in common dominion over things, and consequently every man has the power to use those things which have been given in common. It might seem, then, that the institution of private property and of laws against theft either constitute an infringement of the natural law or indicate that the natural law is subject, in some cases at least, to human power. Suárez answers that the law of nature did not positively forbid the division of common property and its appropriation by individuals; the institution of common dominion was 'negative', not positive. Positively considered, the natural law ordains that no one should be prevented from making the necessary use of common property as long as it is common, and that, after the division of property, theft is wrong. We have to distinguish[40] between preceptive laws and the law concerning dominion. There is no preceptive law of nature that things should always be held in common; but there are preceptive laws relating to conditions which are to a certain extent subject to human power. Nature did not divide goods among private individuals; but the private appropriation of goods was not forbidden by natural law. Private property may, therefore, be instituted by human agency. But there are preceptive laws of nature relating to common ownership and to private ownership; and these preceptive laws are not subject to human agency. The power of the State to confiscate property when there is just cause (as in certain criminal cases) must be understood as provided for in the preceptive laws of nature.

In other words, Suárez will not admit that the natural law is subject to human power. At the same time he maintained that Nature gave the things of the earth to all men in common. But it does not follow, he tells us, either that the institution of private property is against the natural law or that it constitutes a change in the natural law. Why not? A matter may fall under the natural law either in a negative sense or in a positive sense (through positive prescription of an action). Now, common ownership was a part of natural law only in a negative sense, in the sense, that is to say, that by virtue of the natural law all property was to be held in common unless men introduced a different provision. The introduction of private property was thus not against the natural law nor did it constitute a change in any positive precept of the natural law.

However, even if men cannot change or dispense from the natural law, has not God the power to do so? In the first place, if God can dispense from any of the precepts of the Decalogue, it follows that He can abrogate the whole law and order those acts which are forbidden by the natural law. Dispensation from the law prohibiting an act would render that act permissible; but, if God can render an otherwise prohibited act permissible, why could He not prescribe it? 'This was the opinion supported by Occam, whom Pierre d'Ailly and Andreas a Novocastro followed.'[41] The opinion is, however, to be rejected and condemned. The commands and prohibitions of God in respect of the natural law presuppose the intrinsic righteousness of the acts commanded and the intrinsic wickedness of the prohibited acts. The notion that God could command man to hate Him is absurd. Either God would be commanding man to hate an object worthy of love or He would have to render Himself worthy of hatred; but either supposition is absurd.

What, then, of Scotus' opinion, that a distinction must be drawn between the precepts of the First Table of the Decalogue and those of the Second Table and that God can dispense in regard to the latter? Suárez observes that, in a sense, it is inaccurate to say that God, according to Scotus, can dispense in the case of certain precepts of the natural law, since Scotus would not allow that all the precepts of the Decalogue belong, at least in the strictest sense, to the natural law. But Suárez rejects the opinion that the precepts of the Second Table do not strictly belong to the natural law. 'The arguments of Scotus, indeed, are not convincing.'[42]

Suárez maintains, then, that God cannot dispense in regard to any of the Commandments. He appeals to St. Thomas, Cajetan, Soto and others.[43] All the Commandments involve one intrinsic principle of justice and obligation. The apparent cases of dispensation of which we read in the Old Testament were not really cases of dispensation at all. For example, when God told the Hebrews to despoil the Egyptians, He was not acting as legislator and giving them a dispensation to steal. He was either acting as supreme lord and transferring dominion over the goods in question from the Egyptians to the Hebrews; or He was acting as supreme judge and awarded the Hebrews proper wages for their work, wages which had been withheld by the Egyptians.[44]

10. Suárez goes on to distinguish the natural law from 'the law of nations' (*ius gentium*). In Suárez' opinion, the *ius gentium* does not prescribe any acts as being of themselves necessary for right conduct, nor does it forbid anything as being of itself and intrinsically evil: such prescriptions and prohibitions pertain to the natural law, and not to the *ius gentium*.[45] The two are not, therefore, the same. The *ius gentium* 'is not only indicative of what is evil but also constitutive of evil'.[46] Suárez means that the natural law prohibits what is intrinsically evil whereas the *ius gen-*

tium considered precisely as such does not prohibit intrinsically evil acts (for these are already forbidden by natural law) but prohibits certain acts for a just and sufficient reason and renders the performance of those acts wrong. From this it follows that the *ius gentium* cannot possess the same degree of immutability as the natural law possesses.

The laws of the *ius gentium* are, therefore, positive (not natural) and human (not divine) laws. In this case, however, does it differ from civil law? It is not sufficient merely to say that civil law is the law of one State, while the *ius gentium* is common to all peoples; for a mere difference between greater and less does not constitute a specific difference.[47] Suárez' opinion is that 'the precepts of the *ius gentium* differ from those of the civil law in that they are not established in written form'; they are established through the customs of all or nearly all nations.[48] The *ius gentium* is thus unwritten law; and it is made up of customs belonging to all, or practically all, nations. It can, indeed, be understood in two ways. A particular matter can pertain to the *ius gentium* either because it is a law which the various peoples and nations ought to observe in their relations with each other or because it is a set of laws which individual States observe within their own borders and which are similar and so commonly accepted. 'The first interpretation seems, in my opinion, to correspond most properly to the actual *ius gentium* as distinct from the civil law.'[49]

Of the *ius gentium* understood in this sense Suárez gives several examples. For example, as far as natural reason is concerned it is not indispensable that the power of avenging an injury by war should belong to the State, for men could have established some other means of avenging injury. But the method of war, which is 'easier and more in conformity with nature', has been adopted by custom and is just.[50] 'In the same class I place slavery.' The institution of slavery (as a punishment for the guilty) was not necessary from the standpoint of natural reason; but, given this custom, the guilty are bound to submit to it, while the victors may not inflict a more severe punishment without some special reason. Again, though the obligation to observe treaties once they have been made proceeds from the natural law, it is a matter pertaining to the *ius gentium* that offers of treaties, when duly made and for a reasonable cause, should not be refused. To act in this way is, indeed, in harmony with natural reason; but it is more firmly established by custom and the *ius gentium*, and so acquires a special binding force.

The rational basis of this kind of *ius gentium* is the fact that the human race, however much it may be divided into different nations and States, preserves a certain unity, which does not consist simply in membership of the human species, but is also a moral and political unity, as it were (*unitatem quasi politicam et moralem*). This is indicated by the natural precept of mutual love and mercy, which extends to all, 'even foreigners'.[51] A given State may constitute a perfect community, but, taken simply by itself, it is not self-sufficient but requires assistance through association and relationship with other States. In a certain sense, then, different States are members of a universal society; and they need some system of law to regulate their relations with one another. Natural reason does not provide sufficiently for this need; but the habitual conduct of nations has introduced certain laws which are in accordance with nature, even if they are not strictly deducible from the natural law.

St. Thomas asserted in the *Summa theologica*[52] that the precepts of the *ius gentium* are conclusions drawn from principles of the natural law and that they differ from precepts of the civil law, which are determinations of the natural law, not general conclusions from it. Suárez interprets this as meaning that the precepts of the *ius gentium* are general conclusions of the natural law, 'not in an absolute sense and by necessary inference, but in comparison with the specific determination of civil and private law'.[53]

11. In the third book of the *De legibus* Suárez turns to the subject of positive human law. He asks first whether man possesses the power to make laws or whether the making of laws by man spells tyranny; and his treatment of this question involves consideration of the State and of political authority.

Man is a social animal, as Aristotle said, and he has a natural desire to live in community.[54] The most fundamental natural society is, indeed, the family; but the family, though a perfect community for purposes of domestic or 'economic' government, is not self-sufficing. Man stands in further need of a political community, formed by the coalition of families. This political community is necessary, both for the preservation of peace between individual families and for the growth of civilization and culture.

Secondly, in a perfect community (Suárez is here speaking of the political community) there must be a governing power. The truth of this principle would seem to be self-evident, but it is confirmed by analogy with other forms of human society, like the family.[55] Moreover, as St. Thomas indicates,[56] no body can endure unless it possesses some principle the function of which is to provide for the common good. The institution of civil magistracy is thus necessary.

Thirdly, a human magistracy, if it is supreme in its own sphere, has the power to make laws in its own sphere, that is to say, civil or human laws. A civil magistracy is a necessity in a State; and the establishment of laws is one of the most necessary acts of a civil magistracy, if it is to fulfil its governmental and regulative function in the life of the State.[57] This power to make laws belongs to the magistracy which possesses supreme jurisdiction in the State: it is an essential factor in political sovereignty.

The State and political sovereignty are thus natural institutions, in the sense that nature demands their establishment. It may be true that empires and kingdoms have often been established through tyranny and force; but historical facts of this kind are examples of human abuse of power and strength, not of the essential nature of political sovereignty.[58] As to St. Augustine's opinion, that the domination of one man over another is due to the state of affairs brought about by sin, this is to be understood, says Suárez,[59] of that form of dominion which is accomplished by servitude and the exercise of coercion. Without sin there would be no exercise of coercion and no slavery; but there still would be government; at least, 'in so far as directive power is concerned, it would seem probable that this would have existed among men even in the state of innocence'.[60] In this matter Suárez follows St. Thomas.[61] In the *De opere sex dierum*[62] Suárez says that since human society is a result not of human corruption but of human nature itself, it appears that men would have been united in a political community even in the state of innocence, had that state continued to exist.

Whether there would have been one political community or more is not a question which one can answer. All one can say is that if all men had continued to live in Paradise, there could have been one single political community. Suárez goes on to say that there would have been no servitude in the state of innocence but there would have been government, as this is required for the common good.[63]

But the fact that civil magistracy and government are necessary and that the supreme magistracy in a State has power to make laws, does not mean that the power to make laws is conferred directly and immediately on any individual or group of individuals. On the contrary, 'this power, viewed solely according to the nature of things, resides, not in any individual man, but rather in the whole body of mankind'.[64] All men are born free; and nature has not conferred immediately upon any man political jurisdiction over another.

When, however, it is said that the power of making laws was conferred by Nature immediately upon mankind ('the multitude of mankind'), this must not be understood as meaning that the power was conferred on men regarded simply as an aggregate, without any moral union. We must understand mankind as meaning men gathered together by common consent 'into one political body through one bond of fellowship and for the purpose of aiding one another in the attainment of a single political end'.[65] If regarded in this way, men form 'a single mystical body' which needs a single head.[66]

It is to be added that the power in question does not reside in mankind in such a way that it is one power residing in all existent men, with the consequence that they would all form one single political community. 'On the contrary, that would scarcely be possible, and much less would it be expedient.'[67] It seems, then, that the power of making laws, if it existed in the whole assemblage of mankind, did so only for a brief time: mankind began to be divided into distinct political communities 'soon after the creation of the world'. Once this division had begun to take place, the power to make laws resided in the several political communities.

This power comes from God as its primary source.[68] But how does He confer it? In the first place, it is given by God 'as a characteristic property resulting from nature'. In other words, God does not confer the power by any special act which is distinct from the act of creation. That it results from nature means that natural reason shows that the exercise of the power is necessary for the preservation and proper government of the political community, which is itself a natural society. In the second place, the power does not manifest itself until men have formed a political community. Therefore the power is not conferred by God without the intervention of will and consent on the part of men, that is to say, on the part of those men who, by consent, form themselves together into a perfect society or State. However, once they have formed the community the power is resident therein. It is rightly said, then, to have been immediately conferred by God. Suárez adds[69] that the power does not reside in a given political community in such a way that it cannot be alienated by the consent of that community or forfeited by way of just punishment.

12. It is clear that Suárez regarded political society as originating, essentially, in consent. That a greater or less number of States may have actually originated in other ways is a historical accident, not affecting the essence of the State. But if, to this extent, Suárez may be said to have proposed a theory of the 'social contract', this does not mean that he regarded political society as a purely artificial society, a creation of enlightened egoism. On the contrary, as we have seen, he found the ultimate origin of political society in human nature, that is, in the social character and needs of the human being. The formation of political society is a necessary expression of human nature, even if the formation of a given political community must be said to rest essentially on consent, since nature has not specified what particular communities are to be formed.

Much the same is to be said about his theory of sovereignty or, to restrict oneself to the actual point discussed, the power of making laws which appertains to sovereignty. Nature has not specified any particular form of government, says Suárez;[70] the determination of the form of government depends on human choice. It would be extremely difficult for the whole community as such to make laws directly, and practical considerations point to monarchy as the best form of government, though it is as a rule expedient, given man's character, 'to add some element of common government'.[71] What this element of common government is to be, depends on human choice and prudence. In any case, whoever holds the civil power, this power has been derived, either directly or indirectly, from the people as a community. Otherwise it could not be justly held.[72] In order that sovereignty may justly be vested in a given individual, 'it must necessarily be bestowed upon him by the consent of the community'.[73] In certain cases God has conferred power directly, as on Saul; but such cases are extraordinary and, as far as regards the mode of imparting power, supernatural. In the case of hereditary monarchy the just possessor derived power from the commonwealth.[74] As to royal power obtained through unjust force, the king in this case possesses no true legislative power, though in the course of time the people may come to give their consent to and acquiesce in his sovereignty, thus rendering it legitimate.[75]

Thus, just as Suárez holds that the formation of a given political community depends on human consent, so he holds that the establishment of a certain government depends on the consent of the political community which confers the sovereignty. He may therefore be said to maintain, in a sense, the double-contract theory. But, just as he holds that the formation of political communities is a requirement of nature, so he holds that the establishment of some government is required by nature. He may tend to lay more emphasis on the idea of consent; indeed, he speaks explicitly of a 'pact or agreement' between the king and the kingdom;[76] but political authority and sovereignty are nevertheless necessary for the proper preservation and government of mankind. Political authority is derived ultimately from God, on whom all dominion depends; but the fact that it is conferred on a definite individual derives from a grant on the part of the State itself: 'the principate itself is derived from men'.[77] In other words, political sovereignty is not in itself simply a matter of convention or agreement, for it is necessary for human life; but the conferring of sovereignty on certain individuals does depend on agreement.

It may be noted in passing that Suárez thought in terms of the monarchic state of his time. The mediaeval idea of the imperial power plays little part in his political theory.

In his *Defence of the Catholic and Apostolic Faith*[78] Suárez expressly denies that the emperor has universal temporal jurisdiction over all Christians. It is probable, he says, that the emperor never did possess this power; and, even if he did, he has certainly lost it. 'We assume that there are, besides the emperor, a number of temporal kings, like the kings of Spain, France and England, who are entirely independent of the emperor's jurisdiction.'[79] On the other hand, Suárez evidently did not think that a world-State and a world-government were practical possibilities. History shows that there never has been a truly world-wide government. It does not exist, never did exist, and never could have existed.[80] Suárez maintained as we have seen, that the existence of a single political community for all men is morally impossible and that, even if possible, it would be highly inexpedient.[81] If Aristotle was right, as he was, in saying that it is difficult to govern a very large city properly, it would be far more difficult to govern a world-State.

13. What implications did Suárez draw from his doctrine of the pact between monarch and kingdom? Did he hold in particular that the citizens have a right to depose a tyrannical monarch, one who violates his trust?

According to Suárez,[82] the transfer of sovereignty from the State to the prince is not a delegation but a transfer or unlimited bestowal of the whole power which resided in the community. The prince, then, may delegate the power, if he so chooses: it is granted to him absolutely, to be exercised by him personally or through agents, as he thinks most expedient. Moreover, once the power has been transferred to the monarch, he is the vicar of God; and obedience to him is obligatory, according to the natural law.[83] In fact, the transference of power to the monarch makes him superior even to the State which conferred the power, since the State has subjected itself to the monarchy by making the transference.

The monarch cannot, then, be deprived of his sovereignty, since he has acquired ownership of his power. But Suárez immediately adds the qualification, 'unless perchance he lapses into tyranny, on which ground the kingdom may wage a just war against him'.[84] There are two sorts of tyrants.[85] There is the tyrant who has usurped the throne by force and unjustly; and there is the legitimate prince who rules tyrannically in the use he makes of his power. In regard to the first kind of tyrant, the whole State or any part of it has the right to revolt against him, for he is an aggressor. To revolt is simply to exercise the right of self-defence.[86] As to the second type of tyrant, namely the legitimate prince who rules tyrannically, the State as a whole may rise against him, for it must be supposed that the State granted him the power on condition that he should govern for the common good and that he might be deposed if he lapsed into tyranny.[87] It is, however, a necessary condition for the legitimacy of such a revolt that the king's rule should be manifestly tyrannical and that the norms pertaining to a just war should be observed. Suárez refers to St. Thomas on this matter.[88] But it is only the whole State which is entitled to rise against a legitimate monarch acting tyrannically; for he cannot, without more ado, be an aggressor against all individual citizens in the way that the unjust usurper is an aggressor. This is not to say, however, that an individual who is the subject of actual tyrannical aggression on the part of a legitimate monarch may not defend himself. But a distinction must be drawn between self-defence and defence of the State.

In his *Defence of the Catholic and Apostolic Faith*[89] Suárez considers the particular question of tyrannicide. A legitimate monarch may not be slain by private authority on the grounds that he rules tyrannically. This is the doctrine of St. Thomas,[90] Cajetan and others. A private individual who kills on his own authority a legitimate monarch who acts tyrannically is a murderer. He does not possess the requisite jurisdiction.[91] As to self-defence, a private individual may not kill the legitimate monarch simply in order to defend his private possessions; but if the monarch tyrannically threatens the citizen's life, he may defend himself, even if the monarch's death results, though regard for the common welfare might, in certain circumstances, bind him in charity to refrain from slaying the monarch, even at the cost of his own life.

In the case of a tyrannical usurper, however, it is licit for the private individual to kill him provided that no recourse can be had to a superior authority and provided that the tyranny and injustice of the usurper's rule are manifest. Other conditions added by Suárez[92] are that tyrannicide is a necessary means for the liberation of the kingdom; that no agreement has been freely entered upon by the usurper and the people; that tyrannicide will not leave the State afflicted with the same or greater evils than before; and that the State does not expressly oppose private tyrannicide.

Suárez thus affirms the right of resistance, which logically follows from his doctrine of the origin and transference of sovereignty. He certainly in no way encouraged unnecessary revolts; but it is easily understandable that his work on the Catholic Faith was most obnoxious to James I of England, who believed in the divine right of kings and the principle of legitimacy.

14. In the fourth book of the *De legibus* (*De lege positiva canonica*) Suárez considers canon law; and in the fifth book he treats *de varietate legum humanarum et praesertim de poenalibus et odiosis*. In connection with penal laws he raises the question of their binding force in conscience. First of all, it is possible for the human legislator to make laws which bind in conscience, even though a temporal penalty for transgression is attached.[93] But do such laws bind in conscience when the legislator has not expressly stated his intention of binding the consciences of his subjects? In Suárez' opinion[94] a law which contains a precept binds in conscience unless the legislator has expressed or made clear his intention not to bind the conscience. (Whether the law binds under pain of mortal or venial sin depends on the matter of the law and other circumstances.) Suárez draws the logical conclusion that just taxation laws bind in conscience, 'like the law in Spain taxing the price of wheat'.[95] It is possible, however, for there to be penal laws which do not bind in conscience in regard to the act to be performed. Whether a law is of this kind, that is, whether a law is merely penal, depends on the intention of the legislator. This intention need not necessarily be expressed in so many words, for it may be made clear by tradition and custom.[96] When a penal law does not actually command or prohibit an act but simply states, for example, that if someone exports wheat he will be fined, it can be presumed to be merely penal unless it is clear from some other consideration that it was meant to bind in conscience.

A human penal law can oblige subjects in conscience to

undergo the penalty, even before judicial sentence; but only if the penalty is one that the subject can licitly inflict on himself and provided that it is not so severe or repugnant to human nature that its voluntary performance cannot be reasonably demanded.[97] But it does not follow that all penal laws do so oblige in actual fact. If a penal law simply threatens a penalty, it does not oblige the transgressor to undergo the penalty before sentence, whatever the penalty may be:[98] the legislator's intention to oblige the transgressor in conscience to undergo the penalty on his own initiative must be made clear. As to the obligation to undergo the penalty inflicted by judicial sentence, Suárez holds that if some action or co-operation on the part of the guilty man is necessary for the execution of the penalty, he is bound in conscience to perform that act or give that co-operation, provided that the law which he has broken is a just law and that the penalty in question is not immoderate.[99] In this matter, however, common sense has to be used. No one, for example, is obliged to execute himself.[100]

As already mentioned, Suárez considered that taxation laws, if they are just, bind in conscience. He maintained that 'the laws by which such taxes are ordered to be paid, even if no penalty is attached, certainly cannot be called purely penal'.[101] They therefore bind in conscience; and just taxes must be paid in full, even if they have not been demanded, from oversight, for example, unless the legislator's intention to pass a purely penal taxation law is made clear. Regarded in themselves, taxation laws are true moral laws binding in conscience.[102] As for unjust taxation laws, they never bind in conscience, either before or after the demand for the payment of the tax.[103]

15. The sixth book of the *De legibus* is concerned with the interpretation, cessation and change of human laws. It is not always necessary that a law should be revoked by the sovereign before it can be disobeyed licitly. Apart from the fact that a law enjoining anything wrong, anything impossible of fulfilment or anything devoid of any utility is unjust and null from the start,[104] a law may cease to be valid and binding because the adequate end, both intrinsic and extrinsic of the law, has ceased to exist.[105] For example, if a law is passed imposing a tax solely with a view to obtaining

money for a specific object, the law lapses, as regards its binding force, when the purpose has been achieved, even if the law has not been revoked. But if the end of a law is not purely extrinsic but is also intrinsic (for example, if a good act is indeed commanded with a view to some specific end but in such a way that the legislator would command that act irrespective of the specific end), it cannot, of course, be taken for granted that the law lapses simply because the specified end has been achieved.

16. Suárez writes at length of unwritten law or custom, a matter to which he devotes the seventh book (*De lege non scripta quae consuetudo appellatur*). Custom, considered as a juridical factor, is introduced in default of law: it is unwritten law. But it is only common or public custom which can establish law (that is, custom regarded as law), not private custom, which is the custom of one person or of an imperfect community.[106] Moreover, a custom, to establish law, must be morally good: a custom which is intrinsically evil establishes no law.[107] But the distinction between morally good and bad customs is not the same as that between reasonable and unreasonable customs: a custom might be good in itself, that is, considered simply as a custom, while at the same time it might be unreasonable and imprudent if regarded juridically, namely as establishing law.[108]

For the establishment of a custom a perfect community is required:[109] but it is not necessary for its establishment that it should be observed by literally the whole of the community; it is sufficient if the greater part of the community observes it.[110] How is it established? By a repetition of certain public acts by the people.[111] These acts must, of course, be voluntary acts. The reason for this is that the acts which establish a custom are of effect in doing so only in so far as they manifest the consent of the people.[112] They must, therefore, be voluntary: a custom cannot be validly established by acts done under compulsion or from grave or unjust fear.[113] But it does not follow that the consent of the prince is not necessary for the valid establishment of custom or consuetudinary law. This consent may, however, be given in different ways; either by express consent, or by antecedently permitting the introduction of a custom or by contemporaneous or subsequent confirmation, or by the prince doing nothing to check the custom when he has become aware of it.[114] Tacit consent, then, on the part of the sovereign can be sufficient.

Legitimate custom may have various different effects. It may establish a law; it may serve to interpret an existent law; or it may abrogate a law.[115] As regards the first effect, ten years are necessary and sufficient to establish a legal custom.[116] As to the abrogation of law through custom, a twofold will, the will of the people and the will of the prince, is necessary for the attainment of this effect,[117] though a tacit consent on the prince's part can suffice. Custom can even establish penal law.[118] A custom of ten years' standing is required for the abrogation of civil law; but in the case of canon law a period of forty years is required for a custom to be prescriptive against a law.[119]

In the eighth book of the *De legibus* (*De lege humana favorabili*) Suárez deals with privilege, and in the ninth and tenth books with divine positive law. Passing over these topics I propose to say something on Suárez' view of the relation of Church to State.

17. In his *Defence of the Catholic and Apostolic Faith* Suárez discusses and rejects the view that the pope possesses not only supreme spiritual power but also supreme civil power with the consequence that no purely temporal sovereign possesses supreme power in temporal affairs. He appeals to utterances of popes, and then goes on to argue[120] that no just title can be discovered whereby the pope possesses direct jurisdiction in temporal affairs over all Christian States. And without a just title he cannot possess such jurisdiction. There is no evidence that either divine or human law has conferred such jurisdiction on the pope. Suárez recognized, of course, the temporal jurisdiction of the pope as temporal ruler over the Papal States; but he refused to regard other temporal sovereigns as mere vicars of the Holy See. In other words Church and State are distinct and independent societies, even though the end for which the Church exists is higher than that for which the State exists.

But, although the pope does not possess direct or primary civil jurisdiction over temporal sovereigns, he possesses a directive power over them, not merely as individuals but also as sovereigns. In virtue of his spiritual jurisdiction the pope possesses the power of directing temporal princes with a view to a spiritual end.[121] 'By directive power we do not understand simply the power of advising, warning or requesting; for these are not peculiar to superior authority; but we mean a strict power of obliging.'[122] Temporal monarchs are the spiritual subjects of the pope; and the pope's spiritual authority includes the power of directing the monarch in the use of his temporal authority, 'if in any matter he deviates from right reason, or from faith, justice or charity'.[123] This involves an indirect power on the part of the pope over temporal affairs. There may occur a clash between spiritual good and temporal convenience or expediency; and on such occasions the temporal sovereign must yield to the spiritual.[124] The pope should not attempt to usurp direct temporal jurisdiction; but in cases where it is necessary for spiritual good he may interfere, in virtue of his indirect power.

Suárez thus maintained the doctrine of the pope's indirect, though not direct, jurisdiction in the temporal sphere. He also maintained that the pope possesses 'coercive power over temporal princes who are incorrigibly wicked, and especially over schismatics and stubborn heretics'.[125] For directive power without coercive power is inefficacious. This power extends not only to the infliction of spiritual punishments like excommunication but also to the infliction of temporal punishments, such as, in case of necessity, deposition from the throne.[126] As to heathen monarchs, even if the pope does not possess the power to punish them, he has the power to free their Christian subjects from allegiance to them, if the Christians are in danger of moral destruction.[127]

18. Finally something may be said on the subject of Suárez' doctrine concerning war.

War is not intrinsically evil: there can be a just war. Defensive war is permitted; and sometimes it is even a matter of obligation.[128] But certain conditions have to be observed in order that a war should be just. First of all, the war must be waged by a legitimate power; and this is the supreme sovereign.[129] But the pope has the right to insist that matters of dispute between Christian sovereigns should be referred to himself, though the sovereigns are not bound to secure the pope's authorization before making war, unless the pope has expressly said that they must do so.[130]

The second condition for a just war is that the cause of making war should be just. For example, the suffering of a grave injustice which cannot be repaired or avenged in any other way is a just cause for war.[131] A defensive war should be attempted; but before an offensive war is begun, the sovereign should estimate his chances of victory and should not begin the war if he is more likely to lose than to win it.[132] The reason for this proviso is that otherwise the prince would incur the obvious risk of inflicting great injuries on his State. (By 'offensive war' Suárez means, not an 'aggressive war', but a just war freely undertaken. It is legitimate to declare war freely in order to repair injuries suffered or to defend the innocent.)

The third condition for a just war is that the war must be properly conducted and that due proportion must be observed throughout its course and in victory. Before beginning a war the prince is bound to call the attention of the sovereign of the other State to the existence of a just cause of war and to ask for adequate satisfaction. If the other offers adequate reparation for the injury done, he is bound to accept it; if he nevertheless attacks, the war will be unjust.[133] During the conduct of the war it is legitimate to inflict on the enemy all losses necessary for the attainment of victory, provided that these losses do not involve intrinsic injury to innocent persons.[134] Finally, after the winning of victory the prince may inflict upon the conquered enemy such penalties as are sufficient for a just punishment; and he may demand compensation for all losses his State has suffered, including those suffered through the war.[135] Indeed, after the war 'certain guilty individuals among the enemy may also be put to death with justice'.[136]

As to the 'innocent', 'it is implicit in the natural law that the innocent include children, women, and all unable to bear arms', while, according to the *ius gentium*, ambassadors are included, and, among Christians, by positive law, religious and priests. 'All other persons are considered guilty; for human judgment looks upon those able to take up arms as having actually done so.'[137] Innocent persons as such may never be slain, for the slaying of them is intrinsically evil; but if victory cannot be achieved without the 'incidental' slaying of the innocent, it is legitimate to slay them.[138] Suárez means that it is legitimate, for example, to blow up a bridge or to storm a town, if such acts are necessary for victory, even though the attacker has reason to think that these acts will involve the death of some innocent persons 'incidentally'. It would not, however, be legitimate to do such acts with the purpose of killing innocent people.

A question in connection with war discussed by Suárez[139] is the question how far the soldiers partaking in it are morally obliged to ascertain whether it is a just or unjust war. His answer, briefly stated, is as follows. Regular soldiers who are subjects of a prince are not bound to make careful investigation before obeying the summons to war: they can assume that the war is just, unless the contrary is evident. If they have simply speculative doubts about the justice of the war, they should disregard these doubts; but if the soldiers have practical and convincing reasons for thinking that the justice of the war is extremely doubtful they should make further inquiries. As to mercenaries who are not subjects of the prince who proposes to make war, Suárez argues that, although the common opinion seems to be that they are bound to inquire into the justice of war before enlisting, he himself finds no difference in actual fact between subjects and non-subjects. The general principles are, (*a*) that if the doubt which arises about the justice of a war is purely negative, it is probable that soldiers may enlist without making any further inquiry; and (*b*) that if the doubt is positive, and if both sides advance plausible arguments, those about to enlist should inquire into the truth. If they cannot discover the truth, let them aid him who is probably in the right. In practice 'inquiry' for an ordinary soldier means consulting 'prudent and conscientious men' but if the soldiers form an organized body, they can leave the inquiry and decision to their commander. As to the sovereign who wishes to make war, he is bound, of course, to inquire diligently into the justice of his cause; and he may not go to war if the other side is more probably in the right, let alone if it is morally certain that justice rests with the other side.[140]

Chapter Twenty-four

A BRIEF REVIEW OF THE FIRST THREE VOLUMES

Greek philosophy; the pre-Socratic cosmologies and the discovery of Nature, Plato's theory of Forms and idea of God, Aristotle and the explanation of change and movement, neo-Platonism and Christianity – The importance for mediaeval philosophy of the discovery of Aristotle – Philosophy and theology – The rise of science.

1. In the first volume of this *History of Philosophy* I dealt with the philosophy of Greece and Rome. If one regards Greek philosophy as starting in the sixth century B.C. and ending with Justinian's closing of the Athenian Academy in A.D. 529, one can say that it lasted for about a thousand years and that it formed a definite period of philosophic thought with certain more or less well-defined phases.

(i) According to the traditional division, the first phase was that of pre-Socratic philosophy; and it has been customary to depict this phase as characterized predominantly by cosmological speculation. This view has, of course, the authority of Socrates in the *Phaedo*; and Aristotle, who interpreted the thought of previous philosophers largely in terms of his own theory of causes, speaks of the early Greek philosophers as busying themselves with the 'material cause' and of thinkers like Empedocles and Anaxagoras as considering the source of motion or efficient cause. I think that this view of pre-Socratic philosophy, namely that it was predominantly, though certainly not exclusively, cosmological in character, is obviously reasonable and sound. One can express it perhaps by saying that the pre-Socratic philosophers discovered 'Nature', that is, they formed the idea of a cosmos, an organized physical system governed by law. That the cosmos was looked on as divine in some sense, and that one can discern in the theories of the pre-Socratics mythical elements, the connection of which with older cosmogonies can be traced, is true; but there is a world of difference between the mythical cosmogonies and the cosmologies of the pre-Socratic philosophers. There is connection, but there is also difference. The play of imagination and phantasy began to retreat before the reflective work of the mind, based to some degree on empirical data.

It is, I think, important to remember that the pre-Socratic cosmologists represent a pre-scientific phase of thought. There was then no distinction between philosophy and the empirical sciences; nor, indeed, could there have been. The empirical sciences had to attain a certain stage of development before the distinction could well be made; and we may recall that even after the time of the Renaissance 'natural philosophy' or 'experimental philosophy' was used as a name for what we would call 'physical science'. The early Greek philosophers aimed simply at understanding the nature of the world, and their attention was centred on certain problems which aroused their interest and curiosity or, as Aristotle puts it, 'wonder'. Some of these problems were certainly what we would call 'scientific problems', in the sense that they can be profitably dealt with only by the use of scientific method, though the pre-Socratics tried to solve them by the only means in their power, namely by reflection on casual observations and by speculation. In some instances they made brilliant guesses which anticipated scientific hypotheses of a much later date. Anaximander appears to have put forward an evolutionary hypothesis about man's origin, while the atomic theory of Leucippus and Democritus is a notable example of a speculative anticipation of a later scientific hypothesis. According to Aristotle, men first felt wonder at the more obvious things and later raised difficulties and questions about more important matters; and he mentions questions about the sun and the moon and the stars and about the generation of the universe. This statement by Aristotle is worth reflecting on. The 'wonder' of which he speaks was the fountainhead of both philosophy and science. But in the beginning they were not distinguished, and it is only in terms of a later distinction to which we have become thoroughly accustomed, that we classify questions about the sun and moon and stars as scientific questions. It is obvious enough to us that if we wish to learn about the stars, for example, we have to turn to the astronomer for information: we would hardly go to the speculative philosopher for our information. Similarly, we do not think that questions about the physical constitution of matter or about the mechanism of vision (a subject in which Empedocles, for example, interested himself) can be answered by means of arm-chair reflection.

If I were to rewrite the sections about the pre-Socratics in my first volume, I would wish, I think, to give more attention to these aspects of their thought, namely the fact that a number of the questions which they raised were what we would regard as scientific questions and that a number of the theories which they put forward were speculative anticipations of later scientific hypotheses. At the same time it would be incorrect to suggest that the pre-Socratics were nothing but would-be scientists who lacked the method and the requisite technical means for pursuing their real vocation. One might perhaps say something like this about Thales and Anaximenes; but it would be a strange thing to say about Parmenides or even, I think, about Heraclitus. It seems to me that the pre-Socratics, or some of them at least, raised a number of problems which have generally been considered properly philosophical problems. Heraclitus, for example, appears to have raised moral problems which cannot be answered by empirical science. And it is arguable that the drive behind the intellectual activity of some of them was the desire to 'explain' the universe by reducing multiplicity to unity and by discovering the nature of 'ultimate reality', and that they had this drive in common with later speculative philosophers.

I do not think, then, that one is justified in interpreting the pre-Socratics as nothing more than speculative forerunners of science. To do this is to be guilty of a rather cavalier and hasty generalization. At the same time it is only right to draw attention to the fact that some of the main questions which they raised were not questions which can be answered in the way in which the pre-Socratics (unavoidably) tried to answer them. And in this sense it is true to say that they were forerunners of science. It is, I think, also true to say that they were predominantly 'cosmologists' and that a good deal of the field of their cosmological speculation has now been taken over, as it were, by science. But though one can say if one likes that their assumption that Nature is an organized cosmos was a scientific hypothesis, one can just as well say that it was a philosophic hypothesis which lies at the root of all scientific work and research.

(ii) If the early cosmologists discovered Nature, the Sophists, Socrates and Plato discovered Man. It is true, of course, that this statement is inaccurate and exaggerated in at any rate two ways. In the first place, Man was not discovered by the Sophists or by Socrates in the sense that a hitherto unknown island is discovered by an explorer. Nor, for the matter of that, was Nature discovered in this sense by the pre-Socratics. And in the second place, pre-Socratic philosophers, like the Pythagoreans, had theories about Man, just as Plato had theories about Nature. None the less at the time of Socrates there occurred a shift in philosophic interest and emphasis. And that is why some historians say, and are able to make out a reasonable case for saying, that Greek philosophy began with Socrates. In their view, pre-Socratic philosophy should be regarded as primitive science, not as philosophy at all. Philosophy began with the Socratic ethical analysis. This is not my view of the situation; but it is an arguable position.

But it is not my purpose to say anything further here about the shift of interest from Nature to Man. That there was such a shift of interest in the case of Socrates would not be denied; and I dwelt on this theme in my first volume. What I want to do now is to draw attention to a topic which I did not sufficiently emphasize in that volume, namely the part played by analysis in the philosophies of Socrates and Plato. It might be better, however, to say that I wish now to emphasize the part played by analysis in the philosophy of Plato, since it is an obvious enough fact that Socrates was concerned with analysis. (In saying this I am assuming the truth of the view, represented in my first volume, that Socrates did not invent the theory of Forms or Ideas.)

It seems to me that Plato's theory of values was based very largely on an analysis of ethical propositions and value-statements. And though statements of this kind do seem to me to imply belief in the objectivity of values in some sense, it does not follow that values possess the kind of objectivity which Plato appears to have attributed to them. If one may borrow the language of Husserl, one can say perhaps that Plato carried on a phenomenological analysis of 'essences' without observing the *epoche*, thus confusing descriptive phenomenology with metaphysics. Again, it is a feature of Plato's thought that he drew attention to the differences in logical meaning between different types of sentences. He saw, for example, that in some sentences names are used which do not denote any definite individual thing and that there is a sense in which such sentences can be true even if there are no individual things in existence which correspond to those names. On this basis he developed his theory of Forms in so far as it was extended to generic and specific terms. In doing so he was misled by language and confused logic with metaphysics.

In saying this I am very far from suggesting that Plato's idea of the Good and his theory of exemplarism were worthless and that his theory of Forms was no more than the result of a confusion of logic with metaphysics. His remarks about the Good, obscure though they may be, scarcely lend support to the notion that he postulated the Good simply and solely because he was misled by our use of the word 'good'. But the fact remains that Plato's dialectical and logical approach to the metaphysics of 'Forms' or 'Ideas' is open to very serious objections; and in my first volume I did not, I think, bring out sufficiently either the element of 'linguistic analysis' in Plato's philosophy or his confusion of logic with metaphysics.

But it is possible, I think, to place too much emphasis on the theory of Forms or Ideas in Plato's thought. There is no real evidence, so far as I know, that he ever abandoned this theory; indeed, it seems to me that the available evidence prohibits any such supposition. But at the same time I think that it is true to say that the idea of mind or soul came to play an increasingly important part in Plato's thought. The subject of Plato's theology is notoriously obscure; but it is at least clear that he was the real founder of natural theology. That he attached great importance to the idea of a divine Mind or Soul in the universe is made obvious in the *Laws;* and it is equally clear from the *Timaeus*, even if one has to allow for the 'mythical' character of the contents of that dialogue. This is not to say, of course, that Plato had any clear theistic philosophy: if he had, he certainly did not reveal the fact to his readers. If one means by 'God' the God of Judaeo-Christian monotheism, the evidence would suggest that Plato arrived by different lines of thought at two aspects of God; but it does not suggest, or at least it gives us no solid ground for asserting, that Plato combined those two aspects of Deity, attributing them to one personal Being. Thus the Good may be said to represent what the Christian philosopher calls 'God' under the aspect of exemplary cause, though it does not follow, of course, that Plato would have called the Good 'God'. And the Demiurge of the *Timaeus* and the divine Mind or Soul of the *Laws* may be said to represent God under the aspect of efficient cause, provided that one understands by efficient cause in this connection not a Creator in the full sense but an explanatory cause of the intelligible structure of the empirical world and of the orderly movements of the heavenly bodies. But there is no compelling evidence that Plato ever identified the Good with the being represented by the Demiurge of the *Timaeus*. Nevertheless it is clear that if his theory of Forms was his answer to one problem, his doctrine of a divine Mind or Soul was his answer to another problem; and it would appear that this latter doctrine came to occupy a more important position in his thoughts as time went on.

(iii) In regard to Aristotle, one must emphasize, I think, his attempt to give a rational account of the world of experience and, in particular, his preoccupation with the business of rendering observable change and movement intelligible. (It should be remembered that 'movement' did not mean for Aristotle simply locomotion: it included also quantitative and qualitative change.) One certainly ought not to eliminate or to brush aside the Platonic elements or the metaphysical elements in Aristotle's philosophy, as though they were simply relics of a Platonist phase in his development which he forgot to discard; but it is significant that the

God of the *Metaphysics*, the first unmoved mover, was postulated as an explanation of movement in terms of final causality. The God of the *Metaphysics* tends to appear as an astronomical hypothesis.

If one bears in mind Aristotle's preoccupation with the explanation of change and movement, it becomes much easier to account for his radical criticism of the Platonic theory of Forms. As I have already said, Plato's theory certainly lies open to serious objections on logical grounds, and I doubt if his approach to the theory can stand up to criticism, however much value one may wish to attribute to the theory considered in itself and revised. On the other hand, several of Aristotle's criticisms seem to be singularly unimpressive as they stand. Aristotle tended to assume that what Plato was getting at in his theory of Forms was what he, Aristotle, understood by 'forms'; and he then objected that Plato's Forms did not fulfil the function which his own forms fulfilled and that consequently the Platonic theory was absurd. This line of criticism is not a happy one, since it rests on the assumption that Plato's theory was supposed to fulfil the same function which Aristotle's theory of formal causality was intended to fulfil. But if, as I have suggested, one bears in mind Aristotle's preoccupation with the explanation of change and movement and his 'dynamic' outlook, his hostility towards the Platonic theory becomes understandable. His fundamental objection was that the theory was too 'metaphysical'; it was useless, he thought, for explaining the mixture, as it were, of change and stability which we find in things: it was not a hypothesis which had its roots in the empirical data or which was capable of contributing to the explanation of the empirical data or which was verifiable. I do not wish to suggest that Aristotle was a positivist. But if the word 'metaphysical' is understood as it sometimes is today, namely as referring to altogether unverifiable and gratuitous hypotheses, it is clear that Aristotle considered the Platonic theory to be too 'metaphysical'. I certainly do not think that the theory of exemplary causality has no explanatory function; but it can hardly possess any such function except in connection with the idea of a divine being capable of an activity of which the God of Aristotle's *Metaphysics* was not capable. If one looks at the matter from Aristotle's point of view, one can easily understand his attitude to the Platonic theory. One can also understand how St. Bonaventure in the Middle Ages was able to look on Aristotle as a natural philosopher but not as a metaphysician.

(iv) Plato's Demiurge formed the empirical world, conferring on it an intelligible pattern according to an external exemplar or model: Aristotle's God was the ultimate explanation, as final cause, of movement. For neither of them was God the creator, in the full sense, of empirical beings. The nearest the Greek philosophers came to the idea of creation and to a consideration of the problem of finite existence as such was in neo-Platonism.

But the point about neo-Platonism which I wish to emphasize here is its character as the synthesis of Greek philosophic thought and as a system in which philosophy, ethics and religion were combined. It presented itself as a 'way of salvation', even if as a highly intellectual way of salvation which could appeal only to comparatively few minds. In pre-Socratic Pythagoreanism we can already discern the conception of philosophy as a way of salvation, though this aspect of Pythagoreanism may have tended to retreat into the background in proportion as the mathematical studies of the School developed. With Socrates and his theory of virtue as knowledge one can see clearly the idea of philosophy as a way of salvation, and in the thought of Plato the idea is also prominent, though it tends to be overshadowed by the logical and mathematical aspects of his philosophy. Plato was, of course, no pragmatist; but it does not require any great knowledge of his writings in order to realize the importance he attached to the possession of truth for the life of the individual and for society in general. But it is in the later phases of Platonism, especially in neo-Platonism, that the idea of philosophy as a way of salvation becomes so obvious. One has only to think of Plotinus' doctrine of the ethical and religious ascent of man, culminating in ecstatic union with the One. When Porphyry expounded neo-Platonism as a Greek and supposedly intellectually superior rival to Christianity, he was able to do this because in neo-Platonism Greek philosophy had taken on the character of a religion. Stoicism and Epicureanism were both presented as ways of salvation; but though the Stoic ethic certainly possessed a striking nobility, neither system was of a sufficiently high intellectual order to enable it to play the part in the final stages of Greek thought which was actually played by neo-Platonism.

The fact that early Christian writers borrowed terms and ideas from neo-Platonism may tend to make one emphasize the continuity between Greek and Christian thought. And this was the line I took in my first and second volumes. I have no intention of renouncing the validity of this line of thought now; but it is as well to emphasize the fact that there was also a sharp break between Greek and Christian thought. A neo-Platonist like Porphyry realized very clearly the difference between a philosophy which attached little importance to history and for which the idea of an incarnate God was unthinkable and a religion which attached a profound importance to concrete historical events and which was founded on belief in the Incarnation. Moreover, the Christian acceptance of Christ as the Son of God and of a divine revelation in history meant that for the Christian philosophy as such could not be the way of salvation. Christian writers like Clement of Alexandria interpreted philosophy in the literal sense as 'love of wisdom' and regarded Greek philosophy, especially Platonism in a wide sense, as a preparation for Christianity which fulfilled for the Greek world a function analogous to that fulfilled for the Jews by the Law and the Prophets. One is therefore struck by the friendly attitude shown towards Greek philosophy by a Clement of Alexandria as contrasted with the attitude shown by a Tertullian. But if one considers the former attitude a little more closely one will see its implications, namely that the rôle of Greek philosophy has been taken over in a definite manner by the Christian religion. And in point of fact when philosophy really developed in the Christian mediaeval world it tended to be 'academic', a matter for universities and professional logicians. No Christian philosopher really looked on philosophy as a way of salvation; and when mediaeval thinkers are reproached with paying too much attention to logical subtleties it is often forgotten that for them philosophy could not well be anything else than an 'academic' pursuit. When in the modern era one finds the conception of philosophy as a 'way of salvation' showing itself again the conception usually originates either in a disbelief in Christian theology and the desire to find a substitute or, if it is shown by Christian thinkers, in the desire to find an acceptable approach to those who are no longer Christians. The believing Christian looks to religion to be the inspiration of his life and his guide to conduct rather than to philosophy, however interested he may be in the latter.

2. In my second volume I traced the history of philosophy in the Christian world up to the end of the thirteenth century, though I included John Duns Scotus (d. 1308), whose philosophy belongs rather with the great thirteenth-century systems than with the *via moderna* of the fourteenth century. The volume thus covered the Patristic period, the early mediaeval period and the period of constructive metaphysical thinking on the grand scale. The next period, that is to say, the late mediaeval period, has been sketched in the first part of the present volume.

This fourfold division of Christian philosophic thought from the beginning of the Christian era to the close of the Middle Ages is a traditional division, and it is, I think, justified and useful. But it is possible to make an even simpler division by saying that mediaeval philosophy falls into two main periods, the period preceding and the period following the introduction of the Aristotelian *corpus* to western Christendom. In any case I think that it is hardly possible to exaggerate the philosophic importance of this event, namely of the rediscovery of Aristotle. I am speaking primarily as a historian. Philosophers may differ in their evaluations of Aristotelian theories, but there is, I think, no ground for dispute concerning the importance of the rediscovery of Aristotle, considered as a historical event. Apart from the system of John Scotus Eriugena, of which little notice was taken, the early mediaevals possessed nothing which we should be likely to call a philosophical system; and in particular they had no intimate knowledge of any system which owed nothing to Christianity. But the rediscovery of Aristotle and the translation of the leading Islamic thinkers in the second half of the twelfth century and the first part of the thirteenth brought to the knowledge of the Christian mediaeval thinkers for the first time a developed system which was the work of a pagan philosopher and which owed nothing to Christianity.

Aristotle therefore naturally tended to mean for them 'philosophy'. It is a great mistake to allow the obstinacy with which some Renaissance Scholastics clung to the physical and scientific ideas of Aristotle to make one think of the discovery of Aristotle as a philosophical disaster. In the Middle Ages Aristotle was, indeed, known as 'the philosopher', and he was so named because his system was for the mediaevals 'philosophy' to all intents and purposes. But his system meant for them 'philosophy' not so much because it was Aristotelian, in the sense in which we distinguish Aristotelianism from Platonism, Stoicism, Epicureanism or neo-Platonism, as because it was the one great system of philosophy of which they possessed an extensive knowledge. It is important to realize this fact. If we speak, for example, of the attempt of St. Thomas to reconcile Aristotelianism with Christian theology, one will realize the nature of the situation better if one makes the experiment of substituting the word 'philosophy' for the word 'Aristotelianism'. When some of the theologians in the thirteenth century adopted a hostile attitude to Aristotle and regarded his philosophy as being in many respects an intellectual menace, they were rejecting independent philosophy in the name of the Christian faith. And when St. Thomas adopted in great measure the Aristotelian system, he was giving a charter to philosophy. He should not be regarded as burdening Christian thought with the system of a particular Greek philosopher. The deeper significance of his action was that he recognized the rights and position of philosophy as a rational study distinct from theology.

It is as well, too, to remind oneself of the fact that the utilization of the new learning in a constructive manner was due to men like St. Thomas and Duns Scotus who were primarily theologians. The rediscovery of Aristotle raised the problem of the relation between theology and philosophy in a form far more acute than it had previously assumed in the Middle Ages. And the only people in the thirteenth century who made a serious attempt to cope with the problem constructively were the theologians. Those professors of the faculty of arts who are often known as the 'Latin Averroists' tended to accept the entire philosophy of Aristotle, as it stood or as interpreted by Averroes, in a slavish manner. And when taxed with the fact that some of Aristotle's doctrines were incompatible with Christian theology, they answered that the philosopher's business is simply to report philosophical opinions. If they were sincere in giving this answer, they equated philosophy with the history of philosophy. If they were not sincere, they accepted Aristotle in an uncritical and slavish manner. In either case they adopted no constructive attitude. Theologians like St. Thomas on the other hand endeavoured to synthesize Aristotelianism, which, as I have said, meant to all intents and purposes 'philosophy', with the Christian religion. This was not, however, a mere attempt to force Aristotle into a Christian mould, as some critics imagine: it involved a rethinking and development of the Aristotelian philosophy. St. Thomas's work was not a work of ignorant distortion but of original construction. He did not assume the truth of Aristotelianism because it was Aristotelianism and then try to force it into a Christian mould. He was convinced that Aristotelianism, in its main lines, was the result of sound reasoning; and when he attacked the monopsychistic doctrine of the Averroists he attacked it partly on the ground that Averroes had, in his opinion, misinterpreted Aristotle and partly on the ground that monopsychism was false and that it could be shown to be false by philosophic reasoning. It is the second ground which is the most important. If a philosophical theory was incompatible with Christian theology, St. Thomas believed that it was false. But he was well aware that from the philosophic point of view it is not sufficient to say that a theory is false because it is incompatible with Christianity. He was also aware that it is not sufficient to argue that it rested on a misinterpretation of Aristotle. His primary task was to show that the theory rested on bad or inconclusive reasoning. In other words, his rethinking of Aristotelianism was a philosophic rethinking: it did not simply take the form of confronting Aristotelian and supposedly Aristotelian theories with Christian theology and eliminating or changing theories which were incompatible with that theology without any philosophical argument. He was quite prepared to meet both the integral Aristotelians and the anti-Aristotelians on their own ground, namely on an appeal to reasoning. In so doing he developed philosophy as a separate branch of study, separate, that is, from theology on the one hand and from a mere reporting of the words of Aristotle on the other.

One can say, then, that it was due to the rediscovery of Aristotle coupled with the work of the thirteenth-century theologian-philosophers that mediaeval philosophy attained adult stature. Knowledge of the metaphysical and physical works of Aristotle widened the mediaevals' conception of philosophy, which could no longer be looked upon as more or less equivalent to dialectic. Aristotelianism was thus a fecundating principle of prime importance in the growth of mediaeval philosophy. It is doubtless regrettable that Aristotelian science, especially Aristotelian astronomy, should have come to be accorded the degree of respect which it won for itself in certain quarters; but this does not alter the fact that Aristotle the philosopher was very far from being a paralysing weight and burden round the necks of the mediaeval thinkers. Without him mediaeval philosophy would scarcely have been able to advance as rapidly as it did. For study of the works of Aristotle not only raised the general standard of philosophic thinking and analysis but also greatly extended the field of study of the mediaeval philosophers. For example, knowledge of Aristotle's psychological and epistemological theories led to a prolonged reflection on these themes. And when Aristotle's general position was accepted, as by St. Thomas, new problems arose or old problems were rendered more acute. For if there are no innate ideas and our ideas are formed in dependence on sense-perception, the question arises, how is metaphysics possible, in so far as metaphysics involves thinking and speaking of beings which transcend matter. And what meaning can be attached to terms descriptive of transcendent beings? St. Thomas was aware of these problems and of their origin and he gave some consideration to them, while Scotus also was aware of the need for providing some theoretical justification of metaphysics. Again it is arguable that Aristotle's 'empiricism' was one of the influences which gave rise in the fourteenth century to lines of criticism which tended to undermine the metaphysical systems which had themselves been built on Aristotle's ideas. In fine, whatever one's estimation of the value of Aristotle's theories may be, it is hardly possible to deny the fact that the mediaevals' knowledge of his philosophy acted as a most powerful and wide-ranging influence in stimulating philosophic thought in the Middle Ages. When his ideas came to have a deadening effect on thought, this was due simply to the fact that the living and creative movement of thought which had originally been stimulated by his writings had spent itself, for the time being at least.

But if one emphasizes the importance of Aristotelianism for mediaeval philosophy, one must also remember that the theologian-philosophers of the thirteenth century deepened it considerably from the metaphysical point of view. Aristotle himself was concerned to explain the *how* of the world, that is to say, certain features of the world, especially change or becoming or 'movement'. With a philosopher like St. Thomas, however, there was a shift of emphasis: the problem of the *that* of the world, the problem that is, of the existence of finite beings, became primary. It is perfectly true, of course, as M. Gilson has shown with his customary lucidity, that the Judaeo-Christian doctrine of creation directed attention to this subject; and this obviously took place long before the time of St. Thomas. But the latter gave expression to the primacy of this problem for the Christian metaphysician in his theory of the distinction between essence and existence (or rather in his use of the distinction, since he did not invent it). It is possible, therefore, to call the philosophy of St. Thomas an 'existential' philosophy in a sense in which one can hardly call Aristotle's philosophy 'existential'.

3. The mediaevals always had some knowledge of the Aristotelian logic. And at the time when philosophy meant for most people little more than logic or dialectic it was perfectly understandable that philosophy should be widely regarded as being, in a famous phrase, 'the handmaid of theology'. Logic, according to Aristotle's own view, is an instrument of reasoning, and in the early Middle Ages there was not very much outside the theological sphere to which this instrument could be applied. Although, then, a distinction was drawn between faith and reason, that is, between truths accepted on authority and believed by faith and truths which were accepted as the result of demonstration, the problem of the relation of philosophy to theology was not acute. But when the Aristotelian system as a whole became known in the Christian universities the province of philosophy was ex-

tended far beyond the sphere of dialectic. The rise of natural or philosophic theology (which had, of course, its roots in the writings of St. Anselm) and of natural philosophy or cosmology, together with metaphysical psychology, introduced the idea of philosophy as a branch of study distinct from theology and from what would now be called 'science'. It followed, therefore, that Christian thinkers had to give their attention to the proper relation of philosophy to theology.

St. Thomas's views on this matter have been outlined in the second volume of this history, and I do not propose to repeat them here. Let it be sufficient to recall that he gave a charter to philosophy and recognized its intrinsic independence. Naturally, St. Thomas, as a believing Christian, was convinced that a philosophic theory which was incompatible with Christianity was false, for he was far from entertaining the absurd idea that two contradictory propositions could be true at the same time. But, given the truth of Christianity, he was convinced that it could always be shown that a philosophic proposition which was incompatible with Christianity was the result of bad or specious arguments. Philosophers as individual thinkers might go wrong in their reasoning and contradict revealed truth; but philosophy itself could not do so. There is no such thing as an infallible philosopher; but, if there were, his conclusions would always be in harmony with revealed truth, though he would arrive at his conclusions independently of the data of revelation.

This was, of course, a very tidy and convenient view of the relation of philosophy to theology. But one must remark in addition that according to St. Thomas the metaphysician, while unable to demonstrate the revealed mysteries of Christianity, like the Trinity, is able to demonstrate or establish with certainty the 'preambles of faith', such as the existence of a God capable of revealing truths to men. In the fourteenth century, however, as we have seen in the first part of the present volume, a number of philosophers began to question the validity of proofs which St. Thomas had accepted as valid proofs of the 'preambles of faith', that is, as demonstrations of the rational foundations of faith. Their right to criticize any given proof could hardly be questioned legitimately; for analysis and criticism are essential to philosophy. If a philosopher thought, for example, that the principle *omne quod movetur ab alio movetur* could not bear the weight laid on it in St. Thomas's first argument for God's existence, he had every right to say so. On the other hand, if a philosopher questioned the validity of all the proofs for God's existence, it was hardly possible to maintain the close relation between philosophy and theology asserted by St. Thomas, and the problems of the rationality of faith became acute. But no really serious consideration was given to this problem in the fourteenth century. A theologian-philosopher like William of Ockham could question the validity of metaphysical proofs for God's existence without going on to inquire seriously either what the true nature of arguments for God's existence is or what is the rational ground of our belief in God if His existence cannot be demonstrated in the traditional manner. Partly because so many of the leading 'nominalists' were themselves theologians, partly because the general mental background was still provided by Christianity, and partly because the attention of many philosophers was absorbed in logical and analytic problems (and, in Ockham's case, in political and ecclesiastical polemics) the problems raised by the nominalist criticism of traditional metaphysics were not fully grasped or sufficiently discussed. Theology and philosophy were tending to fall apart, but the fact was not clearly recognized.

4. In the first part of the present volume we saw how the *via moderna* spread in the fourteenth and fifteenth centuries. We also saw how in the fourteenth century there were anticipations at least of a new scientific outlook, which developed with striking rapidity at the time of the Renaissance. If the pre-Socratic philosophers discovered Nature, in the sense that they formed the idea of a cosmos or law-governed system, the Renaissance scientists discovered Nature in the sense that they developed the use of scientific method in the discovery of the 'laws' which actually govern natural events. To speak of laws governing Nature may well be open to objection; but the point is not that this or that language was used at the time or that this or that language ought to be used but rather that the Renaissance scientists developed the scientific study of Nature in a way in which it had never been developed before. This meant that physical science attained adult stature. It may have been often known as 'natural philosophy'

or 'experimental philosophy', but, terminology apart, the fact remains that through the work of the Renaissance scientists science came to occupy a place of its own alongside theology and philosophy. And with the growth of modern science a great change has gradually taken place in the common estimation of what 'knowledge' is. In the Middle Ages theology and philosophy were universally regarded as 'sciences'; the great figures in university life were the theologians and the philosophers; and it was they who in general estimation were the possessors of knowledge. In the course of time, however, scientific knowledge in the modern sense has come to be popularly regarded as the norm and standard of knowledge; and in many countries neither theologians nor philosophers would be commonly regarded as possessing 'knowledge' in the sense in which scientists are thought to possess it. This attitude towards knowledge has arisen only gradually, of course, and its growth has been fostered by the development of applied and technical science. But the plain fact is that whereas in the Middle Ages philosophy was to all intents and purposes the sole representative of 'scientific' knowledge outside the sphere of theology, in the post-Renaissance world rival claimants have arisen which in the estimation of many people have wrested from philosophy the title to represent knowledge at all. To mention this view of the matter in connection with Renaissance science is, of course, to anticipate, and it would be inappropriate to discuss the matter at length here. But I have mentioned it in order to show the great importance of the scientific development of the Renaissance period or, rather, one of the ways in which it was important for philosophy. If one can find in the rediscovery of Aristotle a dividing-line in mediaeval philosophy, one can also find in the growth of Renaissance science a dividing-line in the history of European thought.

In view of the fact that the older histories of philosophy were inclined to neglect mediaeval philosophy, of which they knew little, and practically to jump from Aristotle to Descartes, later historians have very rightly emphasized the continuity between Greek philosophy and Christian thought and between mediaeval philosophy and that of the post-Renaissance period. That Descartes, for example, was dependent on Scholasticism for many of his philosophical categories and ideas, that the mediaeval theory of natural law was utilized by Hooker and passed from him in a diluted form to Locke, and that the latter was more dependent on Aristotelianism than he probably realized are now matters of common knowledge among historians. But it is, I think, a mistake so to emphasize the element of continuity that the elements of novelty and change are slurred over. The climate of thought in the post-Renaissance world was not the same as that prevailing in the Middle Ages. The change was due, of course, to a number of different factors working together; but the rise of science was certainly not the least important of those factors. The development of science made it much easier than it formerly had been to consider the world from a point of view which had no obvious connection with theology. If one compares, for instance, St. Bonaventure or even St. Thomas with a philosopher like Descartes one finds at once a considerable difference of outlook and interest, in spite of the fact that all three men were believing Catholics. St. Bonaventure was principally interested in creatures in their relationship to God, as *vestigia Dei*, or in man's case, as the *imago Dei*. St. Thomas, owing to his Aristotelianism, shows a greater interest in creatures from a purely philosophical point of view; but he was above all things a theologian and it is obvious that his primary interest was that of a theologian and a specifically Christian thinker. In the case of Descartes, however, we find an outlook which, though it was the attitude of a man who was a Christian, was what one may call 'neutral' in character. In the post-Renaissance period there were, of course, philosophers who were atheists or at any rate non-Christian: one has only to think of some of the figures of the French Enlightenment. But my point is that after the Middle Ages philosophy tended to become 'lay' in character. A man like Descartes was certainly a good Christian; but one would hardly think of his philosophy as a specifically Christian philosophy, in spite of the influence of his religious beliefs on his philosophic thought. The rise of humanism at the time of the Renaissance, followed by the growth of science, produced fresh interests and lines of thought which, though not necessarily incompatible with theology, could be pursued without any obvious association with or relation to it. This is clear enough in the case of science itself, and the growth of science reacted on philosophy. Or perhaps it is better to say that both the science and the philosophy of the time manifested the growth of the new outlook and fostered it.

But if one stresses the difference between the mediaeval and Renaissance worlds in the climate of thought, it is necessary to qualify this emphasis by drawing attention to the gradual and in large part continuous evolution of the new outlook. A comparatively early mediaeval thinker like St. Anselm was chiefly interested in understanding the faith: for him the primacy of faith was obvious, and what we might call his philosophizing was largely an attempt to understand by the use of reason what we believe. *Credo, ut intelligam.* In the thirteenth century the rediscovery of Aristotelianism greatly widened the interests and horizons of Christian thinkers. Acceptance of Aristotle's physics, however erroneous many of his scientific theories may have been, paved the way for a study of the world for its own sake so to speak. A professional theologian like St. Thomas was naturally not interested in developing what we would call science, not because of any hostility towards such studies but because his interests lay elsewhere. But by the rediscovery of Aristotle and the translations of Greek and Arabic scientific works the ground was prepared for scientific advance. Already in the thirteenth century, and still more in the fourteenth century, we can see the beginning of a scientific investigation of Nature. The ferment of Renaissance philosophy, with its mixture of philosophic speculation and scientific hypothesis, further prepared the way for the rise of Renaissance science. One can say, then, that the rediscovery of Aristotle in the Middle Ages was the remote preparation for the rise of science. But one can, of course, go further still and say that the Christian doctrine of the world's creation by God provided a theological preparation for the advance of science. For if the world is a creation, and if matter is not evil but good, the material world is obviously worth scientific investigation. But scientific investigation could not develop until the right method was found; and for that Christian Europe had to wait many centuries.

The foregoing remarks may possibly sound like an endorsement of Auguste Comte's doctrine of the three stages, as though I meant to say that the theological stage was followed by the philosophical and the philosophical by the scientific stage, in the sense that the later stage supplanted the former, both *de facto* and *de iure*. In regard to the historical facts it has been argued that the development of Greek thought proceeded in the very opposite direction to that demanded by Comte's theory.[1] For the movement was from a primitive 'scientific' stage through metaphysics to theology, rather than from theology through metaphysics to science. However, the development of thought in western Christianity can be used to a certain extent in support of Comte's theory, in so far as the historical facts are concerned. For it might be argued that the primacy of theology was succeeded by a stage characterized by 'lay' philosophical systems, and that this stage has been succeeded by a positivist stage. An interpretation of this sort is certainly open to the objection that it is based on aspects of the development of thought which have been selected in order to support a preconceived theory. For it is clear that the development of Scholastic philosophy did not simply follow the development of Scholastic theology: to a great extent the two developed together. Again, the rise of science in the post-Renaissance world was contemporaneous with a succession of philosophic systems. However, it does seem that at any rate a plausible case can be made out in favour of Comte's interpretation of western thought since the beginning of Christianity. It makes some sense at least to distinguish the Age of Faith, the Age of Reason and the Age of Science, if one is speaking of climates of thought. In the Middle Ages religious faith and theology shaped the climate of thought; at the time of the 'Enlightenment' wide sections of the intellectual public placed their trust in 'reason' (though the use of the word 'reason' in this connection stands in need of careful analysis); and in the modern world a positivist climate of thought prevails in a number of countries if one understands 'positivist' and 'positivism' in a wide sense. Yet even if a plausible case can be made out for Comte's theory from the historical point of view, it certainly does not follow that the succession of stages, in so far as there actually was a succession of stages, constitutes a 'progress' in any but a temporal sense of the word 'progress'. In one period theology may be the paramount branch of study and in another period science; but a change in the climate of thought from a theological to a scientific period does not mean that theology is false or that a scientific civilization is an adequate realization of the potentialities of human culture.

It is, however, fairly obvious now that science cannot disprove the validity of faith or of theological beliefs. Physics, for example, has nothing to say about the Trinity or about the existence of God. If many people have ceased to believe in Christianity, this does not show that Christianity is false. And, in general, the relation of science to religion and theology is not one of acute tension: the tension which in the last century was often alleged to exist between them does not really exist at all. The theoretical difficulty arises rather in regard to the relation of philosophy to theology. And this tension existed in germ once philosophy had attained to adult stature. It did not become obvious as long as the leading philosophers were also theologians; but once the rise of science had directed men's thought in fresh directions and philosophers were no longer primarily theologians the tension was bound to become apparent. As long as philosophers thought that they were able to build up a true metaphysical system by a method of their own, the tension tended to take the form of a tension between divergent conclusions and propositions. But now that a considerable number of philosophers believe that the philosopher has no method of his own the employment of which is capable of adding to human knowledge, and that all factual knowledge is derivable from immediate observation and from the sciences, the problem is rather one concerning the rational foundations of faith. In this sense we are back in the situation created in the fourteenth century by the nominalist criticism of traditional metaphysics, though the nature of the problem is clearer now than it was then. Is there such a thing as a valid metaphysical argument? Can there be metaphysical knowledge and, if so, what sort of knowledge is it? Have we 'blind' faith on the one hand and scientific knowledge on the other, or can metaphysics supply a kind of bridge between them? Questions of this sort were implicit in fourteenth-century nominalist criticism, and they are still with us. They have been rendered all the more acute, on the one hand by the constant growth of scientific knowledge since the time of the Renaissance and, on the other hand, by the succession of metaphysical systems in the post-Renaissance and modern worlds, leading to a prevailing mistrust of metaphysics in general. What is the rôle of philosophy? What is its proper relation to science? What is its proper relation to faith and religious belief?

These questions cannot be further developed or discussed now. My object in raising them is simply that of suggesting various points for reflection in considering the later development of philosophic thought. In the next volume I hope to treat of 'modern' philosophy from Descartes to Kant inclusive, and in connection with Kant we shall be faced with an explicit statement regarding these questions and their solution.

Appendix One

Honorific titles applied to philosophers treated of in this volume.

DURANDUS:	Doctor modernus, *later* Doctor resolutissimus.
PETRUS AUREOLI:	Doctor facundus.
WILLIAM OF OCKHAM:	Venerabilis inceptor.
ANTOINE ANDRÉ:	Doctor dulcifluus.
FRANCIS DE MARCIA:	Doctor succinctus.
JOHN OF MIRECOURT:	Monachus albus.
GREGORY OF RIMINI:	Doctor authenticus.
JOHN RUYSBROECK:	Doctor admirabilis.
DENIS THE CARTHUSIAN:	Doctor ecstaticus.
JOHN GERSON:	Doctor christianissimus.
JAKOB BÖHME:	Philosophus teutonicus.
FRANCIS SUÁREZ:	Doctor eximius.

Appendix Two

A SHORT BIBLIOGRAPHY

Chapter Thirteen: The Revival of Platonism

Texts

ERASMUS. *Opera*. 10 vols. Leyden, 1703–6.
Letters. Latin edition by P. S. Allen, H. S. Allen, H. W. Garrod. 11 vols. Oxford, 1906–47.

LEONE EBREO. *The Philosophy of Love*. F. Friedeberg-Sealey and J. H. Barnes (translators). London, 1937.

Marsilii Ficini Opera. 2 vols. Paris, 1641.

PICO DELLA MIRANDOLA, G. *Opera omnia*. 2 vols. Basle, 1573.

The Renaissance Philosophy of Man (Petrarca, Valla, Ficino, Pico, Pomponazzi, Vives). E. Cassirer, P. O. Kristeller, J. H. Randall, Jr. (edit.). Chicago, 1948.

Studies

BURCKHARDT, J. *The Civilization of the Renaissance*. London, 1944.

DELLA TORRE, A. *Storia dell' academia platonica di Firenze*. Florence, 1902.

DRESS, W. *Die Mystik des Marsilio Ficino*. Berlin, 1929.

DULLES, A. *Princeps concordiae. Pico della Mirandola and the Scholastic Tradition*. Cambridge (Mass.), 1941.

FESTUGIÈRE, J. *La philosophie de l'amour de Marsile Ficin*. Paris, 1941.

GARIN, E. *Giovanni Pico della Mirandola*. Florence, 1937.

GENTILE, G. *Il pensiero italiano del rinascimento*. Florence, 1940 (3rd edit.).

HAK, H. *Marsilio Ficino*. Amsterdam, Paris, 1934.
HÖNIGSWALD, R. *Denker der italienischen Renaissance. Gestalten und Probleme*. Basle, 1938.
TAYLOR, H. O. *Thought and Expression in the Sixteenth Century*. New York, 1920.
TRINKAUS, C. E. *Adversity's Noblemen: The Italian Humanists on Happiness*. New York, 1940.
WOODWARD, W. H. *Studies in Education during the Age of the Renaissance*. Cambridge, 1906.

Chapter Fourteen: Aristotelianism

Texts

LAURENTIUS VALLA. *Dialecticae disputationes contra Aristotelicos*, 1499. (*Opera*. Basle, 1540.)
RUDOLF AGRICOLA. *De inventione dialectica*. Louvain, 1515; and other editions.
MARIUS NIZOLIUS. *De veris principiis et vera ratione philosophandi contra pseudophilosophos libri IV*. Parma, 1553 (edited by Leibniz under the title *Antibarbarus philosophicus*. Frankfurt, 1671 and 1674).
PETRUS RAMUS. *Dialecticae partitiones*. Paris, 1543.
Aristotelicae animadversiones. Paris, 1543.
Dialectique. Paris, 1555.
ALEXANDER ACHILLINI. *De universalibus*. Bologna, 1501.
De intelligentiis. Venice, 1508.
De distinctionibus. Bologna, 1518.
PIETRO POMPONAZZI. *Opera*. Basle, 1567.
MELANCHTHON. *Opera*. C. G. Bretschneider and H. E. Bindseil (edit.). 28 vols. Halle, 1824–60.
Supplementa Melanchthonia. Leipzig, 1910– .
MONTAIGNE. *Essais*. Numerous editions, the most complete being by F. Strowski, P. Gebelin and P. Villey (5 vols.), 1906–33.
SANCHEZ. *Tractatus philosophici*. Rotterdam, 1649.

Studies

BATISTELLA, R. M. *Nizolio*. Treviso, 1905.
CASSIRER, E., KRISTELLER, P. O. and RANDALL, J. H. (edit.). *The Renaissance Philosophy of Man (Petrarca, Valla, Ficino, Pico, Pomponazzi, Vives)*. Chicago, 1948.

DOUGLAS, C. and HARDIE, R. P. *The Philosophy and Psychology of Pietro Pomponazzi*. Cambridge, 1910.

FRIEDRICH, H. *Montaigne*. Berne, 1949.

GIARRATANO, C. *Il pensiero di Francesco Sanchez*. Naples, 1903.

GRAVES, F. P. *Peter Ramus and the Educational Reformation of the 16th Century*. London, 1912.

HÖNIGSWALD, R. *Denker der italienischen Renaissance. Gestalten und Probleme*. Basle, 1938.

MOREAU, P. *Montaigne, l'homme et l'œuvre*. Paris, 1939.

OWEN, J. *The Sceptics of the Italian Renaissance*. London, 1893.

PETERSEN, P. *Geschichte der aristotelischen Philosophie im protestantischen Deutschland*. Leipzig, 1921.

Revista Portuguesa de Filosofia (1951; t. 7, fasc. 2). *Francisco Sanchez no IV Centenário do seu nascimento*. Braga, 1951. (Contains Bibliography of writings about Sanchez.)

STROWSKI, F. *Montaigne*. Paris, 1906.

WADDINGTON, C. *De Petri Rami vita, scriptis, philosophia*. Paris, 1849.

Ramus, sa vie, ses écrits et ses opinions. Paris, 1855.

Chapter Fifteen: Nicholas of Cusa

Texts

Nicolai de Cusa Opera Omnia iussu et auctoritate Academiae Heidelbergensis ad codicum fidem edita. Leipzig, 1932– .

Opera. 3 vols. Paris, 1514. Basle, 1565.

Schriften, im Auftrag der Heidelberger Akademie der Wissenschaften in deutscher Uebersetzung herausgegeben von E. Hoffmann. Leipzig, 1936– .

Philosophische Schriften. A. Petzelt (edit.). Vol. 1, Stuttgart, 1949.

De docta ignorantia libri tres. Testo latino con note di Paolo Rotta. Bari, 1913.

The Idiot. San Francisco, 1940.

Des Cardinals und Bischofs Nikolaus von Cusa wichtigste Schriften in deutscher Uebersetzung. F. A. Scharpff. Freiburg i. B., 1862.

Studies

BETT, H. *Nicholas of Cusa.* London, 1932.

CLEMENS, F. J. *Giordano Bruno und Nicolaus von Cues.* Bonn, 1847.

GANDILLAC, M. DE *La philosophie de Nicolas de Cues.* Paris, 1941.

GRADI, R. *Il pensiero del Cusano.* Padua, 1941.

JACOBI, M. *Das Weltgebäude des Kard. Nikolaus von Cusa.* Berlin, 1904.

KOCH, J. *Nicolaus von Cues und seine Umwelt.* 1948.

MENNICKEN, P. *Nikolaus von Kues.* Trier, 1950.

ROTTA, P. *Il cardinale Niccolò di Cusa, la vita ed il pensiero.* Milan, 1928.

Niccolò Cusano. Milan, 1942.

SCHULTZ, R. *Die Staatsphilosophie des Nikolaus von Kues.* Hain, 1948.

VANSTEENBERGHE, E. *Le cardinal Nicolas de Cues.* Paris, 1920.

Autour de la docte ignorance. Münster, 1915 (Beiträge, 14, 2–4).

Chapters Sixteen–Seventeen: Philosophy of Nature

Texts

CARDANO. *Hieronymi Cardani Mediolanensis philosophi et medici celeberrimi opera omnia.* 10 vols. Lyons, 1663.

TELESIO. *De natura rerum iuxta propria principia.* Naples, 1586.

PATRIZZI. *Discussiones peripateticae.* Basle, 1581.

Nova de universis philosophia. London, 1611.

CAMPANELLA. *Philosophia sensibus demonstrata.* Naples, 1590.

Prodromus philosophiae. Padua, 1611.

Atheismus triumphatus. Rome, 1630.

La città del sole. A Castaldo (edit.). Rome, 1910.

BRUNO. *Opere italiane.* G. Gentile (edit.). Bari.

I. *Dialoghi metafisici.* 1907.

II. *Dialoghi morali.* 1908.

Opera latine conscripta. I & II. Naples, 1880 and 1886. III & IV. Florence, 1889 and 1891.

S. GREENBERG. *The Infinite in G. Bruno. With a translation of Bruno's Dialogue: Concerning the Cause, Principle and One*. New York, 1950.

D. W. SINGER. G. *Bruno: His Life and Thought. With a translation of Bruno's Work: On the Infinite Universe and Worlds*. New York, 1950.

GASSENDI. *Opera*. Lyons, 1658, Florence, 1727.

PARACELSUS. *Four Treatises of Theophrastus von Hohenheim called Paracelsus*. H. E. Sigerist (edit.). Baltimore, 1941.

PARACELSUS. *Selected Writings*. Edited with an Introduction by Jolande Jacobi. Translated by Norbert Guterman. London, 1951.

VAN HELMONT, J. B. *Opera*. Lyons, 1667.

VAN HELMONT, F. M. *Opuscula philosophica*. Amsterdam, 1690.

The paradoxical discourses of F. M. van Helmont. London, 1685.

WEIGEL. *Libellus de vita beata*. Halle, 1609.

Der güldene Griff. Halle, 1613.

Vom Ort der Welt. Halle, 1613.

Dialogus de christianismo. Halle, 1614.

Erkenne dich selbst. Neustadt, 1615.

BÖHME. *Werke*. 7 vols. K. W. Schiebler (edit.). Leipzig, 1840–7 (2nd edition).

Works. C. J. Barber (edit.). London, 1909– .

Studies

BLANCHET, L. *Campanella*. Paris, 1920.

BOULTING, W. *Giordano Bruno, His Life, Thought and Martyrdom*. London, 1914.

CICUTTINI, L. *Giordano Bruno*. Milan, 1950.

FIORENTINO, F. *Telesio, ossia studi storici sull 'idea della natura nel risorgimento italiano*. 2 vols. Florence, 1872–4.

GENTILE, G. *Bruno e il pensiero del rinascimento*. Florence, 1920.

GREENBERG, S. See under *Texts* (Bruno).

HÖNIGSWALD, R. *Denker der italienischen Renaissance. Gestalten und Probleme*. Basle, 1938.

MCINTYRE, J. L. *Giordano Bruno*. London, 1903.

PEIP, A. *Jakob Böhme, der deutsche Philosoph*. Leipzig, 1850.

PENNY, A. J. *Studies in Jakob Böhme*. London, 1912.
Introduction to the Study of Jacob Böhme's Writings. New York, 1901.
SIGERIST, H. E. *Paracelsus in the Light of Four Hundred Years*. New York, 1941.
SINGER, D. W. See under *Texts* (Bruno).
STILLMAN, J. M. *Theophrastus Bombastus von Hohenheim, called Paracelsus*. Chicago, 1920.
TROILO, E. *La filosofia di Giordano Bruno*. Turin, 1907.
WESSELY, J. E. *Thomas Campanellas Sonnenstadt*. Munich, 1900.
WHYTE, A. *Jacob Behmen: An Appreciation*. Edinburgh, 1895.

Chapter Eighteen: The Scientific Movement of the Renaissance.

Texts

LEONARDO DA VINCI. *The Literary Works*. J. R. Richter (edit.). Oxford, 1939.
COPERNICUS. *Gesamtausgabe*. 4 vols.
TYCHO BRAHE. *Opera omnia*. Prague, 1611, Frankfurt, 1648.
KEPLER. *Opera omnia*. 8 vols. Frankfurt, 1858–71.
GALILEO. *Opere*. E. Albèri (edit.). Florence, 1842–56.
Le opere di Galileo Galilei. 20 vols. Florence, 1890–1907.
Dialogo sopra i due massimi systemi del mondo. Florence, 1632.
(English translation by T. Salusbury in *Mathematical Collections and Translations*. London, 1661.)
Dialogues concerning Two New Sciences. H. Crew and A. de Salvio (Translators). Evanston, 1939.

Studies

ALIOTTA, A. and CARBONARA, C. *Galilei*. Milan, 1949.
ARMITAGE, A. *Copernicus, the Founder of Modern Astronomy*. London, 1938.
BURTT, E. A. *The Metaphysical Foundations of Modern Physical Science*. New York, 1936.
BUTTERFIELD, H. *Origins of Modern Science*. London, 1949.
DAMPIER, SIR W. C. *A History of Science*. Cambridge, 1929 (4th edition, 1948).

A Shorter History of Science. Cambridge, 1944.

DANNEMANN, F. *Die Naturwissenschaften in ihrer Entwicklung und in ihrem Zusammenhange*. 4 vols. Leipzig, 1910–13.

DREYER, J. L. E. *Tycho Brahe*. Edinburgh, 1890.

DUHEM, P. *Études sur Léonard de Vinci*. Paris, 1906–13.

Les origines de la statique. Paris, 1905–6.

FAHIE, J. J. *Galileo, his Life and Work*. London, 1903.

GRANT, R. *Johann Kepler. A Tercentenary Commemoration of his Life and Work*. Baltimore, 1931.

JEANS, SIR J. H. *The Growth of Physical Science*. Cambridge, 1947.

KOYRÉ, A. *Études Galiléennes*. Paris, 1940.

MCMURRICH, J. P. *Leonardo da Vinci the Anatomist*. London, 1930.

SEDGWICK, W. T. and TYLER, H. W. *A Short History of Science*. New York, 1917 (revised edition, 1939).

STIMSON, D. *The Gradual Acceptance of the Copernican Theory of the Universe*. New York, 1917.

STRONG, E. W. *Procedures and Metaphysics*. Berkeley, U.S.A., 1936.

TAYLOR, F. SHERWOOD. *A Short History of Science*. London, 1939.

Science Past and Present. London, 1945.

Galileo and Freedom of Thought. London, 1938.

THORNDIKE, L. *A History of Magic and Experimental Science*. 6 vols. New York, 1923–42.

WHITEHEAD, A. N. *Science and the Modern World*. Cambridge, 1927 (Penguin, 1938).

WOLF, A. *A History of Science, Technology and Philosophy in the Sixteenth and Seventeenth Centuries*. London, 1935.

Chapter Nineteen: Francis Bacon

Texts

The Philosophical Works of Francis Bacon. J. M. Robertson (edit.). London, 1905.

Works. R. L. Ellis, J. Spedding and D. D. Heath (edit.). 7 vols. London, 1857–74.

Novum Organum. Edited with introduction and notes by T. Fowler. Oxford, 1889 (2nd edition).

The Advancement of Learning. London (Everyman Series).
R. W. GIBSON. *Francis Bacon. A Bibliography*. Oxford, 1950.

Studies

ANDERSON, F. H. *The Philosophy of Francis Bacon*. Chicago, 1948.
FISCHER, KUNO. *Francis Bacon und seine Schule*. Heidelberg, 1923 (4th edition).
NICHOL, J. *Francis Bacon, his Life and Philosophy*. 2 vols. London and Edinburgh, 1901.
STURT, M. *Francis Bacon, a Biography*. London, 1932.

Chapter Twenty: Political Philosophy

Texts

MACHIAVELLI. *Le Opere di Niccolò Machiavelli*. 6 vols. L. Passerini and G. Milanesi (edit.). Florence, 1873–77.
Tutte le Opere storiche e letterarie di Niccolò Machiavelli. G. Barbèra (edit.). Florence, 1929.
Il Principe. L. A. Burd (edit.). Oxford, 1891.
The Prince. W. K. Marriott (translator). London, 1908 and reprints (Everyman Series).
The Discourse of Niccolò Machiavelli. 2 vols. L. J. Walker, S.J. (translator and editor). London, 1950.
The History of Florence. 2 vols. N. H. Thomson (translator). London, 1906.
The Works of Nicholas Machiavel. 2 vols. E. Farneworth (translator). London, 1762. (2nd edition in 4 vols., 1775).
The Historical, Political and Diplomatic Writings of Niccolò Machiavelli. 4 vols. Boston and New York, 1891.
MORE. *Utopia* (Latin and English). J. H. Lupton (edit.). London, 1895. (There are many other versions, including an English text in the Everyman Series.)
L'Utopie ou le traité de la meilleure forme de gouvernement. Texte latine édite par M. Delcourt avec des notes explicatives et critiques. Paris, 1936.
The English Works. London, 1557. This text is being re-edited and two volumes appeared in 1931 (London), edited by W. E. Campbell and A. W. Reed.

There are various editions of the Latin works. For example, *Opera omnia latina*: Louvain, 1566.

HOOKER. *Works*. 3 vols. J. Keble (edit.). Oxford, 1845 (3rd edition).

The Laws of Ecclesiastical Polity, Books I–V. Introduction by Henry Morley. London, 1888.

BODIN. *Method for the Easy Comprehension of History*. B. Reynolds (translator). New York, 1945.

Six livres de la république. Paris, 1566. Latin edition: Paris, 1584. English translation by R. Knolles: London, 1606.

ALTHUSIUS. *Politica methodice digesta*. Herborn, 1603. Enlarged edition; Groningen, 1610. Modern edition by C. J. Friedrich. Cambridge (Mass.), 1932.

GROTIUS. *De iure belli ac pacis*. Washington, 1913 (edition of 1625). English translation by F. W. Kelsey and others. Oxford, 1925. (These two vols. together constitute No. 3 of 'The Classics of International Law.')

Studies

ALLEN, J. W. *A History of Political Thought in the Sixteenth Century*. London, 1928.

BAUDRILLART, H. *Jean Bodin et son temps*. Paris, 1853.

BURD, L. A. *Florence (II), Machiavelli*. (The Cambridge Modern History, vol. 1, ch. 6.) Cambridge, 1902.

CAMPBELL, W. E. *More's Utopia and his Social Teaching*. London, 1930.

CHAMBERS, R. W. *Thomas More*. London, 1935.

CHAUVIRÉ, R. *Jean Bodin, auteur de la République*. Paris, 1914.

D'ENTRÈVES, A. P. *Natural Law. An Introduction to Legal Philosophy*. London, 1951.

FIGGIS, J. N. *Studies of Political Thought from Gerson to Grotius*. Cambridge, 1923 (2nd edition).

FOSTER, M. B. *Masters of Political Thought*. Vol. 1, *Plato to Machiavelli* (Ch. 8, Machiavelli). London, 1942.

GIERKE, O. VON *Natural Law and the Theory of Society*. 2 vols. E. Barker (translator). Cambridge, 1934.

Johannes Althusius und die Entwicklung der naturrechtlichen Staatstheorien. Breslau, 1913 (3rd edition).

GOUGH, J. W. *The Social Contract. A Critical Study of its Development*. Oxford, 1936.

HEARNSHAW, F. J. C. *The Social and Political Ideas of some Great Thinkers of the Renaissance and the Reformation*. London, 1925.

The Social and Political Ideas of some Great Thinkers in the Sixteenth and Seventeenth Centuries. London, 1926.

MEINECKE, F. *Die Idee der Staatsräson*. (Ch. 1, Machiavelli.) Munich, 1929 (3rd edition).

RITCHIE, D. G. *Natural Rights*. London, 1916 (3rd edition).

SABINE, G. H. *A History of Political Theory*. London, 1941.

VILLARI, P. *The Life and Times of Niccolò Machiavelli*. 2 vols. L. Villari (translator). London, 1892.

VREELAND, H. *Hugo Grotius*. New York, 1917.

Chapter Twenty-one: (Scholasticism of the Renaissance) A General View

Texts

A number of titles of works are mentioned in the course of the chapter. Only a very few selected texts will be mentioned here. For fuller biographies the *Dictionnaire de théologie catholique* can be profitably consulted under the relevant names. The standard bibliographical work for writers of the Dominican Order between 1200 and 1700 is *Scriptores Ordinis Praedicatorum* by Quétif-Echard. A photolithographic reprint of the revised Paris edition of 1719–21 is being published by Musurgia Publishers, New York. For Jesuit authors consult Sommervogel-De Backer, *Bibliothèque de la compagnie de Jésus*. Liége, 1852 ff.

CAJETAN. *Thomas de Vio Cardinalis Caietanus. Scripta theologica*. Vol. 1, *De comparatione auctoritatis papae et concilii cum apologia eiusdem tractatus*. V. M. I. Pollet (edit.). Rome, 1936.

Thomas de Vio Cardinalis Caietanus (1469–1534); *Scripta philosophica:*

Commentaria in Porphyrii Isagogen ad Praedicamenta Aristotelis. I. M. Marega (edit.). Rome, 1934.

Opuscula oeconomico-socialia. P. N. Zammit (edit.). Rome, 1934.

De nominum analogia. De conceptu entis. P. N. Zammit (edit.). 1934.

Commentaria in de Anima Aristotelis. Y. Coquelle (edit.). Rome, 1938.

Caietanus . . . in 'De Ente et Essentia' Commentarium. M. H. Laurent (edit.). Turin, 1934.

Cajetan's commentary on Aquinas's *Summa theologica* is printed in the *Opera omnia* (Leonine edition) of St. Thomas.

BELLARMINE. *Opera omnia.* 11 vols. Paris, 1870–91.

Opera oratoria postuma. 9 vols. Rome, 1942–8.

De controversiis. Rome, 1832.

Tractatus de potestate summi pontificis in rebus temporalibus. Rome, 1610.

MOLINA. *De Institia et Iure.* 2 vols. Antwerp, 1615.

Concordia liberi arbitrii cum gratiae donis, divina praescientia, providentia, praedestinatione et reprobatione. Paris, 1876.

VITORIA. *De Indis et de Iure Belli Relectiones.* E. Mys (edit.). Washington, 1917 (Classics of International Law, No. 7).

JOHN OF ST. THOMAS. *Cursus Philosophicus Thomisticus* (edit. Reiser). 3 vols. Turin, 1930–8.

Cursus philosophicus. 3 vols. Paris, 1883.

Joannis a Sancto Thoma O.P. Cursus theologici. Paris, Tournai, Rome, 1931 ff.

Studies

BARCÍA TRELLES, C. *Francisco Suárez, Les théologiens espagnols du XVI siècle et l'école moderne du droit internationale.* Paris, 1933.

BRODRICK, J. *The Life and Work of Blessed R. Cardinal Bellarmine.* 2 vols. London, 1928.

FIGGIS, J. N. See under bibliography for Suárez.

FRITZ, G., and MICHEL, A. Article *Scolastique* (section III) in the Dictionnaire de théologie catholique, vol. 14, cols. 1715–25. Paris, 1939.

GIACÓN, C. *La seconda scolastica.* I, *I grandi commentatori di san Tommaso;* II, *Precedenze teoretiche ai problemi giuridici;* III, *I Problemi giuridico-politici.* Milan, 1944–50.

LITTLEJOHN, J. M. *The Political Theory of the Schoolmen and Grotius.* New York, 1896.

RÉGNON, T. DE *Bañes et Molina.* Paris, 1883.

SCOTT, J. B. *The Catholic Conception of International Law. Francisco de Vitoria, Founder of the Modern Law of Nations: Francisco Suárez, Founder of the Philosophy of Law in general and in particular of the Law of Nations.* Washington, 1934.

SMITH, G. (edit.). *Jesuit Thinkers of the Renaissance. Essays presented to John F. McCormick, S.J.* Milwaukee, Wis., 1939.

SOLANA, M. *Historia de la Filosofia Española en el siglo XVI.* Madrid, 1940.

STEGMÜLLER, F. *Geschichte des Molinismus. Band I, Neue Molinaschriften.* Münster, 1935 (Beiträge, 32).

STREITCHER, K. *Die Philosophie der spanischen Spätscholastik an den deutschen Universitäten des siebzehnten Jahrhunderts* (in *Gesammelte Aufsätze zur Kulturgeschichte Spaniens*). Münster, 1928.

VANSTEENBERGHE, E. Article *Molinisme* (and bibliography) in the Dictionnaire de théologie catholique, vol. 10, cols. 2094–2187. Paris, 1928.

Chapters Twenty-two–Twenty-three: Francis Suárez

Texts

Opera. 28 vols. Paris, 1856–78.

Metaphysicarum Disputationum Tomi duo. Salamanca, 1597. (Many editions, up to that of Barcelona, 1883–4.)

Selections from Three Works of Francisco Suárez, S.J. (*De legibus, Defensio fidei catholicae. De triplici virtute theologica.*) 2 vols. Vol. 1, the Latin texts; Vol. 2, the translation. Oxford, 1944. (Classics of International Law, No. 20.)

Among bibliographies one can mention *Bibliografica Suareciana* by P. Mugica. Granada, 1948.

Studies

AGUIRRE, P. *De doctrina Francisci Suárez circa potestatem Ecclesiae in res temporales.* Louvain, 1935.

ALEJANDRO, J. M. *La gnoseología del Doctor Eximio y la acusación nominalista.* Comillas (Santander), 1948.

BOUET, A. *Doctrina de Suárez sobre la libertad.* Barcelona, 1927.

BOUILLARD, R. Article *Suárez: théologie pratique.* Dictionnaire de théologie catholique, vol. 14, cols. 2691–2728. Paris, 1939.

BOURRET, E. *De l'origine du pouvoir d'après Saint Thomas et Suárez.* Paris, 1875.

BREUER, A. *Der Gottesbeweis bei Thomas und Suárez. Ein wissenschaftlicher Gottesbeweis auf der Grundlage von Potenz und Aktverhältnis oder Abhängigkeitsverhältnis.* Fribourg (Switzerland), 1930.

CONDE Y LUQUE, R. *Vida y doctrinas de Suárez.* Madrid, 1909.

DEMPF, A. *Christliche Staatsphilosophie in Spanien.* Salzburg, 1937.

FIGGIS, J. N. *Some Political Theories of the early Jesuits.* (Translations of the Royal Historical Society, XI. London, 1897.)

Studies of Political Thought from Gerson to Grotius. Cambridge, 1923 (2nd edition).

Political Thought in the Sixteenth Century. (The Cambridge Modern History, vol. 3, ch. 22). Cambridge, 1904.

GIACÓN, C. *Suárez.* Brescia, 1945.

GÓMEZ ARBOLEYA, E. *Francisco Suárez* (1548–1617). Granada, 1947.

GRABMANN, M. *Die disputationes metaphysicae des Franz Suárez in ihrer methodischen Eigenart und Fortwirkung* (*Mittelalterliches Geistesleben*, vol. 1, pp. 525–60). Munich, 1926.

HELLÍN, J. *La analogía del ser y el conocimiento de Dios en Suárez.* Madrid, 1947.

ITURRIOZ, J. *Estudios sobre la metafísica de Francisco Suárez, S.J.* Madrid, 1949.

LILLEY, A. L. *Francisco Suárez. Social and Political Ideas of some Great Thinkers of the XVIth and XVIIth centuries.* London, 1926.

MAHIEU, L. *François Suárez. Sa philosophie et les rapports qu'elle a avec la théologie.* Paris, 1921.

(Replies by P. Descoqs to this work are contained in *Archives de Philosophie*, vol. 2 [pp. 187–298] and vol. 4 [pp. 434–544]. Paris, 1924 and 1926.)

MONNOT, P. Article *Suárez: Vie et œuvres.* Dictionnaire de théologie catholique, vol. 14, cols. 2638–49. Paris, 1939.

PLAFFERT, F. *Suárez als Völkerrechtslehrer.* Würzburg, 1919.

RECASÉNS SICHES, L. *La filosofía del Derecho en Francisco Suárez.* Madrid, 1927.

REGOUT, D. *La doctrine de la guerre juste de saint Augustin à nos jours* (pp. 194–230). Paris, 1934.

ROMMEN, H. *Die Staatslehre des Franz Suárez.* München-Gladbach, 1927.

SCORRAILLE, R. DE. *François Suárez de la Compagnie de Jésus.* 2 vols. Paris, 1911.

SCOTT, J. B. *The Catholic Conception of International Law. Francisco de Vitoria, Founder of the Modern Law of Nations: Francisco Suárez, Founder of the Modern Philosophy of Law in general and in particular of the Law of Nations.* Washington, 1934.

WERNER, K. *Franz Suárez und die Scholastik der letzten Jahrhunderte.* 2 vols. Ratisbon, 1861 and 1889.

ZARAGÜETA, J. *La filosofía de Suárez y el pensamiento actual.* Granada, 1941.

Among the special issues of periodicals and collected articles devoted to the philosophy of Suárez one may mention the following:

Actas del IV centenario del nacimiento de Francisco Suárez, 1548–1948. 2 vols. Madrid, 1949–50. (Contains articles on Suárez' theological, philosophical and political ideas.)

Archives de philosophie, vol. 18. Paris, 1949.

Pensamiento, vol. 4, número extraordinario, Suárez en el cuarto centenario de su nacimiento (1548–1948). Madrid, 1948. (This number of *Pensamiento* contains valuable studies on the metaphysical, epistemological, political and legal ideas of Suárez.)

Razón y Fe, tomo 138, fascs. 1–4, July–October 1948. Centenario de Suárez, 1548–1948. Madrid, 1948. (Suárez is considered both as theologian and philosopher, but mainly as philosopher.)

The two following works deal mainly with theological aspects of Suárez' thought:

Estudios Eclesiasticos, vol. 22, nos. 85–6, April–September,

1948. Francisco Suárez en el IV centenario de su nacimiento. Madrid, 1948.

Miscelánea Comillas, IX. Homenaje al doctor eximio P. Francisco Suárez, S.J., en el IV centenario de su nacimiento, 1548–1948. Comillas (Santander), 1948.

Among the works published in connection with the third centenary of Suárez' death (1917) one may mention:

Commemoración del tercer centenario del Eximio Doctor español Francisco Suárez, S.J. (1617–1917). Barcelona, 1923.

P. Franz Suárez, S.J. Gedenkblätter zu seinem dreihundertjährigen Todestag (25 September 1617). Beiträge zur Philosophie des P. Suárez by K. Six, etc. Innsbruck, 1917.

Rivista di Filosofia Neo-scolastica, X (1918).

Scritti vari publicati in occasione del terzo centenario della morte di Francesco Suárez, per cura del prof. Agostino *Gemelli*. Milan, 1918.

RIVIÈRE, E. M. and SCORRAILLE, R. DE *Suárez et son œuvre. À l'occasion du troisième centenaire de sa mort*, 1617–1917. Vol. 1, La bibliographie des ouvrages imprimés et inédits (E. M. Rivière). Vol. 2, *La Doctrine* (R. de Scorraille). Toulouse-Barcelona, 1918.

NOTES

CHAPTER THIRTEEN

[1] The *De liberorum educatione*, published in 1450 by Aeneas Sylvius Piccolomini, later Pope Pius II, was taken in large part from Quintilian's *De Oratore*, which had been discovered in 1416, and from an educational work attributed to Plutarch.

[2] For some remarks on the value of Marsilius' translations of Plato and Plotinus, see J. Festugière, *La philosophie de l'amour de Marsile Ficin*, Appendix I, pp. 141–52.

[3] In the Greco-Roman world a considerable literature, dealing with religious, theosophical, philosophical, medical, astrological and alchemist topics became known as the Hermetic literature. It was attributed in some way to, or placed under the patronage of, the 'thrice-great Hermes', who was the Egyptian god Thoth, identified by the Greeks with Hermes.

[4] Cf. *De ente et uno*, 4.

[5] *Ibid.*, 5.

[6] *Oratio de hominis dignitate*, ed. E. Garin, p. 104.

[7] *Ibid.*, p. 106.

[8] *Heptaplus*, ed. E. Garin, pp. 186–8.

[9] *Ibid.*, p. 220.

[10] *Ibid.*, p. 244.

[11] *Ibid.*, p. 222.

CHAPTER FOURTEEN

[1] *De voluptate*, 1, 10.

[2] *De immortdlitate animae*, 10; *Apologia*, 1, 3.

[3] *Ibid.*

[4] *De immortalitate animae*, 9.

[5] Cf. *Ibid.*, 9–10.

[6] On the human mind's knowledge of the universal, see, for example, *Apologia*, 1, 3.

[7] *De immortalitate animae*, 4.

8 *De immortalitate animae*, 14.
9 *Ibid.*
10 *Ibid.*, 13–14.
11 *Ibid.*, 14.
12 *Ibid.*
13 *Ibid.*, 10.
14 *De la sagesse*, 2, 5, 29.

CHAPTER FIFTEEN

1 p. 207.
2 p. 211.
3 *De docta ignorantia*, 1, 4.
4 *Ibid.*, 2, 1.
5 *Ibid.*, 1, 5.
6 *Ibid.*, 1, 21.
7 *Ibid.*, 1, 3.
8 *Ibid.*, 1, 12.
9 *De venatione sapientiae*, 14.
10 *Ibid.*, 13.
11 8.
12 *De docta ignorantia*, 2, 3.
13 *Ibid.*, 2, 11.
14 *Ibid.*, 2, 4.
15 *Ibid.*, 2, 2.
16 *Ibid.*, 2, 4.
17 2, 7.
18 12.
19 2, 14.
20 *De docta ignorantia*, 2, 4.
21 *Ibid.*
22 *De venatione sapientiae*, 9.
23 *De ludo globi*, 1.
24 *Ibid.*
25 *Ibid.*, 2.
26 *De docta ignorantia*, 2, 11.
27 *Ibid.*, 2, 12.
28 *Ibid.*
29 *Ibid.*
30 *Ibid.*, 2, 6.
31 *Ibid.*; cf. *De coniecturis*, 21, 3.
32 *De docta ignorantia*, 3, 1.
33 *Ibid.*, 2, 5.
34 *Ibid.*, 2, 6.
35 *Ibid.*, 2, 9.
36 3, 13.

[37] *De docta ignorantia*, 3, 3.
[38] *De ludo globi*, 1.
[39] *Ibid.*
[40] *De docta ignorantia*, 3, 2.
[41] *De visione Dei*, 19–21.
[42] *Ibid.*, 21.
[43] *De docta ignorantia*, 3, 12.

CHAPTER SIXTEEN

[1] *De rerum natura*, 8, 3.
[2] *Dialogo secondo, Opere*, 1, pp. 175–6.
[3] *Ibid.*, p. 179.
[4] *Dialogo quinto*, pp. 247 ff.
[5] *Dialogo primo*, p. 298.
[6] See note 1, Chapter Seventeen, below.
[7] They are the fifth in the series of objections published in the works of Descartes.

CHAPTER SEVENTEEN

[1] It seems probable that at any rate the term 'monad' was adopted by Leibniz from the younger Van Helmont or through a reading of Bruno suggested by Van Helmont.
[2] *Von der Gnadenwahl*, 1, 3.
[3] *Ibid.*, 1, 3–5.
[4] *Ibid.*, 1, 3.
[5] *Ibid.*, 1, 9–10.
[6] *Ibid.*, 8, 8.

CHAPTER NINETEEN

[1] 1, 129.
[2] *De augmentis scientiarum*, 2, 1.
[3] *Ibid.*, 2, 4.
[4] *Ibid.*, 3, 1.
[5] *Ibid.*
[6] *Ibid.*, 2.
[7] *Ibid.*, 4.
[8] *Ibid.*, 5.
[9] *Ibid.*
[10] *Ibid.*, 6.
[11] *Ibid.*, 4.
[12] *Ibid.*, 5, 1.
[13] *Ibid.*, 2.
[14] *Ibid.*, 6, 4.

15 *De augmentis scientiarum*, 7, 2.
16 *Ibid.*, 8, 1.
17 *Ibid.*, 8, 3.
18 *Ibid.*, 3, 4.
19 1, 3.
20 1, 11.
21 1, 12.
22 1, 14.
23 1, 19 ff.
24 1, 31.
25 *Instauratio magna, distributio operis.*
26 *Ibid.*
27 *Ibid.*
28 *Novum organum*, 1, 38–68.
29 *Ibid.*, 1, 40.
30 1, 70.
31 1, 83.
32 1, 100.
33 1, 105.
34 2, 1.
35 2, 4.
36 1, 17.
37 2, 5.
38 *Ibid.*
39 2, 6.
40 2, 7.
41 2, 8.
42 2, 9.
43 2, 10.
44 2, 11.
45 2, 12.
46 2, 13.
47 2, 15.
48 2, 16–18.
49 2, 19.
50 2, 20.
51 2, 21 ff.
52 *Novum organum*, 1, 61.

CHAPTER TWENTY

1 *The Prince*, 18.
2 2, 2.
3 25.
4 *Discourses*, 1, 9, 2.
5 1, 58, 61.

[6] *Discourses*, 1, 58, 8.
[7] *Ibid.*, 1, 29, 5.
[8] *Ibid.*, 2, 2, 3.
[9] *Ibid.*, 1, 55, 7–11.
[10] *The Prince*, 26.
[11] *Discourses*, 1, 12, 6–8.
[12] Cf. *The Prince*, 15.
[13] Cf. *Politics*, 5, 11.
[14] 1, 2.
[15] 1, 3.
[16] 1, 8.
[17] *Ibid.*
[18] *Ibid.*
[19] 1, 10.
[20] *Ibid.*
[21] *Ibid.*
[22] 1, 10.
[23] *Ibid.*
[24] *Ibid.*
[25] *Ibid.*
[26] 1, 15.
[27] 1, 16.
[28] 3, 3.
[29] *Preamble.*
[30] 5.
[31] Enlarged Latin edition, 1584.
[32] 6.
[33] *Ibid.*
[34] *Republic*, 1, 8.
[35] 5.
[36] *De iure belli ac pacis*, 6.
[37] *Ibid.*, 8.
[38] *Ibid.*, 9.
[39] *Ibid.*, 16.
[40] *Ibid.*, 17.
[41] *De iure belli ac pacis*, 21.
[42] *Ibid.*, 23.
[43] *Ibid.*, 25.
[44] *Ibid.*, 28.
[45] *Ibid.*, 50.
[46] *Prolegomena*, 11.
[47] *Ibid.*, 12.
[48] 1, 1, 10, 1.
[49] 1, 1, 10, 5.
[50] 1, 1, 10, 2.
[51] 39.

52 1, 1, 12, 1.
53 2, 23, 1.
54 *De jure naturae et gentium*, 1, 2, 9–10.
55 1, 1, 14, 1.
56 1, 3, 7, 1.
57 1, 3, 7, 3.
58 1, 3, 8, 1.
59 1, 3, 17, 1.
60 1, 3, 17, 2.
61 1, 4, 1, 3.
62 2, 1, 1, 4.
63 2, 22, 5.
64 2, 22, 6.
65 2, 23, 8.
66 2, 22, 12.
67 2, 23, 6.
68 2, 24.
69 2, 24, 8.
70 3, 25, 2.
71 3, 1, 1.
72 3, 19, 1, 2.
73 1, 1, 14, 1.
74 1, 1, 14, 2.
75 *Prolegomena*, 52.

CHAPTER TWENTY-ONE

1 Ch. 1.
2 *Ibid.*
3 Ch. 2.
4 Ch. 3.
5 *Ibid.*
6 Ch. 10.
7 Ch. 11.
8 9, 23.
9 3, 21.
10 *De summo pontifice*, 1581; enlarged as *De potestate summi pontificis*, 1610.
11 The then General of the Jesuits prohibited the teaching by members of the Order of Mariana's doctrine on tyrannicide.
12 *De potestate civili*, 21.
13 *Ibid.*
14 Cf. *De iustitia*, 1, 2, disp. 34–5.
15 Cf. *The Catholic Conception of International Law* by J. B. Scott, Ch. XIII.

CHAPTER TWENTY-TWO

[1] The importance of this change is not diminished, of course, by the fact that we know that Aristotle's *Metaphysics* was not 'a book' but a collection of treatises.

[2] M. Frischeisen-Köhler and W. Moog: *Die Philosophie der Neuzeit bis zum Ende des XVIII Jahrhunderts*, p. 211; vol. III of F. Ueberweg's *Grundriss der Geschichte der Philosophie*, 12th edition.

[3] *Disp. metaph.*, 1, 2, nn. 19–20.

[4] This classification of psychology was in accordance with Aristotle's remarks in his *De anima*.

[5] *Disp.*, 1, 1, 24.

[6] 1, 2, 11.

[7] 1, 2, 24.

[8] *Ibid.*

[9] 1, 2, 5.

[10] 1, 4, 2.

[11] 2, 1, 9.

[12] 2, 1, 9.

[13] 2, 1, 10.

[14] 2, 1, 13.

[15] 2, 2, 8.

[16] 2, 2, 15.

[17] 2, 3, 7.

[18] 2, 4, 4.

[19] 2, 2, 36; 39, 3, 17.

[20] *expressius, per maiorem determinationem.*

[21] 2, 6, 7.

[22] 3, 2, 3.

[23] *Disp.*, 4, 1–2.

[24] 8, 2, 9.

[25] 8, 7, 25.

[26] 8, 7, 28–9.

[27] 10, 1, 12.

[28] 5, 1, 4.

[29] 5, 2, 8–9.

[30] 5, 2, 16.

[31] 5, 3.

[32] 5, 6, 15.

[33] 5, 6, 17.

[34] 28, 1, 6.

[35] 28, 3, 1.

[36] 28, 3, 2.

[37] 28, 3, 11.

[38] 28, 3, 16.

[39] 29, 1, 7.

40 *Disp.*, 29, 1, 8.
41 29, 1, 20.
42 29, 1, 21.
43 29, 1, 25–40.
44 29, 2, 7.
45 29, 2, 21.
46 29, 3, 1.
47 *Ibid.*
48 29, 3, 2.
49 29, 3, 11.
50 29, 3, 31.
51 30, 1, 12.
52 30, 2.
53 30, 3–5.
54 30, 7.
55 30, 8–9.
56 30, 10.
57 30, 11.
58 30, 12.
59 30, 13.
60 30, 14.
61 30, 15.
62 30, 16.
63 30, 17.
64 30, 15, 33.
65 31, 1, 3.
66 31, 1, 11.
67 31, 1, 12.
68 31, 1, 13.
69 31, 6, 9.
70 31, 6, 13–24.
71 31, 13, 7.
72 31, 13, 18.
73 *Ibid.*
74 *Ibid.*
75 32, 1, 4.
76 32, 2, 12.
77 34, 1, 9.
78 34, 1, 13.
79 34, 4, 8.
80 34, 4, 16.
81 34, 4, 24.
82 34, 4, 33.
83 34, 4, 39.
84 34, 5, 1.
85 34, 5, 33.

[86] *Disp.*, 34, 5, 35.
[87] 34, 5, 42.
[88] 34, 5, 36.
[89] 40, 2, 8.
[90] 40, 4, 14.
[91] 47, 1.
[92] 47, 2, 22.
[93] The opinion that there is always a real distinction between a real relation and its foundation is 'the opinion of the old Thomists', like Capreolus and Cajetan (47, 2, 2).
[94] 47, 2, 22.
[95] 47, 3, 3.
[96] 47, 3, 12.
[97] 47, 3, 11.
[98] 47, 4, 2.
[99] 47, 5, 2.
[100] 47, 6, 5.
[101] 47, 6–9.
[102] 47, 4, 2.
[103] 47, 15, 6.
[104] 47, 15, 16.
[105] 47, 15, 17–28.
[106] 54, *introd.*
[107] 54, 1, 6.
[108] 54, 1, 9.
[109] 54, 2, 15.
[110] 54, 2, 18.
[111] 54, 5, 7.
[112] 54, 5, 23.
[113] 54, 6, 8–9.
[114] 31, 13, 18.
[115] 4, 20.

CHAPTER TWENTY-THREE

[1] *De legibus*, 1, 1, 1; cf. St. Thomas, *S.T.*, Ia, IIae, 90, 1.
[2] *De legibus*, 1, 12, 5.
[3] *Ibid.*, 1, 5, 24.
[4] *Ibid.*, 1, 6, 18.
[5] *Ibid.*, 1, 6, 21.
[6] *Ibid.*, 1, 7, 9.
[7] *Ibid.*, 1, 9, 11.
[8] *Ibid.*, 1, 9, 13.
[9] *Ibid.*
[10] *Ibid.*, 1, 2, 5.
[11] *Ibid.*, 1, 3, 2.

[12] *De legibus*, 1, 3, 3.
[13] Chapters 1–4.
[14] *De legibus*, 2, 2, 5.
[15] *Ibid.*, 2, 2, 13.
[16] *Ibid.*, 2, 2, 15.
[17] *Ibid.*, 2, 3, 6.
[18] *Ibid.*, 2, 3, 4.
[19] *Ibid.*, 2, 1, 5.
[20] *Ibid.*, 2, 1, 11.
[21] *Ibid.*, 2, 4, 5.
[22] *Ibid.*, 2, 4, 8–10.
[23] *Ibid.*, 2, 5, 6.
[24] *Ibid.*, 2, 5, 9.
[25] *Ibid.*, 2, 5, 14.
[26] *Ibid.*, 2, 6, 5.
[27] *Ibid.*, 2, 6, 24.
[28] *Ibid.*, 2, 7, 5.
[29] *Ibid.*, 2, 7, 11.
[30] *Ibid.*
[31] Cf. *Ibid.*, 2, 8, 1.
[32] *Tractatus de bonitate et malitia humanorum actuum*, 9, 3, 10.
[33] De Religione, *pars secunda*, 1, 7, 3.
[34] *De legibus*, 2, 8, 7.
[35] *Ibid.*, 2, 13, 1.
[36] *Ibid.*, 2, 13, 2.
[37] *Ibid.*, 2, 13, 8.
[38] *Ibid.*, 2, 14, 8.
[39] *Ibid.*, 2, 14, 16.
[40] *Ibid.*, 2, 14, 19.
[41] *Ibid.*, 2, 15, 3.
[42] *Ibid.*, 2, 15, 12.
[43] *Ibid.*, 2, 15, 16.
[44] *Ibid.*, 2, 15, 20.
[45] *Ibid.*, 2, 17, 9.
[46] *Ibid.*, 2, 19, 2.
[47] *Ibid.*, 2, 19, 5.
[48] *Ibid.*, 2, 19, 6.
[49] *Ibid.*, 2, 19, 8.
[50] *Ibid.*
[51] *Ibid.*, 2, 19, 9.
[52] Ia, IIae, 95, 4.
[53] *De legibus*, 2, 20, 2.
[54] *Ibid.*, 3, 1, 3.
[55] *Ibid.*, 3, 1, 4.
[56] *De regimine principum*, 1, 1.
[57] *De legibus*, 3, 1, 6.

58 *De legibus*, 3, 1, 11.
59 *Ibid.*, 3, 1, 12.
60 *Ibid.*
61 For St. Augustine's opinion see Vol. 2, Part I, of this history, pp. 103–4.
62 5, 7, 6.
63 *De legibus*, 5, 7, 11.
64 *Ibid.*, 3, 2, 3.
65 *Ibid.*, 3, 2, 4.
66 *Ibid.*
67 *Ibid.*, 3, 2, 5.
68 *Ibid.*, 3, 3, 4.
69 *Ibid.*, 3, 3, 7.
70 *Ibid.*, 3, 4, 1.
71 *Ibid.*
72 *Ibid.*, 3, 4, 2.
73 *Ibid.*
74 *Ibid.*, 3, 4, 3.
75 *Ibid.*, 3, 4, 4.
76 *Ibid.*, 3, 4, 5.
77 *Ibid.*
78 3, 5, 7.
79 *Ibid.*
80 *De legibus*, 3, 4, 7.
81 *Ibid.*, 3, 2, 5.
82 *Ibid.*, 3, 4, 11.
83 *Ibid.*, 3, 4, 6.
84 *Ibid.*
85 *Defence of the Catholic and Apostolic Faith*, 6, 4, 1.
86 *De triplici virtute theologica; de caritate*, 13, 8, 2.
87 *Ibid.*
88 *De regimine principum*, 1, 6.
89 6, 4.
90 *De regimine principum*, 1, 6.
91 *Defence*, 6, 4, 4.
92 *Ibid.*, 6, 4, 8–9.
93 *De legibus*, 5, 3, 2.
94 *Ibid.*, 5, 3, 6.
95 *Ibid.*, 5, 3, 10.
96 *Ibid.*, 5, 4, 8.
97 *Ibid.*, 5, 5, 15.
98 *Ibid.*, 5, 6, 4.
99 *Ibid.*, 5, 10, 8.
100 *Ibid.*, 5, 10, 12.
101 *Ibid.*, 5, 13, 4.
102 *Ibid.*, 5, 13, 9.

103 *De legibus*, 5, 18, 12.
104 *Ibid.*, 6, 9, 3.
105 *Ibid.*, 6, 9, 10.
106 *Ibid.*, 7, 3, 8–10.
107 *Ibid.*, 7, 6, 4.
108 *Ibid.*, 7, 6, 7.
109 *Ibid.*, 7, 9, 3.
110 *Ibid.*, 7, 9, 12.
111 *Ibid.*, 7, 10, 1.
112 *Ibid.*, 7, 12, 1.
113 *Ibid.*, 7, 12, 10.
114 *Ibid.*, 7, 13, 6.
115 *Ibid.*, 7, 14, 1.
116 *Ibid.*, 7, 15, 2.
117 *Ibid.*, 7, 18, 5.
118 *Ibid.*, 7, 16, 3.
119 *Ibid.*, 7, 18, 12.
120 *Defence*, 3, 5, 11.
121 *Ibid.*, 3, 22, 1.
122 *Ibid.*
123 *Ibid.*, 3, 22, 5.
124 *Ibid.*, 3, 22, 7.
125 *Ibid.*, 3, 23, 2.
126 *Ibid.*, 3, 23, 10.
127 *Ibid.*, 3, 23, 22.
128 *De triplici virtute theologica; de caritate*, 13, 1, 4.
129 *Ibid.*, 13, 2, 4.
130 *Ibid.*, 13, 2, 5.
131 *Ibid.*, 13, 4, 1.
132 *Ibid.*, 13, 4, 10.
133 *Ibid.*, 13, 7, 3.
134 *Ibid.*, 13, 7, 6.
135 *Ibid.*, 13, 7, 7.
136 *Ibid.*
137 *Ibid.*, 13, 7, 10.
138 *Ibid.*, 13, 7, 15.
139 *Ibid.*, 13, 6, 8–12.
140 *Ibid.*, 13, 6, 2.

CHAPTER TWENTY-FOUR

1 On this subject *The Christian Challenge to Philosophy* by W. H. V. Reade (London, 1951) can profitably be consulted.

INDEX

(A small *n* after a number indicates that the reference is to a note on the page in question.)